# GLOBAL

## LEATHER, FOOTWEAR INDUSTRY EXPORTERS AND IMPORTERS DIRECTORY

### VOLUME 1

### EUROPE LEATHER AND FOOTWEAR INDUSTRY - STRATEGIC INFORMATION AND CONTACTS

**International Business Publications, USA**
Washington, DC USA

# GLOBAL

## LEATHER, FOOTWEAR INDUSTRY EXPORTERS AND IMPORTERS DIRECTORY

### VOLUME 1. EUROPE LEATHER AND FOOTWEAR INDUSTRY

**Global Leather and Footwear Ind Handbook.**
**VOL. 1**. Europe Leather Indsutry
**Global Leather and Footwear Ind Handbook.**
**VOL. 2**. Europe Footwear Industry
**Global Leather and Footwear Ind Handbook.**
**VOL. 2**. Asia
**Global Leather and Footwear Ind Handbook.**
**VOL. 3**. India
**Global Leather and Footwear Ind Handbook.**
**VOL. 4**. Americas

**UPDATED ANNUALLY**

**We express our sincere appreciation to all government agencies and international organizations which provided information and other materials for this directory**

**Cover Design: International Business Publications, USA**



**2018 Updated Reprint International Business Publications, USA**
**ISBN 1-4387-1962-0**



**Printed in the USA**

**For additional analytical, business and investment opportunities information, please contact Global Investment & Business Center, USA at (703) 370-8082. Fax: (703) 370-8083. E-mail: ibpusa3@gmail.com Global Business and Investment Info Databank - www.ibpus.com**

# GLOBAL
# LEATHER, FOOTWEAR INDUSTRY EXPORTERS AND IMPORTERS DIRECTORY

## VOLUME 1.
## EUROPE LEATHER AND FOOTWEAR INDUSTRY

# LEATHER INDUSTRY: STRATEGIC INFORMATION

## THE WORLD LEATHER MARKET

### LEATHER STATISTICS AND SOURCES OF INFORMATION

The following statistics give a broad picture of world leather production and the share of end uses of leather.

The main leather producing countries in the world - accounting for over 70% of finished leather produced are:

**LEATHER PRODUCTION**
**Top 30 Countries**
**( Million square feet )**

| Country | 1997 | 1998 | 1999 | 2000 | 2015 |
|---|---|---|---|---|---|
| | | | | | |
| China | 2964.4 | 3285.3 | 3900 | 4141.8 | 4493.2 |
| Italy | 2149.4 | 1981.6 | 1820 | 2060.4 | 2065.7 |
| India | 1369.3 | 1379.6 | 1392 | 1428.3 | 1423.7 |
| Korea | 1268.8 | 869.2 | 1000 | 1086.4 | 973 |
| USA | 735.5 | 847 | 930.7 | 861 | 831.8 |
| Former USSR | 932 | 926 | 896 | 731.1 | 782.5 |
| Brazil | 672.3 | 705.2 | 725 | 784.6 | 756 |
| Mexico | 632.9 | 673.6 | 668.2 | 619.9 | 568.3 |
| Spain | 558.6 | 534.8 | 500 | 542.2 | 541.2 |
| Argentina | 403.1 | 430.6 | 461.6 | 485.2 | 487.2 |
| Turkey | 550.3 | 509.6 | 556.8 | 410 | 419.2 |
| Pakistan | 343.2 | 343.3 | 370 | 311.8 | 314.4 |

| Leather use by end product 2003 | | Million square feet |
|---|---|---|
| | | |
| Footwear | | 10835 |
| Garments | | 2205 |
| Automotive | | 1220 |
| Furniture | | 2420 |
| Gloves | | 850 |
| Other leather products | | 1820 |
| Total | | 19350 |
| | | % of total |
| | | |
| Footwear | | 56 |
| Garments | | 11.4 |
| Automotive | | 6.3 |
| Furniture | | 12.5 |
| Gloves | | 4.4 |

| | | |
|---|---|---|
| Other leather products | | 9.4 |
| Total | | 100.0 |

Source: Industry estimates

Source: FOA

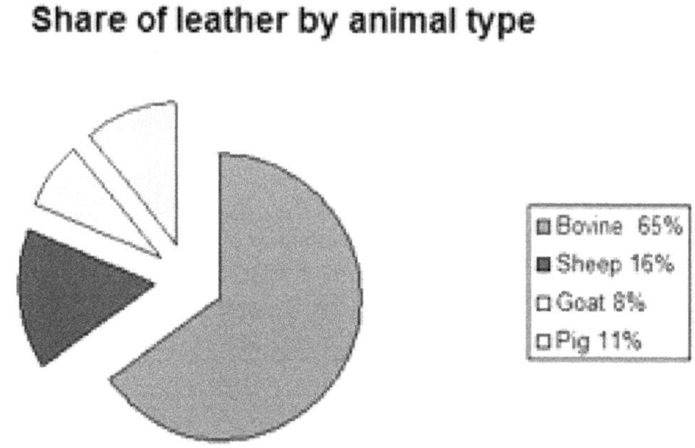


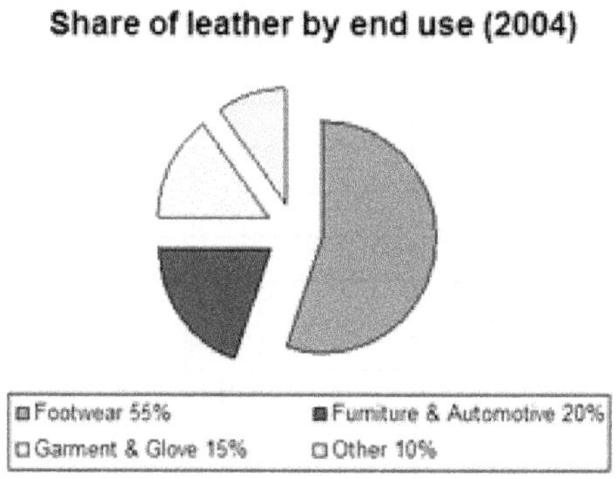


Source: Industry estimates

The best comprehensive source of information on production and trade in the leather sector is the "World statistical compendium for hides, skins, leather and leather footwear," produced every two years by the Food and Agriculture Organisation of the United Nations (FAO) - enquiries to:

Chief, Raw Materials
Tropical and Horticultural Products Service,
Commodities and Trade Division (ESC)
FAO
Viale delle Terme di Caracalla
00100 Rome
Italy

Fax: + (3906) 5705 4495
E-mail: ESC-Registry@fao.org

In the overall food chain, the positive economic importance of the industry taking care of one of its major waste products should not be underestimated or marginalised. As the tanning industry is sometimes criticised on environmental grounds, ponder the alternative hazard of millions of dumped, putrefying hides and skins. Whoever it was who first thought of preserving hides and skins did mankind a tremendous service.

The leather industry in total produces about 18 billion square feet of leather a year, and the total value of this is estimated at about $40 billion. If the by-product of the meat industry, hides and skins, was not used to produce this quantity of leather, then, for example, shoes and upholstery would be manufactured from alternative, non-renewable raw materials such as plastics and other petrochemical based products. Developing countries now produce over 60% of the world's leather, and this proportion is growing.

About 65% of the world production of leather is estimated to go into leather footwear and the global production of footwear is estimated at around 11 billion pairs (worth an estimated $150 billion at wholesale prices).

The value of leather products at retail level would be commensurately higher - and the value of products containing leather, if one counts automobiles and aircraft, would be substantially greater than a straight proportion of the footwear value. The value of leather produced for the automotive industry has been calculated at $1,350 million internationally.

**Trade and employment**

The number of people employed in the tanning industry worldwide is estimated at well over 500,000 and the numbers employed in downstream manufacturing sectors would increase this number substantially. The leather industry is very much an international industry - with raw hides and skins, part processed leather, finished leather, leather components and leather products widely imported and exported. FAO quote figures which demonstrate how important the leather sector is in international trade terms - much bigger than meat and other commonly recognised commodities.

**International Trade**

(Million US Dollars - Average 1994-2010)

| | |
|---|---|
| Raw hides and skins | 5,419 |
| Leather | 13,053 |
| Leather footwear | 24,974 |
| Total | 43,445 |
| | |
| Meat | 17,900 |
| (from cattle, sheep and goats) | |
| Coffee | 10,600 |
| Tea | 1,850 |
| Rice | 6,400 |
| Sugar | 12,300 |
| Rubber | 6,750 |
| Cotton | 8,950 |

Source FAO

On these figures, the value of the international trade in meat, tea, coffee, rice and sugar needs to be added together to surpass the value of the leather and leather footwear sector. At the same time, the table highlights the beneficial economic importance of the industry, adding genuine value to the raw hides and skins which would otherwise be wasted.

Significant steps have been made by the global leather industry with regard to environmental matters. In the manufacturing stages, a high level of quality control ensures that the best use is made of hides and skins and the chemicals required in their conversion into leather. Overall chemical and water use has thus been reduced, reducing the level of waste for treatment.

Many new techniques have evolved specifically to reduce pollution before any form of treatment. Specifically JIT techniques and alternative methods of preservation are used to reduce the use of salt for preservation. Biotechnology is employed in process to reduce the levels of chemicals and energy used. There has been a significant move away from non-biodegradable products, and the phasing out of products suspected of causing environmental damage.

Pollution is also being reduced by making use of previous wastes as a source of new raw materials. Hair, off-cuts, and other manufacturing wastes are being converted in fertilisers, added value products and energy. Products that were not taken up in processing, such as residual chromium from tanning, are being reprocessed to create new tanning materials. Even waste waters from some sections of manufacture are being recycled and used again within manufacture.

The industry is strongly regulated regarding emissions such as waste water, solid wastes and air emissions. Comprehensive effluent treatment systems ensure that waste water discharge limits set by relevant authorities are met. Treated effluents are scrutinised by regulatory authorities, and every tannery needs to meet stringent discharge parameters to both surface waters and sewers. Any solid wastes for landfill from direct manufacture, or from treatment of effluents, are also regulated. Disposal is carefully controlled, with emphasis on alternative uses with gasification techniques and energy generation moving to the fore.

Air emissions have also been closely addressed. The use of solvents has plummeted over the last ten years, being replaced by newly developed water based auxiliaries. For degreasing operations, solvents have been replaced by aqueous degreasing technology. Odour, overspray and air borne particles can all be treated by specialised extraction, chemical and biological treatment systems.

The industry is proactive in addressing environmental issues and in investments in clean technology. The use of best available technology continues to reduce the use of water, chemicals and energy in process, convert waste into new raw materials, and treat residual waste to international standards.

**The issue of chrome**

The use of chromium in the leather industry merits a separate article on its own, and this is planned for a future issue. However, as part of the overview of the industry, the use of chrome is also considered.

Chromium III salts are used extensively in the tanning process. Approximately 90% of the leather manufactured is tanned using chromium III. This is because chromium is the most efficient and versatile tanning agent available, and it is relatively cheap. It has been used in the leather industry for almost 100 years and when it was introduced as an alternative to vegetable tanning extracts from oak bark and similar sources, it heralded a new era for the leather industry. It reduced the time taken within the tanning process from months to days, and offered leathers with properties that were previously unattainable - for example tolerance to heat - without which it would be almost impossible to make leather shoes by mechanical means.

The leather industry only uses chromium in its safest and most stable form - chromium III. However, due to misconceptions about chromium and a failure to recognise the distinctions between chromium III and chromium VI, which is generally understood to be toxic, the tanning industry has often been placed under unwarranted pressure by regulatory bodies with regard to both the use and disposal of chromium and chromium-containing materials. Chromium VI compounds are not used by the tanning industry.

The toxicity of chromium III is similar to that of common salt, and standard chemical references quote: "Chromium III compounds show little or no toxicity." Much of the chromium III used in the tannery is recycled or reused, and most of the chromium III which enters the tannery waste streams is removed on-site by precipitation as the insoluble chromium III hydroxide which may then go to landfill. Chromium will only exist in the environment as chromium III. In soil, chromium VI is rapidly reduced to chromium III by its oxidative action upon organic material.

The EC recently considered and rejected a proposal to include tannery wastes containing chromium in the European Hazardous Waste List on the basis that the wastes did not possess the characteristics necessary for classification as a hazardous waste. In the United States, the Environmental Protection Agency revised substantially upwards its limits for chromium in sludge applied to agricultural land following an action by the industry in the US Court of Appeal, on the basis that there was no scientific justification for the original proposals. The original proposal for a total chromium limit of 12,000mg/kg of dry solids; the revised limit for chromium III was 100,000mg/kg, (after reducing the calculated amount from 2, 400,000mg/kg to 1,000,000 and applying an additional 10-fold safety factor).

A commodity chain encompasses the whole range of activities involved in the design, production, and marketing of a product. The value chain, also called the commodity chain and production-consumption chain, is described as a comprehensive set of activities that are required to bring a product from a concept stage to marketing and consumption of end products (Gereffi1999). It involves a series of components that begin with product design and the selection and purchase of raw materials and intermediate inputs and go through processing, marketing and distribution. The chain continues with the operation of sales of intermediate and end products. The last component of the chain is the consumption of final goods that is regulated by internal and external demands.

The process of globalization has promoted two types of chains through which global production networks manage and operate: the producer-driven and the buyer-driven commodity chains. The first type is characteristic of capital-intensive industries such as automobiles, aircraft, computers, and other advanced technology industrial activities. The buyer-driven commodity chains are organized around labour -intensive industries such as footwear and garments in which the marketing and manufacturing agents (retailers, branded marketing agencies and branded manufacturers) set up global production networks, principally in developing countries. Enterprises in exporting, developing countries produce the finished goods under contract following the specifications, guidelines and technical advice provided by the purchasing agents. Successful examples of buyer driven commodity chains were Japanese in the 50s and 60s, Asian in the 70s and 80s and Chinese in the 90s (Gereffi 1999).

The leather industry utilizes a byproduct of slaughterhouses and transforms the raw materials into various types of leather and manufactured end products. The leather production-consumption chain has three processing stages, each requiring different combinations of material inputs, labour and capital. The first stage is the recovery of raw materials, that has direct links with animal production activities; hides and skins are recovered from dairy, draught animals or animals from slaughter houses. Leather tanning and finishing is the second stage that involves relatively capital-intensive operations while the third stage, which is the production of leather products, is a more labour intensive activity. These three processing stages are linked to key commercial components of the chain, the marketing of intermediate inputs, components and end products, and trade and consumption. Inputs to the chain without which the chain cannot operate under competitive basis are: qualified labour, design and art centers, component production, access to chemicals, technical and administrative support institutions, research and development, training as well as a set of adequate policies.

Marketing is the core of the modern leather product business and the principal main marketing agents have the necessary trade information and have established a wide network of sales channels that allow them to contract production, provide finance and serve the customer on time (within three to five weeks after placing the order) managing the complex mechanism of supply chain within the strategy of buyer-driven commodity chains (Schmel1998, Magretta 2000). There are two markets, the local and the export market; the latter is usually managed within the rules of a buyer-driven commodity chain, supply chain and triangle manufacturing as will be discussed later in this paper.

The support system for investment and innovation is shown in the Diagram as an independent component of the chain but in reality should be present and active in the policy components, services and in all linkages between components of the chain.

**Livestock Slaughter Collection Primary Processing**

**Secondary Processing**

Footwear and Leather Value Chain

## RAW MATERIALS, INDUSTRIAL PROCESSING, TRADE, CONSUMPTION AND DATA

### RAW MATERIALS

This section of the paper refers principally to FAO and UNIDO publications and technical papers.

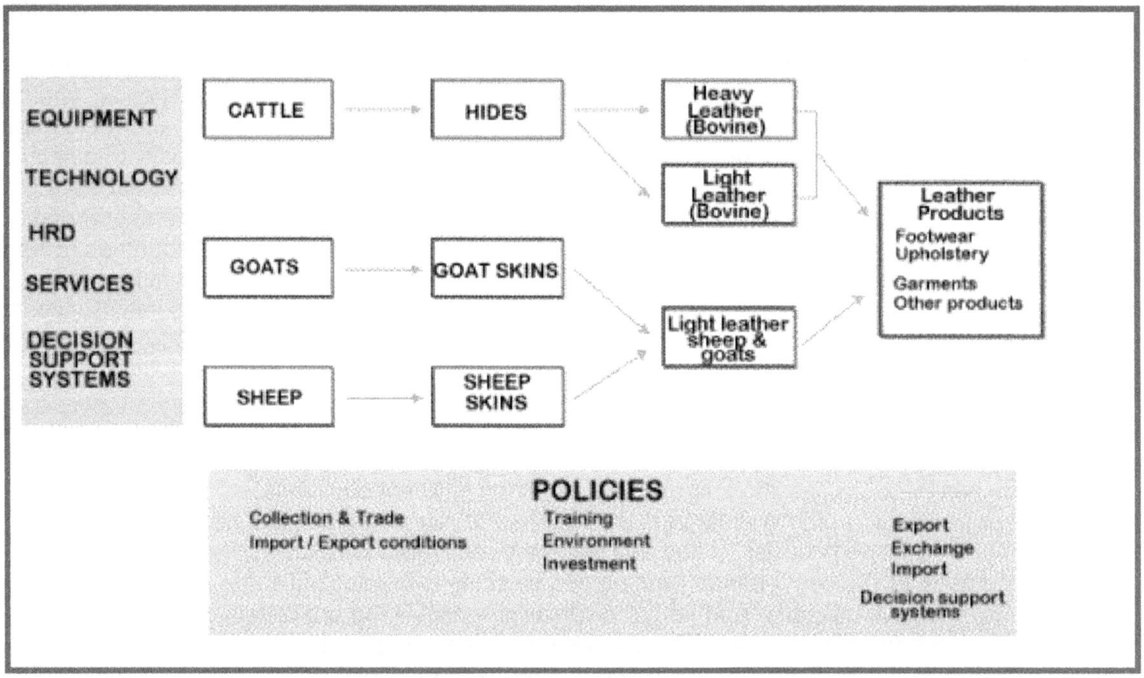


The leather industry depends on the availability of raw materials, which in turn is regulated by the animal population, the off-take ratio and the weight per hide and skin recovered. Between 1994

and 1996, 75% of the bovine herd was located in developing countries, which produce 56% of hides on a numerical basis and 43% of the world hide output by weight.

The largest disparity between population and output of hides occurs in Africa, which holds more than 10% of the worlds cattle but contributed during the period only 4.5% of the total hide output due to low levels of off-take ratio, poor handling in the field and price policies.

In the case of sheep and goatskins, the output coming from developing countries accounted in both cases for similar proportions to their global stock in numerical terms, 59% in sheepskins and 95% in goatskins (FAO 1998).

Sheep and goatskins represent 6% of the total leather supply in the world. Thirty percent of sheepskins come from three countries, New Zealand, Australia and the former Soviet Union. Most of the goatskins (3% of the total leather raw material) come from developing countries, mainly China, India Pakistan and tropical Africa.

In the period 1994-96 the global bovine population of some 1,477 million head yielded approximately 5.5 million tons of raw hides on a wet salted basis. Total production of heavy leather was 460,000 tones and that of light leather 10,138 million square feet. Approximately 65% of the light leather was used for the manufacture of 4,539 million pairs of shoes with leather uppers. The remaining 35% was used for the manufacture of garments, furniture and travel goods including handbags.

621,000 tones of raw skins from sheep and goats yielded 4,140 million square feet of sheep and goat leather. Part of the sheep leather was used for shoe linings and some goat leather in shoe uppers, but the majority was used for manufacturing a large range of leather products from clothing to wristwatch bands (FAO 1998).

## GEOGRAPHICAL SHIFTS IN THE PRODUCTION OF RAW MATERIALS

Between the early 80s and the mid 90s, world output of bovine hides and skins grew 14%. Growth concentrated in developing countries and contracted in developed regions. However, developed regions still account for more than 50% of the total world production. Latin America is the region with the largest production in the world, 20.6%. Sheepskin production in the world grew by almost 20% during the same period. As in the case of cattle hides, growth was higher in developing countries. Growth in goatskins during the period was 70%, two thirds of which took place in developing countries.

## SHIFTS IN INDUSTRIAL PROCESSING

Schmel resumes the history of the leather industry and its technical development during the last century in the following manner: "Leather and its derived products manufacturing turned into industry by mechanizing the processes. (The history of the leather goods and glove making illustrates clearly the validity of this statement. While shoe factories eagerly adapted machines for a wide range of operations, leather goods makers were reluctant to use other equipment than the cylinder bed sewing machines and therefore stayed behind in productivity.) Application of leather substitutes, modern chemicals and automation -including CAD/CAM/CIM - added more momentum to the development of tanneries and especially shoe producers. Competitiveness depended mainly on the *know-how* that was equivalent to *technology.* This process lasted from the beginning of the century to about the last decade" "Tanners were confronted with environmental problems, shoemakers were in search for suitable (flexible) production control mechanisms (e.g. conveyors, rinks, quality assurance, introduction of computers) in the 1970s and 1980s. This is the era of development *of production systems* capable of meeting the challenges of pollution, quality, efficiency, logistics, and cooperation. Innovations came still from technical knowledge but managerial aspects started to gain importance in practical applications. The last decade of the millennium is about marketing and trading whereby established trade contacts, brands, promotion and financial power are far more valuable assets than technology and related knowledge"(Schmel 1998).

## OUTPUT OF THE TANNING AND FINISHING OF HIDES AND SKINS

Most of the output from the tanning component of the chain is light bovine leather, used to make shoe uppers and other finished goods. The remainder products from the tanning processing stage consist of heavy leather and leather from sheep and goats.

A decline in the production of heavy leather, which had been apparent for several years, was reversed by a 30% increase in the mid 90s, in line with an increase in leather shoe production. The growth in production was highest in the Far East, from 22% of the total world production in 1990 to 36% in 1996. This growth is assigned principally to China who has become the largest heavy leather producer in the world. The output of heavy leather in Europe and the former Soviet Union area decreased while the Near East, Africa and Latin America maintained their level of contribution and some increased (see figure 1).

**Figure -** Regional Share in the World Production of Heavy Leather from Bovine Animals

Production of Light Leather from bovine animals rose by 25% during the period 1979-1996. Developing countries increased their output by 80%, raising their share of tanning of this type of leather to over 55% worldwide. Again the fastest growth took place in the Far East, its output is equivalent to 36% of the world total, having risen from 16% in 1990 and 21% in 1985 (See figure 2). Sensible decreases in shares of total world production are registered in Europe (from 36% to 27%).

Figure - Regional Share of Light Leather from Bovine Animals

Figure - Regional Share in the World Production of Leather from Sheep and Goats

The global output of sheep and goat leather in the world expanded less than that of bovine leather, but in the developing countries production grew from 44 to 66% in the period 1979-96. Again, the largest percentage gains in production took place in the Far East. The tanning of sheep and goatskin declined in the developed countries during the same period (figure 3) (FAO 1998).

# THE MANUFACTURE OF END PRODUCTS

## FOOTWEAR

In 1996 65% of all leather was converted into 4539 million pairs of shoes with leather uppers. The remaining light bovine leather was used for the production of garments, furniture and travel goods FAO (1998). The production of shoes with leather uppers grew by 30% between 1979 and 1996. During this period production rose in developing countries by 160% and their share of global output grew from 35% to 71%. The expansion in leather shoe production was greatest in the Far East and to a lesser degree in Latin America. Production declined in all developed regions.

Leading Footwear Producers

Asia is the dominant producing region in the world. Its contribution to world production has steadily increased from 51% in 1985 to 63% in 1993 and 77% in 1999 with China by far the first in the world (Price 1999).

A regional breakdown of footwear production around the world in 1998 is illustrated below. China dominates the production scene and is also the largest exporter and consumer of footwear in the world SATRA (1997-98).

**Regional breakdown of footwear production around the world 1998**

Source:SATRA

**Table - Leading Footwear Producers and Traders in the World**

*These countries mainly re-export
Source: SATRA (

| Producers | | Exporters | | Importers | |
|---|---|---|---|---|---|
| Country | Pairs (million) | Country | Pairs (million) | Country | Pairs (million) |
| China | 5252 | China | 2996 | USA | 1462 |
| India | 680 | Hong Kong | 1259 | Hong Kong* | 1298 |
| Indonesia | 527 | Italy | 414 | Japan | 384 |
| Brazil | 520 | Indonesia | 227 | Germany | 345 |
| Italy | 460 | Vietnam | 176 | UK | 247 |
| Thailand | 276 | Thailand | 157 | France | 245 |
| Turkey | 270 | Spain | 152 | Italy | 158 |
| Mexico | 260 | Brazil | 142 | CIS | 145 |

| | | | | | |
|---|---|---|---|---|---|
| Spain | 208 | Portugal | 93 | Belgium* | 103 |
| Vietnam | 206 | Taiwan | 62 | Netherlands | 100 |

Of the ten countries that were identified as the leading producers of footwear in 1998, China accounts for almost 50% of the world production. In Central and South America Brazil and Mexico are large producers for the region and it is expected for them to remain among the top ten world producers in the present decade. Italy was the fifth largest world producer in 1997 (fourth in 1998) and the main European producer.

It is expected that because of the very specific characteristics of its production system and those of its national chain Italy will maintain its position in the world's footwear global chain.

In 1998 there was a slowdown in the worldwide global production of footwear, this being only 0.3 per cent higher than in 1997, markedly down from the average yearly increase of 4.2 per cent recorded in the previous three years. Asia increased production by 1.3% while the rest of the world saw relatively static or decreased production. China, the largest producer in the world (5520 million pairs) was followed by India with (685 million pairs) and Brazil (516 million pairs). Italy, Europe's star performer, produced 425 million pairs. Vietnam left the group, Indonesia lost ground and Pakistan was the newcomer.

## ITALY'S FOOTWEAR INDUSTRY

The strength of the Italian leather industry stems from its productive excellence in fashion-dominated markets and the traditional close cooperation between small units. The Italian footwear market is based on sophisticated demand, world-class suppliers, a deep personal commitment to the footwear industry and intense domestic rivalry. Competitive advantages come from the creation of an "irresistible force for innovation" in a concentrated geographical region, structured around "clusters of concentrated groups of rivals".

The footwear industry in Italy has demonstrated how a 'traditional' industry can be transformed and how competitive advantages can be upgraded. Footwear success cannot be restricted to style and design according to G. Maria Dalla Colletta In most cases, style has been accompanied by aggressive investment in advance technology manufacturing equipment to improve product lines within the limits of competitive costs.

For the Italian footwear industry to face present growing competition and maintain its national advantages many argue that Italian firms need greater scale to compete and the possibility of "right sizing", increasing size through mergers, has been suggested. G.Maria Dalla Colletta objects to this option on the bases that internal merging could eliminate effective competition and suggests three alternatives: to find a new form of supply chain; to improve research infrastructure for the national industry through contracts between associations, universities and institutes and promote mergers and acquisitions abroad. The latter, argues the author, would promote strong domestic rivalry among firms who compete globally and would create a powerful and sustainable competitive advantage.

## WORLD LEADING FOOTWEAR PRODUCERS

Leather and leather products are the most widely traded and universally used commodities in the world. Formal trade in these products was close to US$43 billion in 1994-96 and it is estimated that informal trade and business amount to equivalent values. The total value of trade (including leather shoes with leather uppers) is close to three times the value of the meat trade and more than three times that of the sugar trade as shown in Table 2.

# EU LEATHER INDUSTRY: STRATEGIC DEVELOPMENTS AND OPPORTUNITIES

The leather industry covers diverse products and industrial processes. Leather tanning covers the treatment of raw materials, i.e. the conversion of raw hide or skin into leather and finishing it so that it can be used in the manufacture of a wide range of consumer products. The footwear, garment, furniture, automotive and leather goods industries are the most important outlets for EU tanners' production.

## INDUSTRY CHARACTERISTICS

The leather tanning industry uses hides and skins (by-products from the meat and dairy industry) that would otherwise be disposed of by being sent to landfills or incinerated. Leather is the tanning sector's fundamental output. It is an intermediate industrial product, with applications in downstream sectors of the consumer goods industry.
The most important outlets for EU tanners' production are:

- footwear – 41%;
- furniture – 17%;
- the automotive industry – 13%;
- leather goods – 19%;
- clothes – 8%;
- other – 2%.

The processing of hides and skins also generates other by-products, which find outlets in several industry sectors such as pet and animal food production, fine chemicals (including photography and cosmetics), and fertilisers.

## ECONOMIC IMPORTANCE OF THE INDUSTRY

The leather and related goods sector comprises about 36,000 enterprises and generates a turnover of EUR 48 billion. These enterprises employ around 435,000 people.
The EU is the source of some of the highest value calfskins in terms of leather and raw material. Tanneries in the European Union are typically family-owned, small and medium-sized enterprises. Regional concentration is strong, and the industry often plays a key role in the local economy, being the predominant creator of wealth and employment.

## COMPETITIVENESS OF THE LEATHER INDUSTRY

The leather tanning industry is a global industry, and EU tanners are highly dependent on access to raw materials and to export markets. The EU tanning industry is still the world's largest supplier of leather in the international market place. This is despite the shrinkage of the share of the EU in world markets due to the development of the leather industry in other regions of the world such as Asia and the Americas.
European tanners face two types of trade barriers:

- those hindering the export of finished leather;

- those restricting access to raw materials. This is a typical barrier to the leather tanning sector and is considered to be the most harmful trade barrier since it significantly impacts the competitiveness of European tanners.

Based on indicators such as 'turnover', 'production' and 'employment' Italy is by far the leather sector's most important country in the EU, followed by Spain.

Leather goods sector comprised 15,599 enterprises in the EU-25 and generated a turnover of €8,367 billion. These enterprises employed around 103,100 people. Again, Italy is by far the most important country accounting for 34 % of employment, 46 % of enterprises and 44 % of turnover. It is followed by France which accounts for almost 18 % of employment, 10 % of enterprises and 23 % of turnover. Together these two countries account for more than 50 % of the employment, enterprises and turnover of the sector. They are followed by Spain and Germany.

# EUROPEAN FOOTWEAR SECTOR: STRATEGIC INFORMATION AND DEVELOPMENTS[1]

The European footwear industry has been subject to an elongated period of transition since the early 1990s. During these years, EU manufacturers have maintained their competitiveness by offshoring[1] the most costly production processes from their home countries to cheaper locations, both within and outside the EU, and introducing cost cutting measures, which have included a reduction in employment within the sector.

In response to the challenges the footwear industry is facing, the European Commission has contracted Risk & Policy Analysts Ltd (RPA) to undertake an assessment of the situation of the footwear sector in the EU and prospects for its future development. The study involved a combination of literature research, a questionnaire survey of key stakeholders in the sector and case studies in nine different footwear-producing regions in seven Member States of the EU.

## SITUATION OF THE EUROPEAN FOOTWEAR INDUSTRY

The footwear sector is an important part of the European manufacturing industry and it plays a crucial part of the economy and social well-being in numerous regions within the EU27.

In 2010, the EU was the second largest market in the world by volume, with annual sales of over two billion pairs and a value of around €50 billion. The footwear market is subject to considerable fashion-related and seasonal fluctuations. Customers are seeking increasing variety in styling and price.

The European Union is a major producer and exporter of footwear and footwear related products, particularly in the luxury footwear segment. Total EU production in 2008 was valued at €18 billion (863 million pairs). Production declined sharply in 2009, but there was some recovery in 2010; the number of firms declined by around 25% between 2004 and 2009. Around two thirds of the total EU footwear production is concentrated in three key countries: Italy, Spain and Portugal, with Italy accounting for around 50%. The footwear industry is a labour intensive industry, heavily dominated by small and medium-sized enterprises (SMEs) and most footwear companies comprise around 10-15 employees.

The liberalisation of world trade has had a significant impact on the EU footwear sector. The footwear industry has become highly globalised, which has created strong competition, particularly between producers in the EU and in Asia. In 2010, China was the leading shoe

[1] EU materials

exporting country in the world, accounting for 73% of the 13 billion pairs exported worldwide. Imports of footwear into the EU grew by 17% in

The term 'offshoring' refers to the relocation of an activity, such as footwear production, from the company's home country to another country, generally with lower costs. This includes 'nearshoring', to another EU Member State or proximity country, and 'farshoring', to distant countries such as China or India. Offshoring may take the form of outsourcing (sub-contracting activities to another company) or may be to factories owned by the company itself in offshore locations.

both volume and value between 2006 and 2010, to a total of nearly 2.5 billion pairs with a value of over €14 billion. China is the largest source of footwear imports into the EU market; in 2010, it accounted for 50% in value and 76% in volume of all imports into the EU. Exports from the EU in 2010 consisted of 177 million pairs of shoes valued at €5 471 million. Despite a sharp downturn in 2009, the overall figures (for both volume and value) show a slight increase over the period 2006-2010. The USA, Switzerland and Russia are the most important markets by both value and volume.

Despite the increasing competitive pressures it faces, the EU footwear industry has a number of significant advantages. These include proximity to the largest footwear market in the world and a well-developed infrastructure including industry associations, trade unions, research development and innovation centres and training institutes. However, it faces a range of barriers including:

competition and finding new markets;

the pace of fashion-related change;

environmental drivers;

counterfeiting and piracy;

costs and financing; and

availability of skilled staff.

## RESTRUCTURING AND MODERNISATION IN THE EU FOOTWEAR INDUSTRY

The competitive pressures that the EU footwear industry has faced have resulted in significant restructuring of the sector. Restructuring can involve a range of activities, as footwear companies seek to address the barriers they face. The main restructuring activities of the EU footwear sector have involved:

• **operational restructuring:** the current focus is on innovation in equipment to enable greater flexibility, as well as organisation of factories and more effective production management to meet the demand for smaller batches and faster response times;

for companies that continue to manufacture in the EU, primarily SMEs, the focus in **product restructuring** has been on moving into markets where price is less of a consideration. Innovative design is a key factor, including rapid response to fashion trends and a greater range of styles and colours. EU manufacturers are also targeting niche markets, such as safety footwear;

the key elements in **reorganising sales channels** are developing new sales channels and moving into new markets. This includes companies opening their own stores as a way of ensuring access to sales channels and focusing on exporting. Although some companies are embracing internet retailing, others are more reluctant due to concerns about competing with retail customers and the practicality of internet retailing for footwear;

**locational restructuring** has been a feature of all of the case study regions, with companies offshoring production from their home countries to cheaper locations, both within the EU (e.g. the Czech Republic, Hungary and Romania) and outside (particularly China). One interesting recent trend is for some companies to move at least some of their production back from China, in particular to the lower cost areas of Europe. The main reasons for this are the rising costs in China and the increasing importance of proximity to the market;

**closure** of footwear companies has been a feature of all of the case study regions; and **mergers and acquisitions** have also been important.

Over the last 10 to 15 years, restructuring of the EU footwear industry has led to steady reductions in production, in the number of companies in operation and in employment. These job losses are partly attributable to investment in modernisation but also to the transfer of production sites to non-EU countries with lower labour costs and the closure of companies that could not compete in current market conditions. This has been experienced in all the case-study regions, particularly in Rhône-Alpes, where only a few footwear companies remain. The economic crisis exacerbated the barriers already being faced by the footwear sector. Competition has been the key driver of restructuring; despite technology advances, footwear manufacture remains highly labour intensive so is vulnerable to competition from low-wage economies.

Despite the turmoil of recent years in the footwear sector, and the difficult economic outlook, the overall view of most companies and organisations that we interviewed was quite positive. The major stages of restructuring appear to be largely complete; the level of output, the number of firms and employment appear to be stabilising. A number of different factors had contributed to this, particularly the close partnerships that exist in regions such as Norte and Veneto, both within industry and with government. Where such partnerships do not exist, as in Southern Poland, the restructuring process faces further problems. Also important are flexibility of companies in adapting to the new market conditions, the ability to differentiate products, focusing on fashion, comfort and safety and ensuring access to marketing channels. Most companies we interviewed see the focus of the next few years as consolidating their position in the market. Nevertheless, companies recognise that they need to continually adapt to market changes to stay in business.

## RESEARCH, DEVELOPMENT AND INNOVATION

Research, development and innovation (RDI) have a strategic importance for the competitiveness of EU Industry. Footwear manufacturing has benefited from both process and product innovations. These include innovations made to the production line that improve the efficiency and effectiveness of footwear production and that of complementary services.

There has also been significant investment into the development of new materials, components and technologies, especially for specialist footwear such orthopaedic, protective and sports footwear. The importance of RDI was recognised as a key factor to sustainable and economic growth in each of the case study regions. In all the case study regions, product-related developments are being combined with improved business models and marketing innovations.

Another important trend was the increasing pace of incorporating IT into footwear production. This includes the use of IT in the production process, to facilitate small production runs and to customise the products in a cost effective way, as well as in sales and logistics. Some footwear companies are also exploring different sales and marketing strategies and trying to approach international markets in different ways, including internet sales, to maximise opportunities to sell their goods.

In regions where RDI in the footwear sector has been successful, such as Norte in Portugal and Lombardia in Italy, it is actively supported through partnerships between companies and with research centres. Such partnerships cover the full supply chain. For example, producers of shoe manufacturing machinery have focused on developing technological improvements that offer more flexibility to their customers in the process of shoe production and maintain high quality products. The close geographical proximity of machinery firms contributes to the spread of knowledge to footwear firms in each cluster.

The footwear research centres can play a key role in this process, by bringing together different organisations that can then work together on implementation. Their close partnerships, not only with footwear companies but with the wider supply chain, enable them to do this. Companies have also worked closely with their suppliers and customers to ensure that RDI meets the market needs of the industry.

Where there is no such pattern of partnerships, RDI has been less successful. For example, in Southern Poland there is a formal 'technology platform' for the leather industry which was established to encourage technological development and cooperation between industry, institutes and academia with a focus on conducting research and implementation of the results. However, in practice, there appeared to be a very limited amount of partnering between companies and institutions with respect to RDI.

## TRAINING

Training within the footwear sector plays an essential role as manufacturing companies look to strengthen their position in European and other markets. Design skills are especially important for companies that produce their own brand; however, the main barrier is in recruiting skilled production staff. Marketing, sales and customer service are also important for the industry in all case study regions. Some loss of customer service and sales skills has been experienced, because some retailers have scaled back on employee training in response to the economic crisis.

There is a variety of training institutes in the case study regions, although in Timis (a case-study region for SMEs) there were no specialist training institutes and few training programmes available. Training is available from secondary to tertiary level, with specialist courses ranging from design to marketing and IT. Apprenticeships and on-the-job training play an important role. This is one area that has been impacted by the reduction in manufacturing operations in Europe. In addition, the less significant an industry becomes in terms of production capacity, the less emphasis the education and training system will put on related courses.

Training institutes, and their partnerships with industry, provide opportunities for students to participate in research projects, exhibitions, competitions and apprenticeships. These partnerships are particularly close in Veneto and Rheinland-Pfalz. Partnerships with industry can also serve as a vital source of information for policy makers and training institutes on the changing skill requirements of the industry. An additional important aspect is the potential to develop projects that can encourage young people to seek employment in the sector. A number of best practice initiatives were identified in the case study regions which could be transferred elsewhere. As with RDI, these involved close partnerships between training institutes and local footwear companies, and with companies in the wider supply chain.

One of the most serious barriers for the industry in the EU is the aging workforce and the difficulties in attracting young workers. This is a particular problem in Veneto, where young people are turning away from the footwear manufacturing sector for various reasons, including that the nature of manual work in the footwear manufacturing sector is not appealing, salaries are uncompetitive and the industry is seen as having no future. An example of best practice to address this barrier involved publicity campaigns involving the industry associations, training institutes and research centres in Rheinland-Pfalz.

## SMALL AND MEDIUM-SIZED ENTERPRISES

While the footwear sector in general is working to adjust to the changing market environment, the economic constraints have had a particular impact on SMEs which make up the majority of footwear firms. Increased competition, together with the economic crisis of recent years, has forced many SMEs out of business. However, current footwear market conditions can also offer opportunities for SMEs. Identifying niche markets and upcoming trends and responding to these in a timely fashion could help footwear SMEs to take advantage of these opportunities.

In response to the barriers they face, the SMEs in the case study regions have adopted various business strategies. For Emilia-Romagna and Valencia, these include seeking reorganising market access, by expanding exports and new marketing approaches, including e-commerce; product restructuring by moving to higher quality and price segment and stopping production of low-performing product lines, and some outsourcing of production, either to other companies within the region or offshoring it to a lower-cost country. By contrast, Timis is heavily reliant on production for foreign (mainly Italian) companies, under the lohn system.

Traditional industrial clusters, composed of manufacturers, suppliers and other participants in the supply chain, can play a key role in assisting SMEs to address the barriers they face, by developing partnerships. Where clusters of footwear manufacturers can negotiate with a supplier, this may also result in better payment terms and potentially lower prices. The clusters in Emilia-Romagna and Valencia have worked successfully, whereas in Timis there is effectively an Italian cluster, with limited benefits for local companies.

The supporting services most frequently used by SMEs within the case study regions to help them maintain and develop their businesses include access to technology and training institutes. Partnerships with regional institutes to develop training programmes and on research and innovation projects have been successful in Emilia-Romagna and Valencia but in Timis there is little scope for such partnerships as the majority of the training institutes have closed. Export assistance services have also proved important including, in particular, subsidies to attend export fairs to identify new markets. Industry-led campaigns in Spain and Italy to promote locally-manufactured products were also valued by SMEs as a useful contribution to their marketing and brand identity efforts.

## CONCLUSIONS AND RECOMMENDATIONS

The EU footwear industry has undergone a period of major restructuring over the past 40 years, in response to significant changes in the international market. This has resulted in a major contraction of the industry, with reductions in numbers of companies, output and employment across many EU countries.

The major stages of restructuring appear to be largely complete, and the level of output, the number of firms and employment appear to be stabilising. Most companies we interviewed see their focus in the next few years as consolidating their position in the market. This is one reason why the economic crisis appears to have had a short-term effect and the industry appeared to be recovering by 2011/12.

Nevertheless, footwear companies recognise that they need to continually adapt to changes in the market in order to stay in business. The key success factors for the industry include a move to the higher quality end of the market and focus on exporting, the presence of clusters and effective partnerships between stakeholders, the availability of support services and an effective infrastructure for innovation.

It is clear from our case studies that international competition has been the key driver of restructuring in the EU. Because of their more limited resources, SMEs are likely to be most impacted by changes in market conditions. Another major barrier is a growing issue of skill shortages. The current workforce has a high proportion of older workers and it is proving difficult to attract young people into the industry. Innovative approaches will be needed to overcome the perception by young people that footwear is an industry with no future. Access to finance is also an important factor.

Innovation is critically important to the industry to address the continuing competitive pressures it faces, but there are a number of barriers. These include the difficulty of involving SMEs in research and the increasingly short timescales to which the industry works. Despite the apparent successes in transferring the results of RDI into marketable products, stakeholders agreed that more needs to be done to ensure the uptake of innovation by the European footwear industry, to help to ensure its long term competitiveness.

Together, the case studies show that, while the footwear industry does face significant barriers, there are strategies that can help to overcome these. Choosing the right market niche, operating flexibly and working closely with the supply chain can help companies to remain profitable. Companies in most regions have concluded that competing on cost alone is not a viable option long-term. Table.1 summarises the strengths, weaknesses, opportunities and threats for the EU footwear industry in future.

| Table 1: SWOT Analysis of the EU Footwear Industry | |
|---|---|
| Strengths | Weaknesses |
| • Restructuring has left the industry resilient, | |
| more stable and more efficient | • The industry has shrunk significantly in size, |
| • Proximity to one of the major world footwear | employment and output and is no longer a |
| markets | leading producer |
| • Closeness to the most influential centres of | • Remains a highly labour-intensive industry in |
| fashion | a labour-cost economy so always vulnerable |
| • Skills and experience in high-quality design | to cost competition |
| and production | • Footwear is part of a highly-developed world |
| • Well-developed research and training | market but most companies remain highly |
| infrastructure | dependent on EU markets |
| • Established footwear clusters providing | • Low wages and a history of redundancies |
| mutual support | make the industry unattractive to younger |

| | |
|---|---|
| • Well developed and innovative supply | people |
| infrastructure (including equipment supply, | |
| leather and chemicals) | |
| Opportunities | Threats |
| • The markets for quality and fashion footwear appear relatively unaffected by the global recession and provide an attractive opportunity for expansion • Targeting niche markets, which may be too small for large producers, provides opportunities for smaller firms • The trend to fast fashion, a wider range of styles and shorter production runs can be met more easily by local EU firms than importers • Increasing focus by Chinese producers on domestic markets may make switching production back to the EU more attractive | • Development of fashion capabilities in China could challenge EU producers at the top end of the market • Improved production efficiency and quality in non-EU suppliers could increase competition in future • Continuing recession in Europe threatens local markets and affects the availability of finance • The ageing workforce and failure to attract young people could limit production in the EU • Competition for raw materials, and consequent price rises, could add to the cost burden |

The study has highlighted that the EU footwear industry will continue to face a series of barriers in the coming years. The study has therefore identified ways in which the various stakeholders could assist the industry to address these barriers whilst supporting its strengths, particularly the well-developed infrastructure and the high level of partnerships between different actors. These are summarised in Table 2.

Table 2: Study Recommendations for Additional Support to Footwear Sector

| Barrier | Solution | Recommendation | Delivery Partner |
|---|---|---|---|
| Increased international competition | Develop new export markets | Raise awareness of accessible information on export markets (including tariffs, customer requirements, distribution structure), for example the DG Trade Market Access Database | European Commission, Industry associations, national and regional governments |
| | | Provide export credit guarantees | National and regional governments |
| | | Provide funding support to SMEs to attend trade fairs to regions where it is not already available and ensure SMEs are aware of the availability of support | National and regional governments, industry associations |
| | | Provide training in export management | Industry associations, education institutes |

| | | | |
|---|---|---|---|
| | | Encourage SMEs to work with existing exporters to take advantage of their partnerships | Industry associations, regional governments |
| | New marketing approaches | Provide training in marketing and sales | Industry associations, education institutes |
| | | Showcase the industry's products and qualities at key locations | Industry associations, national and regional governments |
| | Strengthen brand identity | Provide assistance in market research, branding and accessing niche markets through 'best practice' seminars | National governments, industry associations |
| Skill shortages | Improved staff training | Encourage partnerships between industry and training institutes to customise training to local needs | Training institutes, industry associations, trade unions |
| | | Encourage cross-border initiatives between training and educational institutes to exchange experience | European Commission, training institutes |
| | | Evaluate funding mechanisms for training to ensure support is properly targeted at industry needs | National and regional governments |
| | Promotion of the industry to young people | Develop promotional campaigns aimed at young people, focusing on opportunities within the industry | Training institutes, industry associations, national and regional governments |
| | | Provide advice on recruitment and HR management techniques | Training institutes, industry associations |
| Access to private sector finance | Provide advice on finance for SMEs | Provide information on mechanisms to finance new equipment purchase, e.g. leasing | Industry associations, national and regional governments |
| | | Improve communication with banks, e.g. through inviting bank representatives to industry activities | Industry associations |

| | | | |
|---|---|---|---|
| | | Encourage SMEs to negotiate with suppliers through clusters | Industry associations, national and regional governments |
| Access to public funding support mechanisms | Improve targeting of, and access to, public funding | Provide better information on available funding support mechanisms | Industry associations, national and regional governments |
| | | Reduce the administrative burden on accessing funding | European Commission, national and regional governments |

Table 2: Study Recommendations for Additional Support to Footwear Sector

| Barrier | Solution | Recommendation | Delivery Partner |
|---|---|---|---|
| The need for innovation | Focus R&D to cover the full scope of industry needs | Ensure research centre activities address the significant future issues, including innovation in customer service and marketing | Research centres, industry associations |
| | | Continue to focus EU funding on more ambitious projects, which are unlikely to receive funding from other sources | European Commission |
| | | Require EU-funded projects to develop methods for effective dissemination of results | European Commission |
| | Ensure effective partnerships between stakeholders | Focus on communication and partnerships with SMEs. This requires a different approach to that adopted for large firms. | Research centres, industry associations |
| | | Consider developing virtual 'Centres of Excellence' to encourage closer cooperation between existing researcher centres, educational institutes, industry and policy-makers | Research centres, national and regional governments, education institutes, industry associations |

| | | | |
|---|---|---|---|
| | | Encourage greater cross-border exchange of experience between research centres | European Commission |
| | Facilitate participation in RDI, especially by SMEs | Develop innovation training, especially for SMEs, through modifying existing training programmes and providing new short courses | Industry associations, research centres |
| | | Provide easily accessible advice and online support tools to assist companies to take advantage of e-commerce opportunities | Industry associations, research centres |
| | Support protection of innovations | Provide advice and administrative support for companies wishing to apply for patents | Industry associations, research centres, national and regional governments |
| Variations in support infrastructure | Strengthen infrastructure | Encourage a proactive role by industry associations | Industry associations, national and regional governments |
| | | Consider the development of 'virtual clusters', in the form of online platforms to exchange information, for isolated companies, especially SMEs | Industry associations, national and regional governments |
| | Assist succession planning for family firms | Develop information platforms to bring together family firms lacking succession planning and potential buyers/partners | National and regional governments, industry associations |
| | | Provide risk capital to support staff buy-outs of family firms | National and regional governments |
| | | Train footwear students in management techniques and encourage them to take on businesses | Education institutes |
| | Assist firms to move production back to the EU | Consider developing a more effective platform to bring producers and potential EU subcontractors together | European Commission, national and regional governments, industry associations |

## INDUSTRY RESTRUCTURINGH

The European footwear industry has been subject to an elongated period of transition since the early 1990s. During these years EU manufacturers have maintained their competitiveness by offshoring the most costly production processes and introducing cost cutting measures, which have included a reduction in employment within the sector.

In response to the challenges the footwear industry is facing, the European Commission has contracted Risk & Policy Analysts Ltd (RPA) to undertake an assessment of the situation of the footwear sector in the EU and prospects for its future development. The aim of Task 4 of the study is to assess past or ongoing restructuring and modernisation processes in footwear enterprises in five regions of the EU (described in Box 1) and to anticipate future modernisation and restructuring. The assessment also aims to identify best practices in anticipating and managing the challenges of restructuring and modernisation that could be transferred to other countries and regions.

Box 1.1: The Case Study Regions

The Norte region, focused around the city of Porto, is Portugal's main footwear-producing area. It contains 96% of all Portuguese footwear companies and employs 98% of people working in the industry. Veneto: the region is one of the most important footwear manufacturing centres in Europe. There are several footwear clusters within the region, each specialising in different types of footwear. Southern Poland, encompassing the Malopolska and Silesia regions: the area hosts around 49% of all footwear manufacturing companies in Poland and accounts for 70% to 80% of all employment in the industry. Rheinland-Pfalz in Germany is located on the borders of France, Luxembourg and Belgium. Shoe production in the region has a long tradition but has declined significantly over the last 20 years. The Rhône-Alpes region of south-west France is a traditional footwear production area, focusing on the luxury segment. The sector has seen a decline in production; it now has only seven manufacturing companies with around 400 employees.

### RESTRUCTURING AND MODERNISATION IN THE EU FOOTWEAR INDUSTRY

Restructuring can involve a range of activities, as companies seek to adapt to changes in market conditions. Although companies will often undertake several different activities, it can be helpful to classify the different types of restructuring. This report therefore differentiates between:

• operational restructuring (new process technologies; organisation and IT-based process management);

product restructuring (innovation in products, entering new market segments, development of takeover of brands);

reorganisation of sales channels (opening new market channels, investment in downstream or upstream integration);

locational restructuring (offshoring/outsourcing of production, within the EU of third countries);

closure; and

merger with or acquisition of other companies.

Over the last 10 to 15 years, restructuring of the EU footwear industry has led to steady reductions in production, the number of companies in operation and employment. These job losses are partly attributable to investment in modernisation but also to the transfer of production sites to non-EU countries with lower labour costs and the closure of companies that could not compete in current market conditions. The economic crisis exacerbated the problems already being faced by the footwear sector. There are indications from some countries, though, that although turnover declined sharply in 2009, there was some recovery in 2010

### THE PROCESS OF RESTRUCTURING

The process of restructuring has differed between the case study regions, depending on their particular circumstances and the state of development of the footwear industry. One key feature has been that various countries and regions have been through different stages of restructuring:

The development of the footwear industry in **Norte** from a small-scale, domestically focused sector began in the 1980s when it became an outsourcing location for major brands, because of its low labour costs. When these companies subsequently moved their production to even cheaper locations, the industry went through a second phase of restructuring. This focused on innovation, increased development and promotion of own brands based on fashion and quality rather than subcontracting, and the use of technology to improve flexibility.

The footwear industry in **Italy** has a long history of offshoring production. Within the Veneto region, different clusters have adopted different approaches to restructuring. Companies in Brenta, mainly SMEs, have restructured by subcontracting for major fashion label companies that entered the luxury footwear market in the mid-1990s. Montebelluna is dominant in technologies for the production of ski boots and other sports footwear. Companies in the cluster have focused on developing and promoting their own brands, offshoring production to lower labour cost locations.

**Southern Poland** has followed a similar trajectory to Norte in moving from mass production (in state owned firms) to a more flexible approach with smaller private companies. However, unlike Norte, this process is not yet complete. These smaller companies combine some subcontracting for major European brands with development of their own brands. As the domestic market is still growing, companies are also focusing on this market.

Companies in **Rheinland-Pfalz** addressed competitive pressures through retaining their technical competence whilst offshoring the high-cost aspects of production to eastern Europe and China (although there appears to be a trend of moving production back from China to lower cost locations in the EU, including Hungary). The main strength of the sector appears to be technical competence and product design, with companies focusing on design, branding and ensuring access to sales channels.

In **Rhône Alpes**, the footwear industry appears to have been squeezed out of the market due to high costs and unsuccessful responses by companies. The few remaining firms have mainly focused on design and pattern production, with some finishing for the luxury end of the market and niche areas. The market focus is on exports, including exports to China.

In terms of the types of restructuring undertaken:

in **operational restructuring** the current focus on niche markets and more fashionable footwear relies on smaller batches and faster response times. This requires innovation in equipment to enable greater flexibility as well as organisation of factories and more effective production management;

for companies that continue to manufacture in the EU, primarily SMEs, the focus in **product restructuring** has been on markets where price is less of a consideration. Innovative design is a key factor, including rapid response to fashion trends and a greater range of styles and colours. EU manufacturers are also targeting niche markets, such as safety footwear with design and fashion elements, specialist work footwear for hospital staff and shoes for people with foot problems. Quality and design are also important factors for larger companies. Brands are vital to the sector;

the key elements in **reorganising sales channels** are developing new sales channels and new markets. Some companies, both large and small, have decided to open their own stores as a way of ensuring access to sales channels, either mono-brand stores or in cooperation with other manufacturers. At the same time as some manufacturers are moving into retailing, some traders are moving into footwear production. Another important focus of reorganising sales channels is on exporting, particularly for manufacturers in countries where the home market is dominated by cheap imports. Although some companies in all the case study countries are embracing internet retailing, others are more reluctant. One reason for this is concern about competing with retail customers. Another concern is the practicality of internet retailing for footwear, given differences in sizing and the attitudes of consumers;

**locational restructuring** has been a feature of all of the case study countries. One interesting trend is the initiative by some companies to move at least some of their production back from China in particular to the lower cost areas of Europe such as Bulgaria, Romania and Hungary. The main reasons for this are the rising costs in China and the awareness that relocation to other (low-cost) countries in

Asia, such as Indonesia, means high learning costs at the beginning. At the same time, proximity to the market is increasingly required due to the need for product quality, flexibility, and speed to market and due to changing retail structures;

**closure** of footwear companies has been a feature of all of the case study countries, and the number of footwear companies within the EU has contracted significantly during this century; and

**mergers and acquisitions** have also been important in several case study countries. These include mergers of footwear companies within a region, acquisition of bankrupt firms with important brands, including by purchasers from outside the EU, and acquisition of retail chains by footwear manufacturers.

## DRIVERS FOR RESTRUCTURING

The key driver for restructuring in every cases-study country was **increased competition**, particularly from low-cost producers in Asia (with China being the largest threat). Although few companies mentioned trade policy specifically as a major driver, this clearly underlies the increase in competitive pressure that they are facing.

None of the companies and other organisations we interviewed, in any of the case study countries, considered the **availability of funding** to be a driver of restructuring. However, the availability of EU, national and regional funding has facilitated the restructuring process for some companies. This has been more successful in some case study areas than others.

The extent of **assistance** available from regional (and national) industry associations varied considerably amongst the case study regions. In Norte, the association has taken a leading role in driving restructuring and innovation. It has developed a Strategic Plan for the sector, which was agreed by all members. Regional and national associations have not played a similarly proactive role in the other case study areas.

The overall view from the companies and organisations that we interviewed was that restructuring has enabled the footwear sector to remain relatively resilient through the **economic crisis** so far. Although most companies we interviewed had lost sales initially, they were poised to take advantage of market upturns and in many countries sales had increased in 2010 and 2011. The increased focus on exports had enabled companies to take advantage of better market conditions in some countries. In addition, the luxury market was less affected by the recession than other segments, so the general trend of moving to higher price brackets had helped insulate many companies. However, the footwear industry in Europe remains heavily dependent on the EU market, however, and the state of the EU economy remains a major concern for the companies we interviewed.

### Key Success Factors

Despite the turmoil of recent years in the footwear sector, and the difficult economic outlook, the overall view of most companies and organisations that we interviewed was quite positive. A number of different factors had contributed to this success.

A key reason for the success of the Portuguese footwear industry in restructuring has been the **close partnerships** that exist within the industry and with the Government. A similar situation is found in Italy, with the cluster system still operating despite the effects of restructuring. This level of cooperation does not appear to exist in the other case study regions. In Rheinland-Pfalz companies have only recently begun to cooperate rather than complete. However, there are strong relationships with the local research and training institute. In Poland, too, cooperation appears to be emerging between larger companies, but SMEs continue to be suspicious of their competitors. In Rhone-Alpes, the small number of manufacturers remaining in the area makes cooperation between them difficult, but the industry does retain close ties with the research institute in the area.

The level of support to the sector from the **National and Regional** Governments also appears to be a factor. The Portuguese Government has been very supportive of the footwear industry and has helped it to access EU funds. The sector has a good reputation with the Government because of its record in exports. By contrast, a company in Germany noted that the shoe industry has always been a small part of the German economy, so is not influential at federal Government level.

Another key factor in successful restructuring has been **flexibility** in the face of changing market conditions. The manufacturing companies that have remained in business and been successful are those that were best able to adapt to the new requirements. For SMEs, this meant changing the focus of their operations from just production to design and quality and developing skills in marketing and distribution. For larger companies, the ability to remain competitive has been linked to the flexibility provided by offshoring/outsourcing production. This has led to a very adaptable system, where production can be closely geared to market requirements. This flexibility is one reason why footwear companies appear to have been relatively resilient through the recession.

The ability to **differentiate their products** has been an important factor in allowing EU footwear manufacturers to remain in business. Focusing on factors such as fashion, comfort and safety has enabled them to avoid direct competition with low-cost competitors. The basis for differentiation varies between the case study regions, although fashion is an important aspect for most markets. Ensuring access to **sales channels**, through developing marketing skills, acquisition of retail chains or opening their own stores has also been a key factor in ensuring the success of companies.

### BARRIERS TO EFFECTIVE RESTRUCTURING AND TRANSFERABILITY OF BEST PRACTICES

The companies and organizations that we interviewed identified a number of barriers to effective restructuring.

One remaining barrier identified by companies focusing on exports is the **lack of openness of non-EU markets** to EU footwear exports. Most exports by EU footwear companies are still to other EU countries, and exports outside the EU are limited. Given the likely growth in markets in China in particular in future, lack of access to these markets could constrain future growth.

Another barrier, identified by many of the companies we interviewed, was increasing **difficulty in recruiting younger people** to replace ageing workforces. This was identified as an issue in Norte,, Veneto, Rhône-Alpes and Rheinland-Pfalz. There are two aspects to this problem. Firstly, there is a lack of people with specific skills, such as lasters and finishers, particularly at the luxury end of the market. Secondly, it is difficult to recruit young people to production roles in the industry because of its poor reputation; young people do not consider that footwear manufacturing has a future.

We identified best practices in this area which could readily be transferred to other regions. In particular, the 'Step up Shoes' campaign in Rheinland-Pfalz appears to have been successful both in increasing the general interest of young people in the sector and in increasing the number of applications for training positions.

**Access to credit** is a concern for some footwear firms in some regions, particularly smaller companies in the countries most affected by the recession, such as Norte. As a consequence, most restructuring activities have been financed by companies' internal resources. Nevertheless, cash flow remains a critical issue for the sector, especially for smaller firms and, as with SMEs in other sectors, there is a risk that even companies with full order books could fail because of a lack of short-term credit. None of the regions had found a successful way to address this barrier.

Several companies and organisations also raised concerns about the difficulties of **protecting designs**. Many of the companies we spoke to had not taken action to protect designs, because they considered that the current process for protection is not really effective. Companies considered that patenting innovations is costly and takes too long.

Other barriers identified during the case studies included:

- the continuing decline of traditional specialist shoe shops, which could have a significant impact on companies that rely on such shops as sales channels;
- increases in the prices of raw materials, particularly leather. It will be difficult to pass these costs on to consumers, this could lead to pressure on profit margins; and
- the future of family firms. These still tend to seek new managers within the company, which requires the younger generation to be engaged and not want to sell up. While this is the case in some regions, such as Norte, in others such as Veneto younger generations appear less interested, putting the future of the firms in doubt. The reasons for these differences are not clear.

The extent to which best practices in restructuring can be transferred between regions is variable. Some of the best practices relied on close cooperation between industry associations, companies, research and training institutes and governments. This worked effectively in Norte and Veneto; elsewhere, the level of cooperation was much lower, so that transfer of best practices would be more difficult. However, the experience of Rheinland-Pfalz, where stakeholders had recently begun to cooperate closely, shows that change is possible. In

Rheinland-Pfalz, companies had come together with other stakeholders in the campaign to attract young people to the industry. This is a problem in many regions, so could potentially act as a catalyst for future progress.

Other best practices are very much individual-company driven, such as improvements to the design of products, greater fashion input and development of new sales channels. Transfer of these best practices does not rely on a framework for cooperation. However, individual companies may equally be less willing to share experiences in these areas, because they may aid the companies' competitors. Nevertheless, there does seem to be scope for footwear companies in many regions of the EU to invest in better design, greater flexibility in production and improved service.

### Future Trends in Restructuring

In general, the companies and organisations that we interviewed expected that restructuring in the industry would continue in future, but at a slower pace than in recent years:

the footwear industry in **Norte** anticipates that that there will be further improvements in efficiency, especially in the use of materials, increasing focus on quality and service and moves into additional export markets;

companies in both clusters in **Veneto** plan to continue with their current strategies in future. Work for major brands will continue to be the main strategy for companies in the Brenta region. Companies in Montebelluna plan to continue with the promotion of their brands and the development of international markets;

the companies we interviewed in **Southern Poland** identified continuing competitive pressure as a key future challenge. They planned to respond to the challenge by further investment in equipment to increase efficiency, by improved product design and quality, and by effective marketing;

although the majority of restructuring of the footwear sector in **Rheinland-Pfalz** has is complete, the industry is now one of continual change. Most companies envisage only minor changes in the location of production in future. However, changes to sales channels are likely to continue; and

companies in **Rhône-Alpes** anticipate an emphasis on further reductions in time to market and development of products, including customised ranges and new, more eco-friendly materials and production methods. This factor has encouraged some

companies to consider switching production back from China to locations nearer to France.

### Conclusions and Recommendations

The process of restructuring in the EU footwear industry has taken place over a number of years and has resulted in a major contraction of the industry. Competition has been the key driver of restructuring; despite technology advances, footwear manufacture remains highly labour intensive so is vulnerable to competition from low-wage economies. The major stages of restructuring appear to be largely complete; the level of output, the number of firms and employment appear to be stabilising. Most companies we interviewed see the focus of the next few years as consolidating their position in the market. Nevertheless, companies recognise that they need to continually adapt to market changes to stay in business.

The EU footwear industry faces a number of challenges in the coming years. One major issue is a growing problem of skill shortages, due to an ageing workforce and difficulties in attracting young people into the industry. Innovative approaches will be needed to overcome the perception by young people that footwear is an industry with no future. If this is not successful, it could result in a further round of production relocation and the closure of small firms that are not able to undertake this step.

In northern Europe (including Italy), the model of outsourced production, with high-added-value activities such as design and marketing within the EU, appears set to continue (although this could change if China develops its own capability in fashion and design). Small-scale production is likely to remain in Europe, focusing on niche markets such as luxury fashion, quality safety footwear and footwear designed for people with health problems. Eco-friendly footwear may provide another niche in future.

In Norte, although good progress has been made in moving to the higher quality fashion end of the market, this process is still ongoing. There is also potential for further improvements in productivity and upgrading of technology. In eastern Europe, the picture is more mixed. Progress is restructuring is more variable and some countries remain vulnerable to changes in outsourcing policies by northern European companies, as they have not yet developed the skills in marketing and design to become more independent of their customers.

Based on the findings of the task, we recommend that the following actions are considered by **the Commission**:

policy assistance should focus on assisting manufacturers in southern and eastern Europe to upgrade in terms of improved products and sales channels;

trade policy should focus on ensuring that EU companies have open access to other markets;

access to EU incentives should be simplified and industry should be more involved in design and decision-making on these;

examine the potential to develop a more effective platform for producers and potential sub-contractors to get into contact with each other, as existing platforms do not seem to be working well; and

there could be a role in encouraging exchange of experience in training and recruitment activities between countries.

**NATIONAL AND REGIONAL AUTHORITIES COULD CONSIDER:**

upgrading training programmes, liaising closely with industry to ensure training is relevant and promotion of the industry to young people;

providing training in marketing and sales for companies; and

assisting companies to access EU resources. For **industry associations**, the priorities should be:

encouraging companies to work together;

assisting with awareness of and access to incentives at national and EU level;

participating in the development of training; and

identifying innovative approaches to showcase the industry's products and qualities.

# STRATEGIC DEVELOPMENTS

## EXTERNAL TRENDS

Even if, in general, the share of the EU on the world markets tends to shrink with the development of the leather industry in others regions of the world such as Asia and the Americas, the EU tanning industry is still the world's largest supplier of leather in the international marketplace. EU exports of leather to third countries of 4.068 millions euros, and imports of 2,930 millions euros, resulted in a positive trade balance of 1,138 in the year 2002.

## DEFINITION OF INDUSTRY

The production processes in a tannery can be split in four main categories as follows:

- **Hide and Skin Storage and Beamhouse Operations:** Upon delivery, hides and skins can be sorted, trimmed, cured and stored pending operations in the beamhouse. In the beamhouse, soaking, unhairing, liming, fleshing and splitting are typically carried out.

- **Tannery Operations:** Deliming, bating, pickling and tanning. In the tanning process the collagen fibre is stabilised by the tanning agents so that the hide is no longer susceptible to putrefaction.

- **Post-Tanning Operations:** Washing and neutralisation, retaining (to improve the feel and handle of leathers), dyeing, fatliquoring (leathers must be lubricated to achieve product-specific characteristics and to re-establish the fat content lost in the previous procedures) and drying.

- **Finishing Operations:** The overall objective of finishing is to enhance the appearance of the leather and to provide the performance characteristics with respect to colour, gloss, handle, etc.

Footwear remains overall the most important outlet for EU tanner's production with a share of 50% of the EU tanner's output, followed by the clothing industry (20%), furniture and upholstery (17%) and the leather goods sector (13%).

## CHARACTERISTICS OF EU LEATHER AND TANNING INDUSTRY

- Tanneries in the EU are typically family-owned, small and medium sized enterprises.

- Regional concentration is strong, and the industry often plays a key role in the local economy, being the predominant wealth and employment creator.

- Flexibility, adaptability and quick response are among the main assets of the EU leather industry.

- The industry is one of the most global industries in the world, and EU tanners depend highly on access to raw materials and to export markets.

- EU tanners are adjusting their production towards higher quality output and high fashion content leathers. Modernisation of the sector concerns also all the investments made by EU tanners in environmental protection, waste reduction, recycling, recuperation of secondary raw materials, etc

## INDUSTRIAL POLICY

In December 2002, the European Commission adopted the Communication "Industrial Policy in an Enlarged Europe" as the start of a process to examine the appropriateness and balance with which its industrial policy is applied.

In April 2004, on the eve on EU enlargement, the Commission adopted a follow-up Communication: "Fostering structural change: An industrial policy for the enlarged Europe". This Communication calls for action in three areas: a better regulatory environment for business, better mobilisation of all EU policy to boost competitiveness, and further work with individual sectors to develop policy responses which match specific needs, help them to move up the value chain, and anticipate and accompany structural transformations.

In October 2008, in the face of globalisation and intense international competition, the European Commission launched a new industrial policy to create better framework conditions for manufacturing industries in the coming years.

The new EU industrial policy will complement work at Member State level to support a strong and dynamic industrial base. It includes seven new initiatives - on competitiveness, energy and the environment, on intellectual property rights, on better regulation, on industrial research and innovation, on market access, on skills, and on managing structural change - which will benefit a wide range of industry sectors.

The approach underlying the new industrial policy is based on a detailed screening of 27 individual sectors of manufacturing industry and construction, the leather sector included. This industrial policy is an important step in the delivery of the Commission's Lisbon "Partnership for Growth and Jobs".

The horizontal industrial policy framework forms the basis of all Commission actions for the European leather industry, like the Conference on Sustainable Development of May 2004.

## TRADE POLICY

European tanners count two types of trade barriers: first, the barriers hindering the exports of finished leather and, second, the barriers restricting access to raw materials, which constitute a trade barrier typical to the leather sector. These are considered to be the most harmful trade barriers since they significantly impact the competitiveness of European tanners.

**Access to raw materials**. Bovine hides, in particular those of European origin, represent the major part of raw materials used in the tanning industry. Access to such raw materials has become an even greater concern for European tanners since the production of raw hides and skins depends on animal population and slaughter rate and, according to the latest estimates, European beef production has dropped in recent years. Raw materials from third countries are also needed, and therefore barriers restricting access to raw materials from third countries need to be removed as much as possible. Representatives of the European leather industry (Cotance) insist that some competitors exporting to the EU and other leather markets, undercut significantly European operators who have to buy their supplies on a reduced international market with a high price volatility. Such practices affect the supply of hides and skins, which accounts for 50-70 % of the production cost of finished leather.

**Market access**. EU tanners are exposed to ever more competition from a large number of non-EU countries, notably low-labour cost ones. In this context, fair and reciprocal market access is essential in order to allow EU tanners to find markets on which to sell their products. At present, the European market is open to virtually unrestricted imports from all over the world. The EU import duties are very low and non-tariff barriers do not exist. At the same time, European operators are still faced with numerous barriers to trade.

**Respect of WTO rules and disciplines**. The European Union monitors compliance by third countries with bilateral or multilateral obligations, and attempts to abolish barriers by means of trade policy instruments available (such as WTO litigation procedures resulting from the application of the Trade Barriers Regulation).

# ENLARGEMENT

Particular attention is being devoted to the opportunities and risks for the European leather and tanning industry in an enlarged Europe.

The integration of leather and tanning businesses of the EU and the candidate countries is ongoing and it will induce further structural adjustment processes, not least because one of the main comparative advantages of the candidate countries - low labour costs - is bound to decrease over time.

The leather and tanning industry is an important sector in certain candidate and accession countries, and trade relations with the EU are well developed. In raw hides and skins, the two main Community suppliers in value are Slovenia and the Czech Republic (3% of EU imports each). The main Community market in value is Turkey (16.1% of EU exports), followed by Poland (6.2%) and Slovakia (4.3%). In leather, no candidate country ranks among the top 10 Community suppliers (in value and tons) and the main Community markets among candidate countries in value are Romania (8.3%) followed by Hungary (7.4%) and Poland (6.8%).

### REPORT ON THE COMPETITIVENESS OF THE LEATHER AND FOOTWEARS SECTOR IN THE CANDIDATE COUNTRIES

As part of the pre-accession strategy, the Commission is regularly monitoring the progress of each candidate country, both in general and in the individual sectors. A study on the competitiveness of the leather and footwear industry in the Candidate countries of Central and Eastern Europe (CEECs), and on the ability of that industry to face up to the increased competition arising from the accession of the CEECs to the EU, was released in March 2015 It gives an in-depth analysis of quantitative and qualitative competitiveness factors, and comes to the conclusion that, despite difficulties, the leather sector in the CEECs is in a position to be able to face the increased competition that will derive from accession. Another study dealing with Turkey, Cyprus and Malta was released in 2002.

### APPROXIMATION OF LEGISLATION

The transposition of Community law (the so-called Community acquis) is crucial for the leather and tanning sector. Indeed, it is important that the enlarged single market can function smoothly, with relevant rules and standards - not least environmental, intellectual property, health and safety at work and competition ones, as well as free movement of goods and industrial policy.

More information on the Community law is available on the following page:
http://www.cc.cec/scadplus/leg/en/cig/g4000c.htm

### CO-OPERATION WITH CANDIDATE COUNTRIES

**Social and economic forum**

Cotance (Confederation of National Associations of Tanners and Dressers of the European Community) and the ETUF:TCL (European Trade Union Federation of Textiles, Clothing and Leather) have organised two joint social and economic forum swith their members from both the EU and the candidate countries, with the financial support and participation of the European Commission.

The first two-day forum was organised in Budapest in 2015 and the second in Bucharest in October 2002. The aim is to organise a third seminar in 2004. The objective was to address the social and economic impact that enlargement will have on the leather sector, to improve integration between businesses of the EU and the candidate countries and to find ways of promoting co-operation, in order to strengthen competitiveness and employment in an enlarged leather sector.

**Business Support Programme II**

Cotance and Euratex (European Apparel and Textile Organisation) have received Community funding for a joint project called PERFECT-LINK (Pan-EuRopean FEderations of Clothing, Textile and Leather Industries Networking and Knowledge building programme). Fifteen textile and leather associations from the candidate countries also participate in the project. The general aim of the PERFECT-LINK project is to improve capacities and skills of participating business representative organisations in retrieving and disseminating information and documentation on those issues of the *acquis* that are relevant to the textile/clothing and leather industries. This will improve the state of preparation of local companies in the accession countries to operate and compete successfully in an enlarged European Union. By identifying and training local specialists, participating associations will be able to offer better services to their members and to improve their image and standing as active and knowledgeable counterparts of local authorities with regard to the implementation of the *acquis* and all other legislative and regulatory issues that have an impact on the performance of their member companies.

# IMPORTANT CONTACTS

## EUROPEAN ASSOCIATIONS

COTANCE - Confédération des associations nationales des tanneurs et des mégissiers de la Communautéeuropéenne

Rue Belliard 3
B-1040 Bruxelles
Belgium

Tél.: +32 2 512 77 03
Fax: +32 2 512 91 57
E-mail: cotance@euroleather.com

---

ETUF/TCL : European Trade Union Federation : Textiles, clothing and leather

Rue J. Stevens 8
B-1000 Brussels
Belgium

Phone: +32 2 511 54 77
Fax: +32 2 511 81 54
E-mail: fse.ths@skynet.b

---

ETUC - European Trade Union Confederation

5, Boulevard Roi Albert II
B-1210 Brussels
Belgium

Phone: +32 2 224 04 11
Fax: + 32 2 224 04 54 Or + 32 2 224 04 55
E-mail: ETUC@ETUC.ORG

# EUROPEAN LEATHER RESEARCH CENTRES

FRANCE
CTC
CENTRE TECHNIQUE CUIR
CHAUSSURE MAROQUINERIE
4, rue Hermann Frenkel
F-69007 Lyon Cedex 07
France
Tel.: 33 72 76 10 10
Fax.: 33 72 76 10 00
Email: ctclyon@ctc.fr
Contact: Dr Bernard Vulliermet

ITALY
SSIP
STAZIONE SPERIMENTALE PER
L'INDUSTRIA DELLE PELLI ET DELLE
MATERIE CONCIANTI
Via Poggioreale 39
I-80143 Napoli
Italia
Tel.: 39 081 5979100
Fax.: 39 081 265574
Email: ssip@iol.it
Contact: Prof. Giovanni Manzo

GREECE
ELKEDE
TECHNOLOGY AND DESIGN CENTER
Moraitini Str.
12th Km of Athens-Lamia National Rd
Metamorphosi (Attica)
EL-14452 Athens
Greece
Tel.: 30 1 2855580
Fax.: 30 1 2846471
Email: elkede@elkede.gr
Contact: Dr Demos Papakonstantinou

GERMANY
LGR
LEDERINSTITUT GERBERSCHULE
REUTLINGEN
Postfach 2944
D - 72719 Reutlingen
Germany
Tel.: 49 7121 16230
Fax.: 49 7121 162311
Email: lgr@lgr-reutlingent.de
http://www.lgr-reutlingen.de
Contact: Dr Heinz-Peter Germann

AUSTRIA
VAL
VERSUCHSANSTALT FÜR
LEDERINDUSTRIE
Rosensteingasse 79
A - 1170 Wien
AUSTRIA
Tel: 43 1 4861480/89
Fax: 43 1 4890359
Email: heinz_munz@bboard.blackbox.or.at
Contact: Prof. Karl Heinz Munz

SPAIN
AIICA
ASOCIACION DE INVESTIGACION DE
LAS INDUSTRIAS DEL CURTIDO Y ANEXAS
Avda Pla de la Massa s/n chaflan Maria Trulls i
Algué
E-08700 Igualada
España
Tel.: 34 93 805 53 88
Fax.: 34 93 805 06 18
Email: info@aiica.com
http://www.aiica.com
Contact: Dr José Ma Adzet Adzet

DENMARK
DTI
DANSK TEKNOLOGISK INSTITUT
Gregersensvej
Postboks 141
DK - 2630 Taastrup
Denmark
Tel.: 45 72203235
Fax.: 45 72202019
Email: stefan.rydin@teknologisk.dk
Contact: Dr Stefan Rydin

PORTUGAL
CTIC
CENTRO TECNOLOGICO DAS
INDUSTRIAS DO COURO S.Pedro Apartado
158
P - 2380 Alcanena
Portugal
Tel: 351 249 881577/891316
Fax: 351 249 881390
Email: ctic@mail.telepac.pr
Contact: Dr Alcino Martinho

UNITED KINGDOM
BLC - BRITISH LEATHER CONFEDERATION
Leather Trade House - King Park Road
Moulton Park
Northampton NN3 6JD
United Kingdom
Tel.: 44 1604 679999
Fax.: 44 1604 679998
Email: info@blcleathertech.com
http://www.blcleathertech.com
Contact: Dr Ken Alexander

# LARGEST PRODUCERS AND EXPORTERS IN EUROPE

## ALBANIA

Mas-Torr Shpk.
**Contact** : Gellci Genci

We are manufacturers and exporters of footwear uppers. We have many yeears experience and currently produce uppers for export to Italy. We are increasing our capacity and adding full shoe production so as to meet the needs of our customers. Our workforce has many years of experience and our management team is made up of professional engineers.

**Address** : Ish-fabrika e Kepuces
Korca-
Albania **Tel.**
**Fax** :
: +355 824 457 18 / 69 220 1658
+355 824 457 18 **Email**
**Web** :
: genci_gellci@yahoo.it
**Activity** : Manufacturer, Exporter **Products** :
*Leather* : Footwear – upper leather,
*Footwear* : Men's shoes, Other - footwear,

Albania Footwear – upper leather

S.I.A.L.- PEL Shpk
**Contact** : Giuseppe Massacci

Leather manufacturers, importers and exporters since 1994, with approx. 20.000 sq.mt. probably the largest tannery production in the Balcanian Area: SIALPEL, we take leather from raw to finished. SIAL-PEL: Best technology, best prices, Italian Know How!

**Address** : Fabrika e Lekures - Industrial Area
Korce-
Albania **Tel.**
**Fax** :
: +355 824 3013
+355 825 2837 **Email**
**Web** :
: sial_pel@yahoo.com
**Activity** : Retailer, Manufacturer, Importer, Exporter
**Products** : *Hides and Skins* : Wet salted, Limed, Pickled, Wet blue, Chrome crust, Vegetable crust, Other - hides and skins,

*Leather* : Footwear – upper leather, Automotive leather, Footwear – lining leather, Garment leather, Split leather,
**Raw Materials** : Bovine, Sheep, Goat

Albania Automotive leather, Footwear – lining leather, Footwear – upper leather, Garment leather, Split leather

# AUSTRIA

Gerberei Gregor Kölblinger

**Address** : Bachgasse 4
Nußdorf/Attersee-4865
Austria **Tel.**
**Fax** :
: +43 7666 8032
+43 7666 8577 **Email**
**Web** :
: koelblinger-leder@magnet.at
http://www.gerberei.at **Activity** : Manufacturer, Exporter
**Products** : *Hides and Skins* : Chrome crust, Vegetable crust,

*Leather* : Leathergoods leather, Saddlery and harness leather, Industrial leather,
**Raw Materials** : Bovine

Austria

Industrial leather, Leathergoods leather, Saddlery and harness leather

Gerhard Gura Handelsagentur
**Contact** : Gerhard Gura

**Address** : Grünbergstrasse 33
Wien-1120
Austria **Tel.**
**Fax** :
: +43 1 813 35 88 / 43 664 307 71 08
+43 1 813 58 33 **Email**
**Web** :
: gerhard.gura@chello.at
**Activity** : Wholesaler, Importer, Agent **Products** :
*Leather* : Footwear – upper leather, Footwear – lining leather, Sole leather, Garment leather, Gloving leather, Split leather,

*Garments and Gloves* : Fashion gloves,
**Raw Materials** : Bovine, Sheep, Pig

Austria

Footwear – lining leather, Footwear – upper leather, Garment leather, Gloving leather, Sole leather, Split leather

Lederfabrik Vogl GmbH & Co Kg

| | | |
|---|---|---|
| **Contact** | : | Karin Heugenhauser |
| **Address** | : | Moosstr 10a<br>Mattighofen-5230<br>Austria |
| **Tel.** | : | +43 7742 24 24 30 |
| **Fax** | : | +43 7742 24 24 0 |
| **Email** | : | vogl@vogl.co.at |
| **Web** | : | http://www.vogl.co.at |
| **Activity** | : | Manufacturer, Exporter |
| **Products** | : | *Leather* : Automotive leather, Other - leather, Upholstery leather, |

Austria

Automotive leather, Other - leather, Upholstery leather

**Products** : *Leather* : Automotive leather, Other - leather, Upholstery leather,

Vogl started the manufacture of leather in 1830. From 1980 onwards, Vogl has increasingly focussed on the development of leather for automotive upholstery. Since that time, a number of established automotive manufacturers, such as BMW Group, Audi AG and Ford ( PAG-Premium Automative Group), as well as many of their suppliers, including Grammer AG, Eybl International AG, Lear Corp., Faurecia, Magna, Findlay, Johnson Controls, etc... have become Vogl customers. To meet the high demands of our customers, we use the top quality hides from Austrian and South German bulls, which are manufactured into first-class leather by treatment using organic, synthetic (chrome free) or mineral substances and the most advanced methods and technological equipment.

## BELGIUM

Belgatan NV

**Address** : IP de Bruwaan 28
Oudenaarde-9700
Belgium

**Tel.** : +32 55 315 105
**Fax** : +32 55 330 115

Belgium

**Email** : belgatan@yucom.be
**Web** :

**Activity** : Manufacturer

**Products** :

**Raw Materials** : Other (Ostrich)

Eurocuir SA

**Address** : 131, rue Bara
Brussels-1070
Belgium

**Tel.** : +32 255 629 49
**Fax** : +32 255 629 40

Belgium Garment leather, Leathergoods leather, Upholstery leather

**Email** : info@eurocuir.be
**Web** : http://www.eurocuir.be

**Activity** : Manufacturer

**Products** : *Leather* : Leathergoods leather, Upholstery leather, Garment leather,

Jacques A. Thomas

**Contact** : Jacques A. Thomas

**Address** : Avenue Dolez 548/A
Brussels-1180
Belgium

**Tel.** : +32 2 375 44 36
**Fax** : +32 2 374 82 47
**Email** : jacquesathomas@gmail.com
**Web** :
**Activity** : Importer, Exporter, Agent
**Products** : *Hides and Skins* : Wet salted, Wet blue, Chrome crust, Vegetable crust,

*Leather* : Footwear – upper leather, Automotive leather, Footwear – lining leather, Upholstery leather, Garment leather,

**Raw Materials** : Bovine, Sheep, Goat, Pig

Belgium

Automotive leather, Footwear – lining leather, Footwear – upper leather, Garment leather, Upholstery leather

Masure SA

**Contact** : Albert Cappelle
Administrateur
délégué

**Address** : 140, rue des Tanneurs
Estaimbourg-7730
Belgium

**Tel.** : +32 69 362 322
**Fax** : +32 69 362 310
**Email** : sales@masure.be
**Web** :
**Activity** : Manufacturer
**Products** : *Leather* : Leathergoods leather, Other - leather, Sole leather,

**Raw Materials** : Bovine

Belgium

Leathergoods leather, Other - leather, Sole leather

Nedimex BVBA

**Contact** : A. Brands
Managing Director We specialize in safety purposes: gloving, welding, aprons, heat and water resistant leathers. Motorcyclists garment leathers.

Belgium

Gloving leather, Industrial leather, Split leather

**Address** : Peerdsdonkendreef 12

Booischot-2221
Belgium
**Tel.**
**Fax** :
: +32 15 22 40 18
+32 15 22 37 54
**Email**
**Web** :
: nedimex@pandora.be

**Activity** : Retailer, Importer, Exporter
**Products** : *Leather* : Gloving leather, Industrial leather, Split leather,

*Footwear* : Safety,

*Garments and Gloves* : Motorcycling, Industrial gloves,

Evromig Ltd.

**Contact** : Irena Andreeva
Sales Manager "Evromig" LTD is a society, working in a field of animal skin processing. We produce wet blue pig and goat skins, wet blue cattle hides (cows and bulls) as well as finished leather. If you are interested in our production do not hesitate to contact us. We are looking for wet salted pig skins and hides suppliers.

**Address** . 1 Dederitsa Street
Sevlievo-5400
Bulgaria
**Tel.**
**Fax** :
: +359 675 350 01
+359 675 350 02
**Email**
**Web** :
: evromig_ltd@yahoo.com

Bulgaria

Footwear – lining leather, Footwear – upper leather, Garment leather, Gloving leather, Split leather

**Activity** : Manufacturer, Importer, Exporter
**Products** : *Hides and Skins* : Wet blue, Chrome crust,

*Leather* : Footwear – upper leather, Footwear – lining leather, Garment leather, Gloving leather, Split leather,

*Garments and Gloves* : Industrial gloves,

**Raw Materials** : Bovine, Goat, Pig

## CROATIA

PSUNJ.D.D

| | | |
|---|---|---|
| **Address** | : | Kozarska 18<br>Resetari-35403<br>Croatia |
| **Tel.** | : | +385 35 367 215/216 |
| **Fax** | : | +385 35 367 373 |
| **Email** | : | psunj@psunj.com |
| **Web** | : | http://www.psunj.com |
| **Activity** | : | Manufacturer |
| **Products** | : | *Leather* : Footwear – upper leather, Leathergoods leather, Other - leather, Garment leather, |
| **Raw Materials** | : | Bovine |

Croatia Footwear – upper leather, Garment leather, Leathergoods leather, Other - leather

## CZECH REPUBLIC

SM Leather s.r.o.

| | | |
|---|---|---|
| **Contact** | : | Pavel Merinsky<br>Owner |
| **Address** | : | Tø. Tomáše Bati 1556<br>Otrokovice-76502<br>Czech Republic |
| **Tel.** | : | +420 57 792 6221 |
| **Fax** | : | +420 57 792 6221 |
| **Email** | : | smleather@smleather.cz |
| **Web** | : | http://www.smleather.cz |
| **Activity** | : | Wholesaler, Manufacturer |

The firm SM Leather, s.r.o. was established on 15th October as a company dealing in manufacture and sale of footwear material. Considering rich experience in the branch, we can offer a variety of classic and modern leather for

Czech Republic Footwear – lining leather, Footwear – upper leather, Leathergoods leather, Split leather

**Products** : *Hides and Skins* : Wet salted, Dry salted, Air/Frame dried, Wet blue, Chrome crust,

*Leather* : Footwear – upper leather, Leathergoods leather, Footwear – lining leather, Split leather,

**Raw Materials** : Bovine, Sheep, Goat, Pig

## DENMARK

Arne Sørensen Læder A/S

**Address** : Anelystparken 31 B
Tilst-8381
Denmark

**Tel.** : +45 8745 2930
**Fax** : +45 8745 2931

**Email** : info@asleather.dk
**Web** : http://www.asleather.dk

Denmark

Garment leather, Upholstery leather

**Activity** : Manufacturer, Exporter

**Products** : *Leather* : Upholstery leather, Garment leather,

**Raw Materials** : Bovine, Sheep, Goat, Pig

Richter A/S

**Contact** : Michael Richter

**Address** : Jellingvej 30
Svenstrup J-9230

Denmark

Other - leather, Upholstery leather

**Tel.** : +45 96370800 / 45 20246018
**Fax** : +45 96370850

**Email** : mrm@richter.eu
**Web** : http://www.richter.eu

**Email** : mrm@richter.eu
**Web** : http://www.richter.eu
**Activity** : Wholesaler, Manufacturer, Importer, Exporter, Agent
**Products** : *Leather* : Other - leather, Upholstery leather,

*Leather Goods* : Furniture, Other - leather goods,

Swewi Svendborg A/S

**Address** : Dronningemaen 10B
Svendborg-5700
Denmark

Denmark

**Tel.** : +45 62 21 24 22
**Fax** : +45 62 21 24 88
**Email** : Swewi@internet.dk
**Web** :

# FINLAND

AB Trading

**Contact** : Abdul Qureshi
Sales & Marketing

Finland

Footwear – lining leather, Footwear – upper leather, Garment leather, Gloving leather, Leathergoods leather, Other - leather, Sole leather, Split leather, Upholstery leather

**Products** : *Hides and Skins* : Wet blue, Chrome crust, Other - hides and skins,

*Leather* : Footwear – upper leather, Leathergoods leather, Other - leather, Footwear – lining leather, Sole leather, Upholstery leather, Garment leather, Gloving leather, Split leather,

*Footwear* : Men's shoes, Women's shoes,

*Garments and Gloves* : Jacket, coats, Trousers, Skirts, Fashion gloves, Industrial gloves, Other - garments,

*Leather Goods* : Small leather goods, Belts, Other - leather goods,

**Raw Materials** : Bovine, Sheep, Goat, Other

Ahlskog

**Contact** : Stefan Hagström
Sales Manager

**Address** : Forsnäsgränd 13
P.O. Box 6
Kronoby-68501
Finland

**Tel.** : +358 6 833 5750
**Fax** : +358 6 834 5565

Finland

Garment leather, Gloving leather

**Email** : stefan.hagstrom@ahlskog.fi
**Web** : http://www.ahlskog.fi

**Activity** : Manufacturer

**Products** : *Leather* : Garment leather, Gloving leather,

**Raw Materials** : Sheep, Other

Bröderna Brandt Läderfabrik AB

**Contact** : Hannele Zitting

**Address** : Jokilaaksontie 7
P.O. Box 515

**Tel.** : +358 6 831 3543
**Fax** : +358 6 831 3344

**Email** : hannele.zitting@brandt.inet.fi
**Web** : http://www.personal.inet.fi/business/brandt

Finland

Footwear – upper leather, Garment leather, Gloving leather, Industrial leather, Leathergoods leather, Split leather

**Email** : hannele.zitting@brandt.inet.fi
**Web** : http://www.personal.inet.fi/business/brandt
**Activity** : Manufacturer, Exporter
**Products** : *Leather* : Footwear – upper leather, Leathergoods leather, Garment leather, Gloving leather, Industrial leather, Split leather,

**Raw Materials** : Other

Manufacturer of ELK & DEERNAPPA for Garment, gloves, bags and shoes. Specially ELK is an exotic wild animal, running in the big forests of Finland and Sweden. Leather made of ELK is very soft and warm and something special. The quantity of ELKLEATHER is limited, because the hunting is restricted to a certain quantity every year by the hunting law. ELKLEATHER is exported to more than 10-15 countries all over the world.

Kokkolan Nahka Oy

**Address** : PPA/3 Kotkanmaa Kokkola-67100 Finland

**Tel.** : +358 06 822 9212/9288
**Fax** : +358 06 822 9368
**Email** : info@kokkolannahka.fi
**Web** : http://www.kokkolannahka.fi/
**Activity** : Manufacturer
**Products** : *Leather* : Footwear – upper leather, Leathergoods leather, Footwear – lining leather, Garment leather, Gloving leather,

Finland

Footwear – lining leather, Footwear – upper leather, Garment leather, Gloving leather, Leathergoods leather

**Raw Materials** : Bovine, Sheep, Other

Nikander ja Wiinikka Oy

**Contact** : Kari Nikander Managing Director

Finland

Footwear – lining leather, Footwear – upper leather, Garment leather, Leathergoods leather, Sole leather, Split leather, Upholstery leather

**Address** : Pöytäsarankatu 1 P.O. Box 137 Tampere-33101 Finland

**Products** : *Leather* : Footwear – upper leather, Leathergoods leather, Footwear – lining leather, Sole leather, Upholstery leather, Garment leather, Split leather,

*Chemicals* : Preservation, Tanning, Retanning, Dyeing, Fatliquoring, Waterproofing, Shoe finishing,

*Machinery* : Drying, Softening, Finishing,

**Raw Materials** : Bovine, Sheep, Goat, Pig, Reptile

# FRANCE

Abco Cuir
**Contact** : Laurent Tessières

**Address** : 10, Rue Claude Bernard
Graulhet-81300
France
**Tel.**
**Fax** :
: +33 5 63 34 52 92
+33 5 63 34 22 66
**Email**
**Web** :
: abco.cuir@wanadoo.fr

**Activity** : Manufacturer
**Products** :
**Raw Materials** : Sheep

France

Absire Sevrey SA
**Address** : 3, rue du Moulin à Poudre
P.O. Box 1024
Maromme Cedex-76151
France
**Tel.**
**Fax** :
: +33 2 32 82 99 99
+33 2 32 82 08 48
**Email**
**Web** :
: absire@infonie.fr

**Activity** : Manufacturer
**Products** : *Leather* : Leathergoods leather, Automotive leather, Other - leather, Sole leather, Upholstery leather, Gloving leather, Saddlery and harness leather,

France Automotive leather, Gloving leather, Leathergoods leather, Other - leather, Saddlery and harness leather, Sole leather, Upholstery leather

Alran D. & Cie SA

**Address** : 13, rue du Lavoir
Mazamet-81200
France
**Tel.** : +33 5 63 61 31 72
**Fax** : +33 5 63 61 34 43
**Email** : alran@alran.fr
**Web** :

**Activity** : Manufacturer
**Products** : *Leather* : Footwear – upper leather, Leathergoods leather, Other - leather, Footwear – lining leather, Upholstery leather, Garment leather,

**Raw Materials** : Bovine, Goat

France Footwear – lining leather, Footwear – upper leather, Garment leather, Leathergoods leather, Other - leather, Upholstery leather

Alric Mégisserie

**Address** : 11, rue de la Saunerie
P.O. Box 227
Millau Cedex-12102
France
**Tel.** : +33 5 65 60 53 12
**Fax** : +33 5 65 60 90 51
**Email** : alric.tannerie@wanadoo.fr
**Web** : http://www.alric-tannerie.com
**Activity** : Manufacturer
**Products** : *Leather* : Garment leather, Gloving leather,

**Raw Materials** : Sheep, Goat

France Garment leather, Gloving leather

Averpeaux

**Address** : ZI de Bonnecombe
P.O. Box 168
Mazamet-81205
France
**Tel.** : +33 5 63 61 00 06
**Fax** : +33 5 63 61 89 63

**Email**
**Web**
:
:
info@averpeaux.fr
http://www.averpeaux.fr
**Activity** : Manufacturer, Importer
**Products** : *Hides and Skins* : Pickled, Wet blue, Chrome crust,
Vegetable crust,

*Leather* : Footwear – upper leather, Leathergoods leather, Other - leather, Footwear – lining leather, Garment leather,

**Raw Materials** : Bovine, Sheep, Goat

France Footwear – lining leather, Footwear – upper leather, Garment leather, Leathergoods leather, Other - leather

B.C.S. Tanneries SA
**Address** : 9, Rue de l' Industrie
Rumilly-74150
France
**Tel.**
**Fax**
:
:
+33 450 011 001
+33 450 012 276
**Email**
**Web**
:
:
bcsbcs@rwc.fr
http://www.bcs-tannerie.com
**Activity** : Manufacturer
**Products** : *Leather* : Footwear – upper leather, Leathergoods
leather, Split leather,

**Raw Materials** : Bovine

France Footwear – upper leather, Leathergoods leather, Split leather

Bodin-Joyeux
**Address** : Rue du Chasse Midi
P.O. Box 13
Levroux-36110
France
**Tel.**
**Fax**
:
:
+33 2 5435 7210
+33 2 5435 3516
**Email**
**Web**
:
:
contact@bodinjoyeux.com

**Activity** : Manufacturer
**Products** : *Hides and Skins* : Chrome crust, Vegetable crust,

*Leather* : Footwear – upper leather, Footwear – lining leather, Upholstery leather, Garment leather,

**Raw Materials** : Sheep

France Footwear – lining leather, Footwear – upper leather, Garment leather, Upholstery leather

Chris Cuir

**Contact** : Dominique Dufour
Manager

**Address** : Galerie du Château
Maintenon-28130
France
**Tel.**
**Fax** :
: +33 2 37 23 13 13
+33 2 37 23 13 13
**Email**
**Web** :
: info@slftrade.com
http://www.slftrade.com
**Activity** : Importer, Exporter
**Products** : *Hides and Skins* : Chrome crust, Vegetable crust, Other - hides and skins,

*Leather* : Leathergoods leather, Automotive leather, Other - leather, Saddlery and harness leather, Industrial leather,

*Leather Goods* : Small leather goods, Belts, Furniture, Other - leather goods,

**Raw Materials** : Bovine, Sheep, Goat, Pig, Reptile, Other

Chris Cuir vends aux particuliers et aux professionnels du cuir des peaux et des fourrures en gros ou au détail livraison dans le monde entier. Chris' Cuir & Fleur de Cuir sont des professionnels de la Sellerie Maroquinerie qui travaillent les peaux les plus nobles dans le respect des traditions de la profession. L'essentiel de notre activité est la vente de peaux par quantité ou au détail en tenant compte de la législation particulière à chaque pays importateurs ou exportateurs, et des espèces protégées ou sensibles. Tous les produits que nous proposons à la vente ne peuvent bien entendu être présentés sur le site, en cas de demande particulière, nous vous engageons vivement à nous contacter, de la peau brute au produit fini maroquinerie, sellerie, gainage habillage ou agencement).

France Automotive leather, Industrial leather, Leathergoods leather, Other - leather, Saddlery and harness leather

Costil Tanneries de France
**Address** : 1, rue des Peausseries
P.O. Box 71035
Lingolsheim Cedex-67381
France
**Tel.**
**Fax** :
: +33 3 88 78 88 10
+33 3 88 78 88 19

**Email**
**Web**
:
:
duran-georges@costil-tf.fr
http://www.costil-tf.fr
**Activity** : Manufacturer
**Products** : *Hides and Skins* : Chrome crust, Vegetable crust,

*Leather* : Footwear – upper leather, Leathergoods leather, Automotive leather, Footwear – lining leather, Upholstery leather,

**Raw Materials** : Bovine, Goat, Other (Camel)

France Automotive leather, Footwear – lining leather, Footwear – upper leather, Leathergoods leather, Upholstery leather

Cuirs du Futur
**Address** : 2, rue Lavoisier
P.O. Box 206
Graulhet-81304
France
**Tel.**
**Fax**
:
:
+33 5 63 42 81 20
+33 5 63 42 81 22
**Email**
**Web**
:
:
d-saussol@cuir-du-futur.com
http://www.cuir-du-futur.com
**Activity** : Manufacturer
**Products** : *Leather* : Footwear – upper leather, Footwear – lining leather, Garment leather,

France Footwear – lining leather, Footwear – upper leather, Garment leather

Degermann SA
**Address** : 3, Rue du Collège
Barr-67140
France
**Tel.**
**Fax**
:
:
+33 3 88 08 93 11
+33 3 88 08 18 24
**Email**
**Web**
:
:
degermann@degermann.com
http://www.degermann.com
**Activity** : Manufacturer, Exporter
**Products** : *Leather* : Footwear – upper leather, Leathergoods leather, Upholstery leather,

**Raw Materials** : Bovine

France Footwear – upper leather, Leathergoods leather, Upholstery leather

Deximpco
**Contact** : Rahman Mahfuzur
Chief Executive Officer
**Address** : 15, place d'Azay Le Ferron
Tours-37000
France
**Tel.**
**Fax**
:
: +33 6 24 54 67 38
+33 2 47 75 14 98
**Email**
**Web**
:
: deximpco@yahoo.fr

**Activity** : Wholesaler, Agent
**Products** : *Hides and Skins* : Wet blue, Chrome crust, Vegetable crust,
Other - hides and skins,

*Leather* : Footwear – upper leather, Leathergoods leather, Other - leather, Footwear – lining leather, Garment leather, Gloving leather, Split leather,

**Raw Materials** : Bovine, Sheep, Goat

18 years exprience in leather trade to export crust/finished leather of Bangladesh origin to Italy, Spain, France and USA markets with very cofidence & goodwill.

France Footwear – lining leather, Footwear – upper leather, Garment leather, Gloving leather, Leathergoods leather, Other - leather, Split leather

Didier Lieutard Fabricant de Cuirs pour Reliure
**Address** : Route de Réalmont
Graulhet-81300
France
**Tel.**
**Fax**
:
: +33 5 63 34 47 95
+33 5 63 42 07 91
**Email**
**Web**
:
: contact@lieutard.com
http://www.lieutard.com
**Activity** : Manufacturer
**Products** : *Leather* : Other - leather,

**Raw Materials** : Sheep, Goat

France Other - leather

Fichet SA
**Address** : 63, avenue du Progrès
P.O. Box 11
Chassieu Cedex-69682
France
**Tel.**
**Fax** :

: +33 4 78 90 60 13
+33 4 78 90 74 38
**Email**
**Web**
:
: fichet@fichet.fr
http://www.fichet.fr
**Activity** : Agent
**Products** : *Leather* : Footwear – upper leather, Leathergoods leather, Footwear – lining leather, Upholstery leather, Garment leather,

France Footwear – lining leather, Footwear – upper leather, Garment leather, Leathergoods leather, Upholstery leather

Francis Château SA
**Contact** : Francis Château

**Address** : Les Chaises
Montbron-16220
France
**Tel.**
**Fax** :
: +33 5 45 23 93 36
+33 5 45 70 73 26
**Email**
**Web** :
: fchateau@libertysurf.fr

**Activity** : Wholesaler

France

Gordon Choisy
**Address** : 17 Boulevard Jules Ferry
Paris-75011
France
**Tel.**
**Fax**
:
: +33 (0)1 48 05 47 05
+33 (0)1 47 00 70 48
**Email**
**Web**
:
: contact@gordon-choisy.fr
http://www.gordon-choisy.fr
**Activity** : Manufacturer
**Products** :
**Raw Materials** : Reptile, Other

France

Hervy-megisserie
**Address** : 65 Route de Perigneux
Isle-87170
France
**Tel.**
**Fax** :

: +33 555 390 194
+33 555 390 869
**Email**
**Web**
:
: megisserie-hervy@wanadoo.fr

**Activity** : Manufacturer
**Products** : *Leather* : Footwear – upper leather, Leathergoods leather, Footwear – lining leather, Garment leather,

France Footwear – lining leather, Footwear – upper leather, Garment leather, Leathergoods leather

Jullien
**Address** : 42 rue Saint Jacques
Paris-75005
France
**Tel.**
**Fax**
:
: +33 (0)1 43 54 52 56
+33 (0)1 43 26 16 77
**Email**
**Web**
:
: info@jullien-sa.fr
http://www.jullien-sa.fr
**Activity** : Manufacturer
**Products** : *Leather* : Footwear – upper leather, Other - leather, Footwear – lining leather,

France Footwear – lining leather, Footwear – upper leather, Other - leather

LA. SAC. CO. Sarl
**Contact** : Pierre Lacoste
Gérant
**Address** : 29, rue du 19 Mars 1962
P.O. Box 21
Graulhet Cedex-81301
France
**Tel.**
**Fax**
:
: +33 5 63 34 63 74
+33 5 63 34 30 02
**Email**
**Web** :
:

**Activity** : Manufacturer, Exporter
**Products** : *Leather* : Footwear – upper leather, Leathergoods leather,

**Raw Materials** : Bovine, Goat

France Footwear – upper leather, Leathergoods leather

M&D Consult

**Contact** : Youcef Tounsi
Consultant Relation d'affaires
**Address** : 1324 av. Heidelberg
Montpellier-34080
France
**Tel.**
**Fax** :
: +33 4 67 75 35 09
+33 4 67 75 35 09
**Email**
**Web** :
:

**Activity** : Agent
**Products** : *Hides and Skins* : Wet blue, Vegetable crust,

*Leather* : Footwear – upper leather, Garment leather, Industrial leather,

*Chemicals* : Tanning,

*Footwear* : Men's shoes, Other - footwear, Women's shoes, Boots, Sport,

*Garments and Gloves* : Jacket, coats, Trousers, Fashion gloves,

*Leather Goods* : Belts, Furniture,

**Raw Materials** : Bovine, Other

France Footwear – upper leather, Garment leather, Industrial leather

M. Maison & Cie
**Address** : 15, Avenue Daumesnil
Paris-75012
France
**Tel.**
**Fax** :
: +33 1 43 41 22 22
+33 1 43 41 11 12
**Email**
**Web** :
: contact@maisonfey.com
http://www.maisonfey.com
**Activity** : Manufacturer
**Products** : *Leather* : Other - leather, Upholstery leather,

*Leather Goods* : Small leather goods, Furniture, Other - leather goods,

France Footwear – upper leather, Garment leather, Leathergoods leather, Upholstery leather

Maison Fey
**Address** : 15, Avenue Daumesnil
Paris-75012
France

**Tel.**
**Fax**
:
+33 1 43 41 22 22
:
+33 1 43 41 11 12
**Email**
**Web**
:
contact@maisonfey.com
:
http://www.maisonfey.com
**Activity** : Manufacturer
**Products** : *Leather* : Other - leather, Upholstery leather,

*Leather Goods* : Small leather goods, Furniture, Other - leather goods,

France Other - leather, Upholstery leather

Mégisserie Lauret
**Address** : 34 rue de la Paulèle
Millau-12100
France
**Tel.**
**Fax**
:
+33 5 65 60 42 56
:
+33 5 65 59 04 79
**Email**
**Web**
:
tannerie.lauret@wanadoo.fr
:
http://pro.wanadoo.fr/tannerie.lauret/
**Activity** : Manufacturer
**Products** : *Leather* : Leathergoods leather, Garment leather,

**Raw Materials** : Sheep

France Garment leather, Leathergoods leather

Mégisserie Mercier
**Address** : 13, rue Etienne Delmas
P.O. Box 341
Millau-12103
France
**Tel.**
**Fax**
:
+33 5 65 59 21 40
:
+33 5 65 61 22 09
**Email**
**Web**
:
megisserie.mercier@wanadoo.fr
:
http://www.hervy-mercier.com
**Activity** : Manufacturer, Exporter
**Products** : *Hides and Skins* : Wet salted, Chrome crust, Vegetable crust,

*Leather* : Footwear – upper leather, Leathergoods leather, Garment leather, Gloving leather,

**Raw Materials** : Sheep

France Footwear – upper leather, Garment leather, Gloving leather, Leathergoods leather

Megisserie Moisand

**Contact** : Gérard Blanc
Directeur Général Cuirs pour reliure. Ameublement, Maroquinerie. Parchemins.

**Address** : Z.I de Marclan
Muret-31600
France
**Tel.** : +33 5 61 51 00 39
**Fax** : +33 5 61 5149 98
**Email** :
**Web** :

**Activity** : Manufacturer
**Products** : *Leather* : Leathergoods leather, Other - leather, Upholstery leather, Saddlery and harness leather, Industrial leather,

**Raw Materials** : Sheep, Goat, Pig

France Industrial leather, Leathergoods leather, Other - leather, Saddlery and harness leather, Upholstery leather

OCTAN

**Contact** : Romec Cuirs, Velours, Chèvres et Agneaux

**Address** : 39, rue Colonel Naudy
P.O. Box 127
Graulhet cedex-81303
France
**Tel.** : +33 5 63 34 30 63
**Fax** : +33 5 63 34 30 63
**Email** : cuiroctan@aol.com
**Web** :

**Activity** : Manufacturer, Importer, Exporter
**Products** : *Hides and Skins* : Vegetable crust,

*Leather* : Garment leather, Split leather,

**Raw Materials** : Sheep, Goat

France Garment leather, Split leather

Quadri Group

**Contact** : M. Quadri We are producers for shoe leathers and also leather garments!!!

**Address** : 12, rue Marie de France
Marcq-en-Baroeul-59700
France
**Tel.**
**Fax** :
: +33 328 33 98 98

**Email**
**Web** :
: france@quadrigroup.com

**Activity** : Importer, Exporter
**Products** : *Leather* : Footwear – upper leather, Footwear – lining leather,

**Raw Materials** : Bovine, Sheep, Goat, Other

France Footwear – lining leather, Footwear – upper leather

SA Rouzieres
**Contact** : Rouzieres
Président Directeur Général

**Address** : Carrefour de l'Europe
Graulhet-81300
France
**Tel.**
**Fax** :
: +33 5 63 34 52 29
+33 5 63 34 16 50
**Email**
**Web** :
: jerome.rouzieres@free.fr

**Activity** : Manufacturer
**Products** : *Hides and Skins* : Other - hides and skins,

*Leather* : Leathergoods leather, Sole leather, Garment leather,

**Raw Materials** : Sheep, Goat

France Garment leather, Leathergoods leather, Sole leather

Sarl André Hiriar

**Contact** : André Hiriar
Gérant Hiriar établi depuis 1936 commerce avec: - Peaux d'Agneaux et Moutons picklés France, Uk, Australie - Peaux d'Agneaux, Moutons et Chèvres pour vêtements: plongé, nappa, crispé, antique, vielli, bubble, double face, velours, stretch en diverses finitions. - Peaux pour dessus et doublures chaussures: aniline, pécari, grain arabe... - Peaux sciées pour doublure chaussures, vêtements, reliure, maroquinerie.

**Address** : 18, rue Galibert Pons
P.O. Box 12
Mazamet-81200
France
**Tel.**
**Fax** :
: +33 5 6361 0107
+33 5 6398 6817
**Email**
**Web** :
: hiriar@wanadoo.fr
http://www.cuirsetpeauxhiriar.com
**Activity** : Wholesaler, Exporter
**Products** : *Hides and Skins* : Wet salted, Pickled, Wet blue, Chrome crust, Vegetable crust,

*Leather* : Footwear – upper leather, Leathergoods leather, Upholstery leather, Garment leather, Gloving leather, Split leather,

*Chemicals* : Tanning,

**Raw Materials** : Sheep, Goat

France Footwear – upper leather, Garment leather, Gloving leather, Leathergoods leather, Split leather, Upholstery leather

Sarl Marcel DUMAS et Cie

**Contact** : Frédéric Dumas
Gérant

**Address** : 2, la Combe Du Prieuré
Annonay-07100
France

Parchemins Peaux dc décoration Articles souvenirs Chaussons et moufles en agneau

**Tel.** : +33 4 75.33.47.68
**Fax** : +33 4 75 67 93 73
**Email** : ets.dumas@wanadoo.fr
**Web** : http://www.etsdumas.com
**Activity** : Wholesaler, Manufacturer, Importer, Exporter
**Products** : *Hides and Skins* : Other - hides and skins,

*Leather* : Other - leather, Upholstery leather, Saddlery and harness leather,

**Raw Materials** : Bovine, Sheep, Goat

France Other - leather, Saddlery and harness leather, Upholstery leather

Sarl MR 37

**Contact** : Benchabana
Chief Executive Officer

We are international leather

France Footwear – lining leather, Footwear – upper leather.

**Address** : 26, rue de vilde
Tours-37100
France

**Tel.** : +33 6 60 12 51 97
**Fax** : +33 8 74 51 62 49
**Email** : sarl_mr_37@hotmail.fr
**Web** :
**Activity** : Wholesaler, Agent
**Products** : *Hides and Skins* : Pickled, Wet blue, Chrome crust, Vegetable crust, Other - hides and skins,

*Leather* : Footwear – upper leather, Leathergoods leather, Other - leather, Footwear – lining leather, Upholstery leather, Garment leather, Gloving leather, Split leather,

*Footwear* : Men's shoes, Other - footwear, Women's shoes, Sandals,

*Garments and Gloves* : Jacket, coats, Industrial gloves, Other - garments,

*Leather Goods* : Small leather goods, Large leather goods, Belts, Furniture, Other - leather goods,

**Raw Materials** : Bovine, Sheep, Goat, Other

Garment leather, Gloving leather, Leathergoods leather, Other - leather, Split leather, Upholstery leather

Sibel Leather

**Contact** : Emilie .
Trader

Basé en plein centre de la France. A 2 heures de Lyon - 30 minutes de Clermont Fd Nous disposons de près de 50 000m2 de cuir et chutes de cuir. Lots ou suivis Nous étudions également toutes propositions d'achat. Vous souhaitez destocker des lots de peausseries (fins de collection...) et/ou Vous recherchez du cuir de

France

Automotive leather, Footwear – upper leather, Garment leather, Leathergoods leather, Other - leather, Split leather

**Address** : 9, rue des Percières
Courpière-63120
France

**Tel.** : +33 473 51 28 22
**Fax** : +33 473 531 325



**Email** : sibel63@wanadoo.fr
**Web** :

**Products** : *Hides and Skins* : Chrome crust, Vegetable crust, Other - hides and skins,

*Leather* : Footwear – upper leather, Leathergoods leather, Automotive leather, Other - leather, Garment leather, Split leather,

*Leather Goods* : Small leather goods, Large leather goods,

SOFIC

**Address** : 10, rue Augustin Vincent
Saint André de la Marche-49450
France

**Tel.** : +33 2 41 58 42 82
**Fax** : +33 2 41 71 01 55

**Email** :
**Web** : http://www.sofic-cuir.com

**Activity** : Wholesaler

**Products** : *Hides and Skins* : Chrome crust, Other - hides and skins,

*Leather* : Automotive leather, Upholstery leather, Garment leather, Industrial leather,

*Footwear* : Men's shoes, Women's shoes, Children shoes, Boots,

**Raw Materials** : Bovine, Sheep, Goat, Reptile

France

Automotive leather, Garment leather, Industrial leather, Upholstery leather

SOFIC Paris

**Contact** :

Nous sommes distributeur de cuirs et peaux pour la sellerie automobile, l'ameublement, les tapissiers, les décorateurs, les architectes d'intérieur, la maroquinerie, la chaussure, l'orthopédie et la reliure d'art. Nous commercialisons aussi

France

Automotive leather, Footwear – lining leather, Footwear – upper leather, Industrial leather, Upholstery leather

**Address** : 86 Avenue Ledru Rollin
Paris-75012
France

**Tel.** : +33 1 43 43 79 73
**Fax** : +33 1 43 43 37 83



**Email** :
**Web** : http://www.sofic-cuir.com

**Products** : *Hides and Skins* : Chrome crust, Other - hides and skins,

*Leather* : Footwear – upper leather, Automotive leather, Footwear – lining leather, Upholstery leather, Industrial leather,

**Raw Materials** : Bovine, Sheep, Goat, Reptile

Soperpo Sarl

**Contact** : Assemat
Directeur Commercial

**Address** : 55, rue de Metz
P.O. Box 267
Mazamet Cedex-81208
France

**Tel.** : +33 5 63 61 02 84
**Fax** : +33 5 63 98 54 61

**Email** : sorpepo@aol.com
**Web** :

**Activity** : Wholesaler, Importer, Exporter, Agent

**Products** : *Hides and Skins* : Wet salted, Dry salted, Air/Frame dried, Limed, Pickled, Wet blue, Chrome crust, Vegetable crust, Other - hides and skins,

*Leather* : Footwear – upper leather, Leathergoods leather, Upholstery leather, Garment leather, Gloving leather, Split leather,

**Raw Materials** : Bovine, Sheep, Goat, Pig, Reptile, Other

Courtage, négoce, import, export. Tous cuirs bruts, semi tannés, tannés. Vêtements, chaussures, maroquinerie, fourrure. Perforation à façon petites peaux.

France

Footwear – upper leather, Garment leather, Gloving leather, Leathergoods leather, Split leather, Upholstery leather

STEP-CATANE

France

Footwear – upper leather, Leathergoods leather

Tannerie Ciulli Frères

**Address** : 57, Boulevard Gustave Richard

**Tel.** : +33 2 41 62 21 99

**Email** : hproux@step-catane.com

**Activity** : Agent

France

Footwear – lining leather, Footwear – upper leather, Leathergoods leather, Saddlery and harness leather, Sole leather

**Activity** : Agent
**Products** : *Leather* : Footwear – upper leather, Leathergoods leather,

**Raw Materials** : Bovine, Goat

Tannerie de Callac

**Address** : Z.A. de Kerguiniou
Callac-22160
France

**Tel.** : +33 2 96 45 50 68
**Fax** : +33 2 96 45 95 02
**Email** : vuadelle@armornet.tm.fr
**Web** : http://www.armornet.tm.fr/tcmultimedia/tannerie-de-callac/une.htm
**Activity** : Manufacturer
**Products** : *Leather* : Other - leather, Saddlery and harness leather,

*Footwear* : Other - footwear,

*Leather Goods* : Small leather goods,

**Raw Materials** : Bovine, Sheep, Other (Fish)

France Other - leather, Saddlery and harness leather

Tannerie Garat et Fils SARL

**Contact** : Emmanuel Garat
Gérant

Cuir à semelles Tannage végétal en fosses Cuir équipement

**Address** : Donamaria
Armendaritz-64640
France

**Tel.** : +33 5 59 37 61 57
**Fax** : +33 5 59 37 65 12
**Email** :
**Web** :
**Activity** : Manufacturer
**Products** : *Leather* : Sole leather, Industrial leather,

**Raw Materials** : Bovine

France Industrial leather, Sole leather

Tannerie Valeix

**Contact** : Jacques Valeix
Gérant

**Address** : 92, avenue de Lodève
Bedarieux-34600
France

**Tel.** : +33 4 67 95 05 13
**Fax** : +33 4 67 23 28 33

France Footwear – upper leather, Industrial leather, Leathergoods leather, Other - leather, Saddlery and harness leather, Split leather

**Email** : tannerie.valeix@wanadoo.fr
**Web** :



**Activity** : Manufacturer

**Products** : *Leather* : Footwear – upper leather, Leathergoods leather, Other - leather, Saddlery and harness leather,

**Products** : *Leather* : Footwear – upper leather, Leathergoods leather, Other - leather, Saddlery and harness leather, Industrial leather, Split leather,

**Raw Materials** : Bovine

Tanneries d'Annonay SA

**Contact** : J.P Bardy
Secrétaire Général

Cuir de veau pour chaussures et maroquinerie

**Address** : 5 Rte Roche Pereandre
P.O. Box 53
Annonay-07102
France

**Tel.** : +33 4 75 32 42 80
**Fax** : +33 4 75 67 74 34

**Email** : contact@tannerie-annonay.fr
**Web** : http://www.tannerie.com

**Activity** : Manufacturer

**Products** : *Leather* : Footwear – upper leather, Leathergoods leather,

**Raw Materials** : Bovine

France Footwear – upper leather, Leathergoods leather

Tanneries Darius Fabre

**Address** : 10 boulevard Dr Pontier
Graulhet, Cedex-81301
France

**Tel.** : +33 5 63 42 82 30
**Fax** : +33 5 63 42 82 31

**Email** : darius-fabre@darius-fabre.fr
**Web** :

**Activity** : Manufacturer

**Products** : *Leather* : Footwear – upper leather, Leathergoods leather, Footwear – lining leather,

France Footwear – lining leather, Footwear – upper leather, Leathergoods leather

Tanneries des cuirs d'Indochine et de Madagascar- Roggwiller

**Address** : 24, avenue Hoche
Paris-75008
France

**Tel.** : +33 1 58 56 36 00
**Fax** : +33 1 58 56 36 01

**Email** : tcim@roggwiller.com
**Web** : http://www.roggwiller.com

**Activity** : Manufacturer, Exporter

**Products** : *Leather* : Footwear – upper leather, Leathergoods leather, Automotive leather, Upholstery leather, Garment leather,

**Raw Materials** : Reptile, Other

France Automotive leather, Footwear – upper leather, Garment leather, Leathergoods leather, Upholstery leather

Tanneries du Puy

| | | | | |
|---|---|---|---|---|
| **Contact** | : | Patrick Michoud<br>Directeur Commercial | | |
| **Address** | : | Chadrac<br>P.O. Box 35<br>Le Puy-en-Velay-43001<br>France | | |
| **Tel.** | : | +33 4 71 09 60 44 | | |
| **Fax** | : | +33 4 71 02 81 05 | France | Footwear – upper leather, Garment leather, Leathergoods leather |
| **Email** | : | contact@tanneries-du-puy.fr | | |
| **Web** | : | http://www.tanpuy.com | | |
| **Activity** | : | Manufacturer | | |
| **Products** | : | *Hides and Skins* : Wet blue, Chrome crust,<br><br>*Leather* : Footwear – upper leather, Leathergoods leather, Garment leather, | | |
| **Raw Materials** | : | Bovine | | |

Tanneries Dupire

| | | | | |
|---|---|---|---|---|
| **Address** | : | Rte Juvardeil<br>Chateauneuf Sur Sarthe-49330<br>France | | |
| **Tel.** | : | +33 2 41 69 44 35 | | |
| **Fax** | : | +33 2 41 69 87 54 | | |
| **Email** | : | info@dupire.com | France | Footwear – lining leather, Footwear – upper leather, Leathergoods leather |
| **Web** | : | http://www.dupirc.com | | |
| **Activity** | : | Manufacturer | | |
| **Products** | : | *Leather* : Footwear – upper leather, Leathergoods leather, Footwear – lining leather, | | |

Tanneries Haas

| | | | | |
|---|---|---|---|---|
| **Address** | : | 1, Route du Hohwald<br>Eichhoffen-67140<br>France | | |
| **Tel.** | : | +33 88 08 97 43 | | |
| **Fax** | : | +33 88 08 51 45 | | |
| **Email** | : | contacts@tanneries-haas.com | France | Footwear – lining leather, Footwear – upper leather, Garment leather, Leathergoods leather, Saddlery and harness leather |
| **Web** | : | http://www.tanneries-haas.com/ | | |
| **Activity** | : | Manufacturer, Exporter | | |
| **Products** | : | *Leather* : Footwear – upper leather, Leathergoods leather, Footwear – lining leather, Garment leather, Saddlery and harness leather, | | |
| **Raw Materials** | : | Bovine | | |

Tanneries Nouvelles Pechdo

**Contact** : Barthelemy Marc
Directeur

**Address** : Z I Plaine Coste
Millau-12100
France

**Tel.** : +33 5 65 60 50 20
**Fax** : +33 5 65 60 22 24
**Email** : info@tanneries-pechdo.fr
**Web** : http://www.tanneries-pechdo.fr
**Activity** : Manufacturer
**Products** : *Leather* : Garment leather, Gloving leather,

Cowbelly Leather for safety gloves: Treatments: waterproof, oil resistant, heat resistant... Registered Trade Mark: High Techtan Cowbelly Leather for sport/dress/leisure gloves: For dress, casual gloves For skiing, motorcycling, snowboarding...gloves Registered Trade Mark: Nepskin (high waterproof leather) Special Chrome free Leather: Registered Trade Mark: Ecocuir Cowbellies for garment yokes Washable Leathers (full grain or nubuck) specially meant for trims in combiantion with textile. All our leathers according to the European Norms.

France

Garment leather, Gloving leather

**Raw Materials** : Bovine

Tanneries Rémy Carriat SA

**Contact** : Marie Carriat Hiriart
Président

**Address** : 225, Route d' Itxassou
P.O. Box 1
Espelette-64250
France

**Tel.** : +33 5 59 93 90 88
**Fax** : +33 5 59 93 82 26
**Email** : carriat@carriat.com
**Web** : http://www.carriat.com
**Activity** : Manufacturer
**Products** : *Leather* : Footwear – upper leather, Leathergoods leather, Upholstery leather, Saddlery and harness leather,

La beauté d'un cuir façonné dans la grande tradition française. The beauty of a leather shaped in the French Tradition.

France

Footwear – upper leather, Leathergoods leather, Saddlery and harness leather, Upholstery leather

**Raw Materials** : Bovine

Tanneries Roux - France

**Contact** : Jean- Luc Couvreur
Directeur de Production

**Address** : 2, Avenue Bruno Larat
P.O. Box 66
Romans Cedex-26102
France

**Tel.** : +33 4 750 222 29
**Fax** : +33 4 750 257 92
**Email** : info@tanneries-roux.com
**Web** : http://www.tanneries-roux.com
**Activity** : Tanner

France

Garment leather, Gloving leather, Other - leather, Sole leather

**Products** : *Leather* : Other - leather, Sole leather, Garment leather, Gloving leather,

*Leather Goods* : Small leather goods, Large leather goods

Varcuir

**Contact** : Gérard Blanc

**Address** : 247 Avenue de Tavernes
P.O. Box 10
Barjols-83670
France

**Tel.** : +33 4 94 77 22 01
**Fax** : +33 4 94 77 15 69
**Email** :
**Web** :
**Activity** : Manufacturer, Exporter
**Products** : *Leather* : Footwear – upper leather, Leathergoods leather, Other - leather, Upholstery leather, Saddlery and harness leather, Industrial leather,

**Raw Materials** : Bovine, Sheep, Goat, Pig

Cuirs pour reliure. Cuirs pour instruments de musique. Parchemins. Cuir Végétal. Cuir Megis Blanc.

France

Footwear – upper leather, Industrial leather, Leathergoods leather, Other - leather, Saddlery and harness leather, Upholstery leather

VIDAL René et Cie

**Contact** : Bernard Vidal
Président Directeur Général

**Address** : Usine de la Maylarié
Mazamet-81200
France

**Tel.** : +33 5 63 61 00 79
**Fax** : +33 5 63 61 95 39
**Email** : rene.vidal.leather@wanadoo.fr
**Web** :
**Activity** : Retailer, Manufacturer, Importer, Exporter
**Products** : *Hides and Skins* : Air/Frame dried, Pickled,

*Leather* : Leathergoods leather, Other - leather, Sole leather, Upholstery leather, Saddlery and harness leather,

**Raw Materials** : Sheep

France

Leathergoods leather, Other - leather, Saddlery and harness leather, Sole leather, Upholstery leather

# GERMANY

Alja Lederhandel GmbH

Germany

Garment leather, Sole

leather, Split leather

**Address** : Gutenbergstrasse 8,
Obertshausen-63179
Germany

**Tel.** : +49 6104 70060
**Fax** : +49 6104 700666

**Email** : info@alja-leder.de
**Web** :

**Activity** : Manufacturer

**Products** : *Hides and Skins* : Chrome crust, Vegetable crust,

*Leather* : Sole leather, Garment leather, Split leather,

**Raw Materials** : Bovine, Sheep, Goat, Other

Bavaria Lederveredelung Gmbh

**Address** : Kreuz Str. 51
Groîbottwar-71723
Germany

**Tel.** : +49 7148 96260
**Fax** : +49 7148 962 626

Germany Split leather

**Email** :
**Web** :

**Activity** : Manufacturer

**Products** : *Leather* : Split leather,

**Raw Materials** : Kangaroo

C.R. Rasmuss & Co GmbH

**Contact** : Joachim Haustein
Managing Director

Since more than 50 years we are active as worldwide agents/brokers in the hide, skin and leather business working on

Germany Footwear – upper leather, Garment leather, Gloving leather

**Address** : Schwentinestr. 80
Norderstedt-22851
Germany

**Tel.** : +49 40 52[illegible]3421
**Fax** : +49 40 5291914

**Products** : *Hides and Skins* : Wet salted, Pickled, Wet blue, Chrome crust,

*Leather* : Footwear – upper leather, Garment leather, Gloving leather,

**Raw Materials** : Bovine, Sheep, Goat, Pig, Other

Colonia Leather GmbH & Co KG

**Address** : Hirtenweg 1
Kassel-34128
Germany

**Tel.** : +49 561 988 2610
**Fax** : +49 561 885 499

**Email** : consult@colonia-leather.com
**Web** : http://www.colonia-leather.com

**Activity** : Manufacturer

**Products** : *Hides and Skins* : Chrome crust, Vegetable crust,

*Leather* : Footwear – upper leather, Leathergoods leather, Footwear – lining leather, Garment leather,

**Raw Materials** : Sheep, Goat, Pig, Other (fishes, camels)

Germany — Footwear – lining leather, Footwear – upper leather, Garment leather, Leathergoods leather

Cozium Gmbh

Contact : Ursula Kralle

**Address** : Mühlheimer Str. 23

**Tel.** : +49 06104 42721

**Email** : ursiek@aol.com

**Activity** : Wholesaler, Importer,

**Products** : *Leather* : Leathergoods

**Raw Materials** : Reptile

Germany — Leathergoods leather

**Raw Materials** : Reptile

Dauster Leder & Mode

**Address** : Friedrichstr.
Wiesbaden-65185
Germany

**Tel.** : +49 611 30 30 33
**Fax** : +49 611 30 04 00

**Email** : ddauster@leder-dauster.de
**Web** : http://www.leder-dauster.de

**Activity** : Wholesaler, Retailer, Importer

**Products** : *Leather* : Garment leather,

*Garments and Gloves* : Jacket, coats, Trousers, Skirts, Motorcycling, Fashion gloves, Sport gloves, Other - garments,

*Leather Goods* : Small leather goods, Belts,

**Raw Materials** : Bovine, Sheep, Goat, Pig, Reptile

Germany | Garment leather

Fauck OHG

**Address** : Hegauer Weg 38
Berlin-14163
Germany

**Tel.** : +49 308 015 081
**Fax** : +49 308 022 070

**Email** : info@fauck.de
**Web** : http://www.fauck.de

**Activity** : Importer, Exporter, Agent

**Products** : *Leather* : Footwear – upper leather, Leathergoods leather, Upholstery leather, Garment leather,

**Raw Materials** : Bovine, Sheep, Goat, Pig, Other

Germany | Footwear – upper leather, Garment leather, Leathergoods leather, Upholstery leather

Friedrich Sturm GmbH & CO. KG.

**Contact** : John R. Semmelhaak

**Address** : Bornkamp 2
Osterhorn-25364

: +49 (0)4127 / 97980
: +49 (0)4127 / 979899

Germany | Footwear – upper leather, Garment leather, Leathergoods leather, Split

| | | | | |
|---|---|---|---|---|
| **Tel.** : +49 (0)4127 / 97980<br>**Fax** : +49 (0)4127 / 979899<br>**Email** : sturm@frsturm.com<br>**Web** : http://www.frsturm.com<br>**Activity** : Wholesaler, Manufacturer, Importer, Exporter<br>**Products** : *Hides and Skins* : Wet salted, Wet blue, Chrome crust,<br><br>*Leather* : Footwear – upper leather, Leathergoods leather, Upholstery leather, Garment leather, Split leather,<br><br>**Raw Materials** : Bovine | in raw and wet-blue. Specialities: Wetblue selected grains | | leather, Upholstery leather |

Gebr. Schnittger GmbH & Co

| | | | |
|---|---|---|---|
| **Address** : Wiesbadener Strasse 7<br>Nürnberg-90427<br>Germany<br><br>**Tel.** : +49 911 30300-0<br>**Fax** : +49 911 30300-33<br>**Email** : info@schnittger.com<br>**Web** : http://www.schnittger.com<br>**Activity** : Manufacturer, Exporter<br>**Products** : *Hides and Skins* : Wet blue,<br><br>*Leather* : Split leather | | Germany | Split leather |

Heller Leder GmbH & Co KG

| | | | |
|---|---|---|---|
| **Contact** : Andreas Frenzel<br>International Sales Manager<br><br>**Address** : Hauptstrasse 1<br>P.O. Box 20<br>Hehlen-37619<br>Germany<br><br>**Tel.** : +49 5533 9702-0<br>**Fax** : +49 5533 4947 | Heller Leder is one of the leading tanneries in Middle Europe. A modern wetblue plant along with a biological sewage treatment enables the company | Germany | Footwear – lining leather, Leathergoods leather, Split leather, Upholstery leather |

**Products** : *Hides and Skins* : Wet blue, Chrome crust,

*Leather* : Leathergoods leather, Footwear – lining leather, Upholstery leather, Split leather,

**Raw Materials** : Bovine

InTrade Gmbh

| | | | |
|---|---|---|---|
| **Contact** : Stefan Schöner<br>Manager<br>**Address** : Schwarzwaldstr, 13<br>Rheinstetten-<br>Germany<br>**Tel.** : +49 721 951 06 85 / 639 192 49 81<br>**Fax** : +49 721 951 06 84 / 639 192 49 83<br>**Email** : intrade@tesionmail.de<br>**Web** : http.://www.intrade-germany.com<br>**Activity** : Wholesaler, Manufacturer, Importer, Exporter, Agent<br>**Products** : *Hides and Skins* : Wet salted, Dry salted, Air/Frame dried, Pickled, Wet blue, Chrome crust, Other - hides and skins,<br>*Leather* : Footwear – upper leather, Automotive leather, Footwear – lining leather, Upholstery leather, Garment leather, Gloving leather,<br>**Raw Materials** : Bovine, Sheep, Goat, Pig, Other | As your partner in the leather business and with some succesfull experiences we can offer you our assortment with raw, wet blue, crust and finished cattle, calf, buffalo, lamb, sheep, goat, pig, horse, lama, alpaca, deer and leather scraps. If you have any queries, please do not hesitate to contact us. | Germany | Automotive leather, Footwear – lining leather, Footwear – upper leather, Garment leather, Gloving leather, Upholstery leather |

JP Consulting International Trade Promotion

| | | |
|---|---|---|
| **Contact** : Jurgen Pack<br>**Address** : Brücker Mauspfad 623<br>Cologne-51109<br>**Tel.** : +49 221 844954<br>**Fax** : +49 221 844986<br>: jp-consulting@t-online.de<br>: http://www.ap-consulting.com | Germany | Garment leather |

**Email** : jp-consulting@t-online.de
**Web** : http://www.ap-consulting.com
**Activity** : Consultant
**Products** : *Leather* : Garment leather,

*Footwear* : Men's shoes, Women's shoes, Children shoes, Sport,

*Garments and Gloves* : Jacket, coats, Trousers, Skirts, Fashion gloves, Sport gloves, Industrial gloves,

*Leather Goods* : Small leather goods, Belts,

field of international trade and investment promotion in Cologne/Germany. Since 1989 JP CONSULTING & Associates have been working as responsible Management Consultants for international donor organizations as well as private companies. For leather manufacturers from abroad JP CONSULTING & Associates can offer the following range of services: a. Product Design and Quality Management b. Management and Export Marketing Consulting c. Promotion of Trade and Industrial Investments for Developing Countries d. Trade Fair Consulting e. Information Service/Training and Workshop Activities

Julius Lies GmbH

**Contact** : Roland Lies
**Address** : Olbrichtstr. 16
**Tel.** : +49 6201 14021
**Email** : lies@lies.hd.uunet.de
**Activity** : Importer, Exporter
**Products** : *Hides and Skins* : Wet
**Raw Materials** : Bovine, Sheep, Goat, Pig

Germany Garment leather, Split leather, Upholstery leather

**Raw Materials** : Bovine, Sheep, Goat, Pig

Kromwell GmbH, Division NORIMEX

**Contact** : Werner Baumeister
Geschäftsführer

Sales representative for tanneries in New Zealand and Europe to the: - automotive - clothing - shoe - leathergoods industries

**Address** : Thumenberger Weg 26
P.O. Box 250349
Nürnberg-90128
Germany

**Tel.** : +49 911 580 7650
**Fax** : +49 911 580 7659

**Email** : norimex1@kromwell.de
**Web** :

**Activity** : Agent

**Products** : *Leather* : Footwear – upper leather, Leathergoods leather, Other - leather, Upholstery leather, Garment leather, Split leather,

*Footwear* : Men's shoes, Women's shoes, Children shoes, Boots, Sport,

*Garments and Gloves* : Jacket, coats,

*Leather Goods* : Small leather goods, Large leather goods, Belts,

Germany

Footwear – upper leather, Garment leather, Leathergoods leather, Other - leather, Split leather, Upholstery leather

**Raw Materials** : Bovine, Sheep, Goat, Other

Räuchle (Gebr) GmbH and Co KG

**Address** : Fabrikstrasse 43
Backnang-71522
Germany

**Tel.** : +49 7191 3339-0
**Fax** : +49 7191 3339-29

**Email** : leder@raeuchle.com
**Web** : http://www.raeuchle.com

**Activity** : Manufacturer

**Products** : *Leather* : Footwear – upper leather, Other - leather, Garment leather,

Germany

Footwear – upper leather, Garment leather, Other - leather

Schmenger Leder GmbH & Co

| | | | | |
|---|---|---|---|---|
| **Contact** | : Hans-Georg Potschmela<br>Director | Schmenger Leder is present on all leading leather markets of the world. The programm includes fashionable upper leathers for shoe, upholstery, leather goods and leather garment industries as well as lambskins, lining leathers and wet blues. Major countries of supply are Italy, Spain, India, Indonesia, China and Brazil. Furthermore, the arrangement of shoe and shoe upper productions abroad is constantly gaining importance. The product range is supplemented by cut and sewn upholstery covers made from leather. | Germany | Footwear – lining leather, Footwear – upper leather, Garment leather, Gloving leather, Leathergoods leather, Sole leather, Split leather, Upholstery leather |
| **Address** | : Zweibruecker Str. 29<br>P.O. Box 2661<br>Pirmasens-66953<br>Germany | | | |
| **Tel.** | : +49 6331 879-0 | | | |
| **Fax** | : +49 6331 879-292 | | | |
| **Email** | : info@schmenger.com | | | |
| **Web** | : http://www.schmenger.com | | | |
| **Activity** | : Wholesaler, Importer, Exporter, Agent | | | |
| **Products** | : *Hides and Skins* : Wet blue, Chrome crust, Vegetable crust,<br><br>*Leather* : Footwear – upper leather, Leathergoods leather, Footwear – lining leather, Sole leather, Upholstery leather, Garment leather, Gloving leather, Split leather,<br><br>*Footwear* : Men's shoes, Women's shoes, Children shoes, Sandals, Boots, Safety,<br><br>*Garments and Gloves* : Jacket, coats, Trousers, Skirts, | | | |
| **Raw Materials** | : Bovine, Sheep, Goat, Pig | | | |

TLW-Thüringer Lederfabrik Weida Gmbh

| | | | |
|---|---|---|---|
| **Address** | : Schloßmühlenweg 3<br>Weida-07570<br>Germany | Germany | Automotive leather, Garment leather, Upholstery leather |
| **Tel.** | : +49 366 03 70 212 | | |
| **Fax** | : +49 366 03 70 286 | | |
| **Email** | : info@tlw-leder.de | | |
| **Web** | : http://www.tlw-leder.de | | |
| **Activity** | : Manufacturer, Exporter | | |
| **Products** | : *Leather* : Automotive leather, Upholstery leather, Garment | | |

leather,

Universal Bossert Handelsgessellschaft mbH

| | | | |
|---|---|---|---|
| **Contact** : Petra Bossert<br>Managing Director<br>**Address** : Arnulfstrasse 49<br>P.O. Box 1411<br>Pirmasens-66954<br>Germany<br>**Tel.** : +49 6331 800 244<br>**Fax** : +49 6331 800 266<br>**Email** : info@bossert.de<br>**Web** : http://www.bossert.de<br>**Activity** : Wholesaler, Importer, Exporter, Agent<br>**Products** : *Hides and Skins* : Wet salted, Dry salted, Pickled, Wet blue, Chrome crust, Vegetable crust,<br>*Leather* : Footwear – upper leather, Leathergoods leather, Footwear – lining leather, Sole leather, Upholstery leather, Gloving leather, Saddlery and harness leather, Split leather,<br>**Raw Materials** : Bovine, Sheep, Goat, Pig, Others (Horse) | | Germany | Footwear – lining leather, Footwear – upper leather, Gloving leather, Leathergoods leather, Saddlery and harness leather, Sole leather, Split leather, Upholstery leather |

Weinheimer Leder Gmbh

| | | | |
|---|---|---|---|
| **Contact** : Gerd Knapp<br>Executive director<br>**Address** : Höhnerweg 2-4<br>Industriepark Freudenberg - Bau 5<br>Weinheim-69469<br>Germany<br>**Tel.** : +49 6201 259 97 0<br>**Fax** : +49 6201 259 97 29<br>**Email** : info@weinheimer-leder.de<br>**Web** : http://www.weinheimer-leder.com<br>**Activity** : Manufacturer, Importer, Exporter<br>**Products** : *Leather* : Footwear – upper leather,<br>**Raw Materials** : Bovine | | Germany | Footwear – upper leather |

Worring Leder Gmbh

| | | | |
|---|---|---|---|
| **Address** : | Neckarst 12-16<br>Muelheim An Der Ruhr-45478<br>Germany | Germany | Automotive leather, Footwear – upper leather, Garment leather, Leathergoods leather |
| **Tel.** : | +49 208 52602 | | |
| **Fax** : | +49 208 592071 | | |
| **Email** : | infoleder@web.de | | |
| **Web** : | http://www.worring-leder.de | | |
| **Activity** : | Wholesaler | | |
| **Products** : | *Leather* : Footwear – upper leather, Leathergoods leather, Automotive leather, Garment leather, | | |

## GREECE

Angelos Pelekanos Tannery

| | | | |
|---|---|---|---|
| **Contact** : | Angelos Pelekanos<br>Owner | Greece | Footwear – lining leather, Footwear – upper leather, Garment leather, Gloving leather |
| **Address** : | 8, Karystou Street<br>Saint Anna Rentis<br>Athens-18233<br>Greece | | |
| **Tel.** : | +30 210 345 34 87 | | |
| **Fax** : | +30 210 981 06 94 / 345 10 28 | | |
| **Email** : | pdg1954@otenet.gr | | |
| **Web** : | | | |
| **Activity** : | Manufacturer, Exporter | | |
| **Products** : | *Hides and Skins* : Wet salted, Wet blue, Chrome crust,<br><br>*Leather* : Footwear – upper leather, Footwear – lining leather, Garment leather, Gloving leather, | | |
| **Raw Materials** : | Sheep, Goat | | |

Heriscokid

| | | | | |
|---|---|---|---|---|
| **Contact** : | O.K. Issidorides<br>General Manager | Agent since 1905 for leather and shoemaking accessories and components | Greece | Footwear – lining leather, Footwear – upper leather, Garment leather, Sole leather, Upholstery leather |
| **Address** : | 33 Nikis Street<br>Athens-105 57<br>Greece | | | |

**Tel.** : +30 210 322 2609
**Fax** : +30 210 323 2759
**Email** :
**Web** :
**Activity** : Agent
**Products** : *Leather* : Footwear – upper leather, Footwear – lining leather, Sole leather, Upholstery leather, Garment leather,

**Raw Materials** : Bovine, Sheep, Goat, Pig, Reptile, Other

Mitronikas Leather

**Contact** : E. Mitronikas
General Director
**Address** : 12 Santa & Glezoy
Agrinion-30100
Greece
**Tel.** : +30 264 10 276 02
**Fax** : +30 264 10 252 16
**Email** : mitronika@agr.forthnet.gr
**Web** :
**Activity** : Wholesaler, Manufacturer, Exporter
**Products** : *Hides and Skins* : Wet salted, Wet blue,

*Leather* : Footwear – upper leather, Upholstery leather, Garment leather, Gloving leather,

**Raw Materials** : Sheep, Goat

Greece

Footwear – upper leather, Garment leather, Gloving leather, Upholstery leather

Pieles de Grecia

**Contact** : George Thirianos
**Address** : Karystou Street 8
Saint Anna Rentis
Athens-18233
**Tel.** : +30 210 345 3487
**Fax** : +30 210 981 0694
**Email** : pdg1954@otenet.gr
**Web** :

Wholesaler, Manufacturer, Exporter, Agent

Greece

Footwear – lining leather, Footwear – upper leather, Garment leather, Gloving leather

| | | | | |
|---|---|---|---|---|
| **Activity** : Wholesaler, Manufacturer, Exporter, Agent<br>**Products** : *Hides and Skins* : Wet salted, Wet blue, Chrome crust,<br>*Leather* : Footwear – upper leather, Footwear – lining leather, Garment leather, Gloving leather,<br>**Raw Materials** : Bovine, Sheep, Goat | finish nappa lamb/sheep/goat leather for shoe upper, garments, and lining. | | |

## ICELAND

| | | | |
|---|---|---|---|
| Lodskinn Saudarkroki Ehf<br>**Contact** : Gunnsteinn Bjornsson, General Manager<br>**Address** : Borgarmyri 5, Saudarkroki-550, Iceland<br>**Tel.** : +35 44535600<br>**Fax** : +35 44535105<br>**Email** : lodskinn.office@simnet.is<br>**Web** : http://www.randburg.com/is/lodskinn<br>**Activity** : Manufacturer<br>**Products** : *Leather* : Leathergoods leather, Garment leather,<br>**Raw Materials** : Sheep | Lodskinn Saudarkroki is producer of double face skins in various article from Icelandic raw material. Ready for use in the garment industry. | Iceland | Garment leather, Leathergoods leather |

## IRELAND

| | | |
|---|---|---|
| International Leathers Ltd.<br>**Address** : 39 Shrigley Road, Killyleagh, Downpatrick-BT30 9SS, Ireland<br>**Tel.** : +44 (0)28 44 821 002<br>**Fax** : +44 (0)28 44 821 008<br>**Email** : sales@intleathers.com<br>**Web** : http://www.intleathers.com<br>**Activity** : Manufacturer<br>**Products** : *Leather* : Garment leather, | Ireland | Garment leather |
| Newgrange Leathers Limited | Ireland | Automotive |

| | | |
|---|---|---|
| **Contact** | : | William Carroll<br>Manging Director |
| **Address** | : | Unit 4A<br>Mullaghboy Industrial Estate<br>Navan - Co Meath-<br>Ireland |
| **Tel.** | : | +353 46 902 07 00 / 01 |
| **Fax** | : | +353 46 907 40 60 |
| **Email** | : | info@newgrangeleathers.com |
| **Web** | : | http://www.newgrangeleathers.com |
| **Activity** | : | Wholesaler |
| **Products** | : | *Leather* : Leathergoods leather, Automotive leather, Upholstery leather, |

At Newgrange Leathers we offer a Complete Collection of Quality Leathers for Contract and Residential applications.

leather, Leathergoods leather, Upholstery leather

## ITALY

ABIP SpA

| | | |
|---|---|---|
| **Address** | : | Via Martiri Della Liberta', 18<br>Torbole Casaglia-25030<br>Italy |
| **Tel.** | : | +39 030 215 9511 |
| **Fax** | : | +39 030 215 9595 |
| **Email** | : | abip@abip.com |
| **Web** | : | http://www.abip.com |
| **Activity** | : | Manufacturer |
| **Products** | : | *Leather* : Footwear – upper leather, Leathergoods leather, Footwear – lining leather, Sole leather, Upholstery leather, Garment leather, |
| **Raw Materials** | : | Bovine |

Italy Footwear – lining leather, Footwear – upper leather, Garment leather, Leathergoods leather, Sole leather, Upholstery leather

Accoppiature Toscana Srl

| | | |
|---|---|---|
| **Address** | : | Via Provinciale Francesca, 412/A<br>S. Maria A Monte (PI)-56020<br>Italy |
| **Tel.** | : | +39 0587 706 441 |
| **Fax** | : | +39 0587 706 825/705 540 |
| **Email** | : | consorzio.pisa@offnelson.it |
| **Web** | : | |
| **Activity** | : | Manufacturer |
| **Products** | : | *Leather* : Footwear – upper leather, Leathergoods leather, |

Italy Footwear – upper leather, Leathergoods leather

Adamicom

| | | | | |
|---|---|---|---|---|
| **Contact** | : Lorenzo Vendramin<br>Manager Director | Dear Sir or Madam, Quality Raw leather and wet Blue cowhide is our main business since 1992, we do buy in Eastern Europe to have it tanned here in Vicenza. Our speciality is full thickness (also split) in whole leather, average sqf is about 39-39sqf, our main market is shoesmaker - sportshoes maker. We assest to be umbeatable in the PRICE/QUALITY equation, just because we tann our own hides. If interested in having quotation please provide me the desired Grades and desired quantity, so to work out an estimate. Sample is always available at customer shipping cost. Thanks. | Italy | Automotive leather, Footwear – lining leather, Footwear – upper leather, Leathergoods leather, Other - leather, Split leather, Upholstery leather |
| **Address** | : Treviso<br>Maser-31010<br>Italy | | | |
| **Tel.** | : +393 331 106 829 | | | |
| **Fax** | : +394 233 499 934 | | | |
| **Email** | : wetblue@gmail.com | | | |
| **Web** | : | | | |
| **Activity** | : Wholesaler, Manufacturer, Importer, Exporter | | | |
| **Products** | : *Hides and Skins* : Wet salted, Dry salted, Pickled, Wet blue, Chrome crust,<br><br>*Leather* : Footwear – upper leather, Leathergoods leather, Automotive leather, Other - leather, Footwear – lining leather, Upholstery leather, Split leather, | | | |
| **Raw Materials** | : Bovine | | | |

Adelaide SpA

| | | | |
|---|---|---|---|
| **Address** | : Via S. Rocco 120<br>Fraz. S.Lazzaro<br>Bassano Del Grappa-36061<br>Italy | Italy | Automotive leather, Footwear – lining leather, Footwear – upper leather, Garment leather, Leathergoods leather, Split leather, Upholstery leather |
| **Tel.** | : +39 0424 566 221/2/3 | | |
| **Fax** | : +39 0424 566 121 | | |
| **Email** | : adelaide@keycomm.it | | |
| **Web** | : http://www.adelaidespa.com | | |
| **Activity** | : Manufacturer | | |
| **Products** | : *Leather* : Footwear – upper leather, Leathergoods leather, Automotive leather, Footwear – lining leather, Upholstery leather, Garment leather, Split leather, | | |
| **Raw Materials** | : Bovine | | |

Adige Conceria SpA — Italy — Footwear –

**Address** : Via Eugenia Curiel 1/3
S. Miniato, PI-56024
Italy

upper leather, Leathergoods leather

**Tel.** : +39 571 49185/499002
**Fax** : +39 571 4988 21

**Email** : adige@adige-spa.it
**Web** :

**Activity** : Manufacturer

**Products** : *Hides and Skins* : Chrome crust, Vegetable crust, Other - hides and skins,

*Leather* : Footwear – upper leather, Leathergoods leather,

**Raw Materials** : Bovine

Alaska Conceria SpA

**Address** : Via Degli Orti, 13
Santa Croce Sull'Arno,PI-56029
Italy

**Tel.** : +39 0571 367 163
**Fax** : +39 0571 360 743

**Email** : alaska@leonet.it
**Web** : http://www.leonet.it/leather/alaska

Italy Footwear – upper leather, Leathergoods leather

**Activity** : Manufacturer

**Products** : *Hides and Skins* : Chrome crust, Vegetable crust,

*Leather* : Footwear – upper leather, Leathergoods leather,

**Raw Materials** : Bovine

Alba Gruppo

**Address** : Via Liguria 6
Ponte a Cappiano (FI)-50050
Italy

Italy Footwear – upper leather, Split leather

**Tel.** : +39 0571 295 511
**Fax** : +39 0571 297 258

**Email** : info@albagroup.it
**Web** : http://www.albagroup.it



**Activity** : Manufacturer

**Products** : *Hides and Skins* : Chrome crust, Vegetable crust,

*Leather* : Footwear – upper leather, Split leather,

**Raw Materials** : Bovine, Goat

Albarello Federico Srl

**Address** : Via Serio, 6
Milano-20139
Italy

**Tel.** : +39 02 5523 0217
**Fax** : +39 02 5523 0212
**Email** : info@federicoalbarello.com
**Web** : http://www.federicoalbarello.com
**Activity** : Manufacturer
**Products** : *Leather* : Footwear – upper leather, Leathergoods leather, Upholstery leather, Garment leather,

Italy Footwear – upper leather, Garment leather, Leathergoods leather, Upholstery leather

**Raw Materials** : Bovine, Goat, Reptile, Pig, Other

Albatros Industria Conciaria Spa

**Address** : Agglomerato Industriale
Via Asi Travl II°
P.O. Box 75
Solofra (AV)-83029
Italy

**Tel.** : +39 0825 5321 21
**Fax** : +39 0825 5321 23
**Email** : export@albatrostannery.it
**Web** : http://www.albatrostannery.it
**Activity** : Manufacturer, Importer, Exporter
**Products** : *Leather* : Footwear – upper leather, Garment leather,

Italy Footwear – upper leather, Garment leather

**Raw Materials** : Sheep

Alberto Rosi

**Contact** : Alberto Rosi
Agent

Italy Footwear – lining leather, Footwear – upper leather, Garment leather, Leathergoods

**Address** : Via Lazio 42
P.O. Box 51018
Pieve A Nievole-
Italy

**Address** : Via Lazio 42
P.O. Box 51018
Pieve A Nievole-
Italy

leather, Sole leather, Split leather

**Tel.** : +39 0572 802 85 / 86
**Fax** : +39 0572 951 308
**Email** : info@albertorosi.it
**Web** : http://www.dermafly.com
**Activity** : Importer, Agent
**Products** : *Hides and Skins* : Wet salted, Limed, Pickled, Wet blue, Chrome crust, Vegetable crust,

*Leather* : Footwear – upper leather, Leathergoods leather, Footwear – lining leather, Sole leather, Garment leather, Split leather,

*Footwear* : Men's shoes, Women's shoes, Children shoes, Sandals, Boots, Safety, Military, Shoe components,

*Garments and Gloves* : Jacket, coats, Trousers, Motorcycling, Other - garments,

*Leather Goods* : Small leather goods, Large leather goods,

**Raw Materials** : Bovine, Sheep, Goat, Pig

Aldo E Ivo Portolano Guanti Srl

**Address** : Via Carlo Cattaneo, 1
Melito di Napoli (NA)-80017
Italy

**Tel.** : +39 081 7102 236
**Fax** : +39 081 7114 481
**Email** : airport@tin.it
**Web** :
**Activity** : Manufacturer
**Products** : *Leather* : Footwear – upper leather, Footwear – lining leather, Garment leather, Gloving leather,

**Raw Materials** : Sheep, Goat

Italy Footwear – lining leather, Footwear – upper leather, Garment leather, Gloving leather

Alex Leather Srl Italy Footwear – lining leather, Footwear –

| | | | | |
|---|---|---|---|---|
| **Address** | : | Via Provincial Francesca Nord<br>Loc. Cardero<br>Santa Maria a Monte, PI-56020<br>Italy | | upper leather, Leathergoods leather |
| **Tel.** | : | +39 0587 7051 97 | | |
| **Fax** | : | +39 0587 7051 98 | | |
| **Email** | : | | | |
| **Web** | : | | | |
| **Activity** | : | Manufacturer | | |
| **Products** | : | *Leather* : Footwear – upper leather, Leathergoods leather, Footwear – lining leather, | | |
| **Raw Materials** | : | Sheep, Goat | | |

Alex Pellami Srl

| | | | | |
|---|---|---|---|---|
| **Address** | : | Via Buonarroti 1<br>Castelfranco Di Sotto PI-56022<br>Italy | | |
| **Tel.** | : | +39 0571 478 107/0338 8189555 | | |
| **Fax** | : | +39 0571 478 107 | Italy | Garment leather |
| **Email** | : | alexpellami@libero.it | | |
| **Web** | : | | | |
| **Activity** | : | Agent | | |
| **Products** | : | *Leather* : Garment leather, | | |
| **Raw Materials** | : | Sheep | | |

Ally Projects Srl

| | | | | |
|---|---|---|---|---|
| **Address** | : | Via Calamandrei, 21<br>Pieve a Nievole-51018<br>Italy | | |
| **Tel.** | : | +39 0572 950 980 | | |
| **Fax** | : | +39 0572 951 901 | Italy | |
| **Email** | : | | | |
| **Web** | : | | | |
| **Activity** | : | Importer | | |
| **Products** | : | | | |
| **Raw Materials** | : | Reptile, Other | | |

Ambassador Conceria Spa — Italy — Footwear – lining leather, Footwear –

| | | | | |
|---|---|---|---|---|
| **Address** | : | Via di Pelle, 72<br>Santa Croce sull'Arno-56029<br>Italy | | upper leather, Garment leather, Leathergoods leather |
| **Tel.** | : | +39 0571 30021/35034 | | |
| **Fax** | : | +39 0571 35676 | | |
| **Email** | : | info@ambassadorconceria.it | | |
| **Web** | : | http://www.ambassadorconceria.it | | |
| **Activity** | : | Manufacturer, Exporter | | |
| **Products** | : | *Leather* : Footwear – upper leather, Leathergoods leather, Footwear – lining leather, Garment leather, | | |
| **Raw Materials** | : | Bovine | | |
| Ambra Conceria Srl | | | Italy | Upholstery leather |
| **Address** | : | Via Casette 2<br>Almisano di lonigo (VI)-36045<br>Italy | | |
| **Tel.** | : | +39 0444 436 022 | | |
| **Fax** | : | +39 0444 436 012 | | |
| **Email** | : | roscio.n@ambraleather.com | | |
| **Web** | : | http://www.ambraleather.com | | |
| **Activity** | : | Manufacturer, Exporter | | |
| **Products** | : | *Leather* : Upholstery leather, | | |
| **Raw Materials** | : | Bovine | | |
| Anaconda Srl | | | Italy | Footwear – upper leather, Garment leather, Leathergoods leather |
| **Address** | : | Via M.L. King, 6/8<br>Ponte a Egola. PI-56024<br>Italy | | |
| **Tel.** | : | +39 0571 485 105 | | |
| **Fax** | : | +39 0571 491 10 | | |
| **Email** | : | info@anaconda.it | | |
| **Web** | : | http://www.anaconda.it | | |
| **Activity** | : | Manufacturer, Importer, Exporter | | |
| **Products** | : | *Leather* : Footwear – upper leather, Leathergoods leather, Garment leather, | | |
| **Raw Materials** | : | Reptile | | |
| Antelope Tanning Spa | | | Italy | Footwear – |

| | | | | |
|---|---|---|---|---|
| **Address** | : | Via Del Trebbio Nord<br>P.O. Box 112<br>S.Croce S/A-56029<br>Italy | | upper leather |
| **Tel.**<br>**Fax** | :<br>: | +39 0571 30306/30095<br>+39 0571 30548 | | |
| **Email**<br>**Web** | :<br>: | info@antelopetanning.it<br>http://www.antelopetanning.it | | |
| **Activity** | : | Manufacturer | | |
| **Products** | : | *Hides and Skins* : Chrome crust,<br><br>*Leather* : Footwear – upper leather, | | |
| **Raw Materials** | : | Bovine | | |
| Antiba Conceria SpA | | | | |
| **Address** | : | Via Toscana, 11<br>Santa Croce Sull'Arno. PI-56029<br>Italy | | |
| **Tel.**<br>**Fax** | :<br>: | +39 0571 3812<br>+39 0571 366 486 | | |
| **Email**<br>**Web** | :<br>: | info@antiba.com | Italy | Footwear – upper leather, Leathergoods leather |
| **Activity** | : | Manufacturer | | |
| **Products** | : | *Hides and Skins* : Chrome crust, Vegetable crust,<br><br>*Leather* : Footwear – upper leather, Leathergoods leather, | | |
| **Raw Materials** | : | Bovine, Sheep, Goat | | |
| Antica Manifattura Pelli Srl | | | | |
| **Address** | : | Via Sambuco | | |
| **Tel.** | : | +39 0825 535 292 | | |
| **Email** | : | ancimi@libero.it | | |
| **Activity** | : | Manufacturer | | |
| **Products** | : | *Leather* : Footwear – upper leather, | Italy | Footwear – lining leather, Footwear – upper leather, Garment leather, Leathergoods leather |

**Raw Materials** : Sheep, Goat

Anzolin Conceria Spa

**Address** : Via Roggia Di Mezzo, 53
Montorso-36050
Italy

**Tel.** : +39 0444 474 047
**Fax** : +39 0444 474 054

**Email** : info@conceria-anzolin.it
**Web** : http://www.conceria-anzolin.it

Italy | Footwear – upper leather, Leathergoods leather

**Activity** : Manufacturer

**Products** : *Leather* : Footwear – upper leather, Leathergoods leather,

**Raw Materials** : Bovine

Argos Srl

**Address** : Via di Pelle 68
Santa Croce sull'Arno-56029
Italy

**Tel.** : +39 0571 311 18
**Fax** : +39 0571 366 102

**Email** : info@argostannery.it
**Web** : http://www.argostannery.it

Italy | Footwear – upper leather, Leathergoods leather

**Activity** : Manufacturer

**Products** : *Leather* : Footwear – upper leather, Leathergoods leather,

**Raw Materials** : Bovine

Ariston Srl

**Address** : Via G. Rossini 12
Casoria (NA)-80026
Italy

**Tel.** : +39 081 573 4732
**Fax** : +39 081 573 2377

Italy | Gloving leather, Leathergoods leather

**Email** : info@ariston1.it
**Web** : http://www.ariston.idn.it

**Activity** : Manufacturer

**Products** : *Leather* : Leathergoods leather, Gloving leather,

**Products** : *Leather* : Leathergoods leather, Gloving leather,

**Raw Materials** : Bovine, Sheep, Goat

Arnella SpA

**Address** : Via E. Fermi, 32
Santa Croce sull'Arno.-56029
Italy

**Tel.** : +39 571366 740
**Fax** : +39 571 353 04

**Email** :
**Web** :

Italy Footwear – upper leather, Leathergoods leather

**Activity** : Manufacturer

**Products** : *Hides and Skins* : Chrome crust,

*Leather* : Footwear – upper leather, Leathergoods leather,

**Raw Materials** : Bovine, Sheep, Goat

Arno Conceria SpA

**Address** : Via Della Repubblica 4B
Santa Croce sull'Arno. PI-56029
Italy

**Tel.** : +39 0571366 636
**Fax** : +39 0571366 669

**Email** :
**Web** :

Italy Footwear – upper leather, Leathergoods leather

**Activity** : Manufacturer

**Products** : *Hides and Skins* : Chrome crust, Vegetable crust,

*Leather* : Footwear – upper leather, Leathergoods leather,

**Raw Materials** : Bovine, Goat

Arpel Srl

**Address** : Via Quari DX
Cologna Veneta (VR)-37044

Italy Footwear – upper leather, Garment leather, Leathergoods leather

**Tel.** : +39 333 4243036/437020
**Fax** : +39 0442 411011

**Email** :
**Web** :

**Email** :
**Web** :

**Activity** : Manufacturer

**Products** : *Leather* : Footwear – upper leather, Leathergoods leather, Garment leather,

**Raw Materials** : Other (Deer)

Artigiano del Cuoio Srl

**Address** : Via Romaiano, 12
Ponte a Egola. PI-56024
Italy

**Tel.** : +39 0571 497 228
**Fax** : +39 0571 499 592

**Email** : info@artigiano.it
**Web** : http://www.artigiano.it

**Activity** : Manufacturer

**Products** : *Leather* : Footwear – upper leather, Leathergoods leather, Other - leather, Upholstery leather,

Italy Footwear – upper leather, Leathergoods leather, Other - leather, Upholstery leather

**Raw Materials** : Bovine

Ascot SpA

**Address** : Via di Ripa 49-51
Santa Croce sull'Arno, PI-56029
Italy

**Tel.** : +39 0571 31601/35693
**Fax** : +39 0571 31602

**Email** : info@ascotspa.it
**Web** :

**Activity** : Manufacturer

**Products** : *Hides and Skins* : Vegetable crust,

*Leather* : Footwear – upper leather, Leathergoods leather, Footwear – lining leather, Sole leather,

Italy Footwear – lining leather, Footwear – upper leather, Leathergoods leather, Sole leather

**Raw Materials** : Bovine, Sheep, Goat

Astico Scamosceria SPA

Italy Automotive leather, Footwear – upper leather.

| | | | | |
|---|---|---|---|---|
| **Address** | : | Via Masere, 49<br>Thiene (VI)-36016<br>Italy | | Leathergoods leather, Sole leather, Upholstery leather |
| **Tel.** | : | +39 0445 365 688 | | |
| **Fax** | : | +39 0445 366 711 | | |
| **Email** | : | astico@astico.com | | |
| **Web** | : | http://www.astico.com | | |
| **Activity** | : | Manufacturer, Exporter | | |
| **Products** | : | *Leather* : Footwear – upper leather, Leathergoods leather, Automotive leather, Sole leather, Upholstery leather, | | |
| **Raw Materials** | : | Bovine | | |

Astoria Conceria Srl

| | | | | |
|---|---|---|---|---|
| **Address** | : | Via Bernini 12/B<br>Castelfranco di Sotto PI-56022<br>Italy | | |
| **Tel.** | : | +39 0571 489 408 | | |
| **Fax** | : | +39 0571 489 409 | | |
| **Email** | : | info@conceriaastoria.it | Italy | Footwear – upper leather, Leathergoods leather |
| **Web** | : | http://www.conceriaastoria.it | | |
| **Activity** | : | Manufacturer | | |
| **Products** | : | *Hides and Skins* : Chrome crust, Vegetable crust,<br><br>*Leather* : Footwear – upper leather, Leathergoods leather, | | |
| **Raw Materials** | : | Bovine | | |

Atema Conceria Srl

| | | | | |
|---|---|---|---|---|
| **Address** | : | Via Provinciale Francesca Nord 205<br>Castelfranco di Sollo PI-56022<br>Italy | | |
| **Tel.** | : | +39 0571480 406 | Italy | Footwear – upper leather, Garment leather, Leathergoods leather |
| **Fax** | : | +39 0571480 782 | | |
| **Email** | : | info@conceriaatema.it | | |
| **Web** | : | http://www.conceriaatema.it | | |
| **Activity** | : | Manufacturer | | |



| | | |
|---|---|---|
| **Products** | : | *Hides and Skins* : Vegetable crust,<br><br>*Leather* : Footwear – upper leather, Leathergoods leather, Garment |

*Leather* : Footwear – upper leather, Leathergoods leather, Garment leather,

**Raw Materials** : Bovine

Ausonia Conceria Spa

**Address** : Via San Tommasa, 109
Santa Croce sull'Arno, PI-56029
Italy

**Tel.** : +39 0571 3611
**Fax** : +39 0571 3612 22

**Email** : icuoi@ausonia.it
**Web** :

Italy — Leathergoods leather, Upholstery leather

**Activity** : Manufacturer

**Products** : *Hides and Skins* : Vegetable crust,

*Leather* : Leathergoods leather, Upholstery leather,

**Raw Materials** : Bovine

B.C.N. Concerie SpA

**Address** : Via E. Fermi 25
Santa Croce sull" Arno
Pisa-56029
Italy

**Tel.** : +39 571 311 51
**Fax** : +39 571 356 31

Italy

**Email** : info@bcn.it
**Web** : http://www.bcn.it

**Activity** : Tanner

**Products** : *Hides and Skins* : Chrome crust, Vegetable crust,

B.T. Veneta Pelli Srl

**Address** : Via Sestra Strada 6521

**Tel.** : +39 0444 451 768/451 769

**Email** : btveneta@keycomm.it

**Activity** : Manufacturer

Italy — Footwear – lining leather, Footwear – upper leather, Leathergoods leather

**Activity** : Manufacturer

**Products** : *Leather* : Footwear – upper leather, Leathergoods leather, Footwear – lining leather,

**Raw Materials** : Bovine

Badalassi Carlo Srl — Italy — Leathergoods leather

**Address** : Via Martin Luther King 45 - 49
Ponte A. Egola
San Miniato (PI)-56024
Italy

**Tel.** : +39 571 496 64/498 802
**Fax** : +39 571 499 532

**Email** :
**Web** :

**Activity** : Manufacturer

**Products** : *Hides and Skins* : Vegetable crust,

*Leather* : Leathergoods leather,

Baden Leder Srl — Italy — Footwear – upper leather, Gloving leather, Leathergoods leather

**Contact** : Baldi Pierangelo
Manager

**Address** : Via Madonna Degli Angeli 3/A
Vigevano, PV-27029
Italy

**Tel.** : +39 381 75405
**Fax** : +39 381 72020

**Email** : info@badenleder.com
**Web** : http://www.badenleder.com

**Activity** : Wholesaler, Importer, Exporter

**Products** : *Hides and Skins* : Pickled, Chrome crust, Vegetable crust,

*Leather* : Footwear – upper leather, Leathergoods leather, Gloving leather,

**Raw Materials** : Reptile, Other

Since 1985 we are importer/producer and exporter of exotic leather. We are specialized in peccary leather for gloves, shoes and leather goods. We also deal with crocodile, lizard, deer, kangaroo and other exotics.

Bastianello Conceria SpA — Italy — Upholstery leather

**Address** : Via Bottego 2
P.O. Box 77
Arzignano (VI)-36071
Italy

**Tel.** : +39 0444 675 884
**Fax** : +39 0444 673 373

**Email** : bastianello@keycomm.it
**Web** :

**Activity** : Manufacturer

**Products** : *Leather* : Upholstery leather,

**Raw Materials** : Bovine

BBM International Srl

Italy

Bello Conceria Di Ferrandino Michele & C. Snc

**Address** : Via per Turbigo 1
Castano Primo (MI)-20022
Italy

Italy Garment leather

**Tel.** : +39 0331 877 822
**Fax** : +39 0331 881 178

**Email** : bbm@bbminternational.it
**Web** : http://www.bbminternational.it

Beschin Gino Conceria SpA

**Address** : Via della Concia 20
Arzignano (VI)-36071
Italy

**Tel.** : +39 0444 671 888
**Fax** : +39 0444 450 874

**Email** : beschin@keycomm.it
**Web** : http://www.beschin.it

**Activity** : Manufacturer

**Products** : *Leather* : Footwear – upper leather, Leathergoods leather, Other - leather, Footwear – lining leather, Upholstery leather,

Italy Footwear – lining leather, Footwear – upper leather, Leathergoods leather, Other - leather, Upholstery leather

**Raw Materials** : Bovine

Bisonte Cuoificio SpA

Italy Sole leather

Bizzarro S.R.L.

| | | | | |
|---|---|---|---|---|
| **Address** | : | Via Ascanio Masini 36<br>Santa Croce sull'Amo (PI)-56029<br>Italy | Italy | |
| **Tel.** | : | +39 571 31184/30036 | | |
| **Fax** | : | +39 571 33894 | | |
| **Email** | : | bisonte.cuoificio@tiscalinet.it | | |
| **Web** | : | | | |
| **Activity** | : | | | |
| **Products** | : | *Hides and Skins* : Vegetable crust,<br><br>*Leather* : Sole leather, | | |

Bomar SpA

| | | | | |
|---|---|---|---|---|
| **Address** | : | Via C. Pannocchia 7<br>Ponte a Egola (PI)-56024<br>Italy | Italy | Footwear – lining leather, Footwear – upper leather, Garment leather |
| **Tel.** | : | +39 571 49391 | | |
| **Fax** | : | +39 571 498 870 | | |
| **Email** | : | info@bomar-spa.com | | |
| **Web** | : | http://www.bomar-spa.com | | |
| **Activity** | : | Manufacturer | | |
| **Products** | : | *Hides and Skins* : Chrome crust, Vegetable crust,<br><br>*Leather* : Footwear – upper leather, Footwear – lining leather, Garment leather,<br><br>*Footwear* : Women's shoes,<br><br>*Garments and Gloves* : Jacket, coats, | | |
| **Raw Materials** | : | Goat | | |

Bonistalli & Stefanelli SpA

| | | | | |
|---|---|---|---|---|
| **Address** | : | Via Piemonte 4 | Italy | Sole leather |
| **Tel.** | : | +39 571 33 134/30 287 | | |
| **Email** | : | bonste@leonet.it | | |

**Web** :

**Activity** : Manufacturer

**Products** : *Hides and Skins* : Vegetable crust,

*Leather* : Sole leather,

Brizzi Agenzie Srl

**Address** : Via Valbrona, 4
Milano (MI)-20125
Italy

**Tel.** : +39 02 643 6671
**Fax** : +39 02 643 6355

**Email** :
**Web** :

**Activity** : Manufacturer

**Products** : *Hides and Skins* : Chrome crust, Vegetable crust,

*Leather* : Automotive leather, Garment leather, Split leather,

**Raw Materials** : Bovine, Goat, Other (Horse, Chamois, Elk, Deer, Ostrich)

Italy Automotive leather, Garment leather, Split leather

Brotini Mario & C. Snc

**Address** : Via delle Confina 3-5-7
Castelfranco di Sotto PI-56022
Italy

**Tel.** : +39 571 480 251
**Fax** : +39 571 489 011

**Email** : brotini@sintesi-net.it
**Web** :

**Activity** : Manufacturer

**Products** : *Leather* : Footwear – upper leather, Footwear – lining leather,

*Chemicals* : Tanning,

*Leather Goods* : Small leather goods, Large leather goods,

Italy Footwear – lining leather, Footwear – upper leather

Buran Srl

**Address** : Contrada San Giovanni
Colonnella (TE)-64010

Italy Sole leather

**Tel.** : +39 861 7261
**Fax** : +39 861 726 318

**Tel.** : +39 861 7261
**Fax** : +39 861 726 318
**Email** : daniele.antonini@buran.it
**Web** :
**Activity** : Manufacturer
**Products** : *Leather* : Sole leather,

Byfinco Srl
**Address** : Via S. Rocco 120
Fraz S. Lazzaro
Bassano del Grappa (VI)-36061
Italy
**Tel.** : +39 424 566 221/2/3
**Fax** : +39 424 566 414
**Email** : byfinco@tin.it
**Web** :
**Activity** : Manufacturer
**Products** : *Hides and Skins* : Chrome crust,

*Leather* : Footwear – upper leather, Leathergoods leather, Footwear – lining leather, Upholstery leather, Split leather,

Italy Footwear – lining leather, Footwear – upper leather, Leathergoods leather, Split leather, Upholstery leather

CA. PRI. Suolificio SpA
**Address** : Contrada Campiglione, 20
Fermo (AP)-63023
Italy
**Tel.** : +39 734 628 367/648
**Fax** : +39 734 628 879
**Email** : info@ca-pri.it
**Web** : http://www.ca-pri.it
**Activity** : Manufacturer, Exporter
**Products** : *Leather* : Sole leather,

Italy Sole leather

Calligiana Industria Conciaria SpA.
**Address** : Via del Puntone, s/n
**Tel.** : +39 571 297 766
**Email** : calligiana@calligiana.it
**Activity** : Manufacturer

Italy Footwear – lining leather, Footwear – upper leather, Leathergoods leather

**Activity** : Manufacturer

**Products** : *Hides and Skins* : Vegetable crust,

*Leather* : Footwear – upper leather, Leathergoods leather, Footwear – lining leather,

Calvin Srl

| | | | |
|---|---|---|---|
| **Address** | : Via Privata, 1<br>Santa Croce S. Arno (PI)-56029<br>Italy | Italy | Footwear – lining leather, Footwear – upper leather, Leathergoods leather, Split leather |
| **Tel.** | : +39 571 367 683 | | |
| **Fax** | : +39 571 381 722 | | |
| **Email** | : calvin@internetlibero.it | | |
| **Web** | : | | |
| **Activity** | : Manufacturer | | |
| **Products** | : *Hides and Skins* : Chrome crust,<br>*Leather* : Footwear – upper leather, Leathergoods leather, Footwear – lining leather, Split leather, | | |

Camaleonte SpA Conceria Pellami

| | | | |
|---|---|---|---|
| **Address** | : Via Provinciale Le Francesca Sud 183-185<br>Santa Croce sull'Amo (PI)-56029<br>Italy | Italy | Footwear – upper leather, Leathergoods leather |
| **Tel.** | : +39 0571 31186/34081 | | |
| **Fax** | : +39 0571 366 207 | | |
| **Activity** | : Manufacturer | | |
| **Products** | : *Hides and Skins* : Chrome crust, Other - hides and skins,<br>*Leather* : Footwear – upper leather, Leathergoods leather, | | |

Capital Trading Srl

| | | | |
|---|---|---|---|
| **Address** | : Via Prov. Francesca Nord<br>Castelfranco di Sotto-56024<br>Italy | Italy | Footwear – lining leather, Footwear – upper leather, Leathergoods leather, Sole leather |
| **Tel.** | : +39 571 367 149 | | |
| **Fax** | : +39 571 367 149 | | |
| **Email** | : capitaltrading@netfree.it | | |
| **Web** | : | | |
| **Activity** | : Agent | | |
| **Products** | : *Leather* : Footwear – upper leather, Leathergoods leather, Footwear – lining leather, Sole leather, | | |

Caponi & Caponi Srl

| | | | | |
|---|---|---|---|---|
| **Address** | : | Via N. Bonaparte, 27<br>Fucecchio (FI)-50054<br>Italy | Italy | |
| **Tel.** | : | +39 571 261 891 | | |
| **Fax** | : | +39 571 261 895/6 | | |
| **Email** | : | info@caponi-caponileathers.it | | |
| **Web** | : | http://www.caponi-caponileathers.it | | |
| **Activity** | : | Agent | | |
| **Raw Materials** | : | Bovine, Sheep, Goat | | |

Caponi Giuseppe & Co. Srl

| | | | | |
|---|---|---|---|---|
| **Address** | : | Via A. Gramsci 348<br>Ponte a Egola (PI)-56024<br>Italy | Italy | Footwear – lining leather, Footwear – upper leather, Leathergoods leather, Other - leather, Split leather |
| **Tel.** | : | +39 571 497 080 | | |
| **Fax** | : | +39 571 498 824 | | |
| **Email** | : | conceriacaponi.g@elenet.it | | |
| **Web** | : | | | |
| **Activity** | : | Manufacturer | | |
| **Products** | : | *Hides and Skins* : Chrome crust, Vegetable crust, Other - hides and skins,<br><br>*Leather* : Footwear – upper leather, Leathergoods leather, Other - leather, Footwear – lining leather, Split leather, | | |

Carbi. Pel Srl

| | | | | |
|---|---|---|---|---|
| **Address** | : | Via Segala, 13<br>Zermeghedo (VI)-36050<br>Italy | Italy | Footwear – lining leather, Footwear – upper leather, Gloving leather, Leathergoods leather, Upholstery leather |
| **Tel.** | : | +39 444 685 015 | | |
| **Fax** | : | +39 444 686 094 | | |
| **Email** | : | info@carbipel.com | | |
| **Web** | : | http://www.carbipel.com | | |
| **Activity** | : | Manufacturer | | |
| **Products** | : | *Hides and Skins* : Chrome crust,<br><br>*Leather* : Footwear – upper leather, Leathergoods leather, Footwear – lining leather, Upholstery leather, Gloving leather, | | |
| **Raw Materials** | : | Bovine, Other (Horse) | | |

Carli & Gori SAS — Italy

**Address** : Via Curtatone E. Montanara,10
Santa Croce S. Arno (PI)-56029
Italy

**Tel.** : +39 571 30333
**Fax** : +39 571 261 782

**Email** :
**Web** :

**Activity** : Manufacturer

**Products** :

**Raw Materials** : Goat

Carli Conceria Srl

**Address** : Viale Colombo, 212
Ponte a Cappiano-Fucecchi-50050
Italy

**Tel.** : +39 571 297138
**Fax** : +39 571 297 139

**Email** : carliconc@interfree.it
**Web** :

**Activity** : Manufacturer

**Products** : *Hides and Skins* : Chrome crust,

*Leather* : Footwear – upper leather, Leathergoods leather, Footwear – lining leather,

Italy Footwear – lining leather, Footwear – upper leather, Leathergoods leather

Carlotto Ida Srl Conceria

**Address** : Via Lavoro 71
Arzignano (VI)-36071
Italy

**Tel.** : +39 0444 676 888
**Fax** : +39 0444 671 657

**Email** : carlotto.ida@tin.it
**Web** :

**Activity** : Manufacturer

**Products** : *Hides and Skins* : Chrome crust,

*Leather* : Footwear – upper leather, Footwear – lining leather, Garment leather,

Italy Footwear – lining leather, Footwear – upper leather, Garment leather

Carsten's Suede & Leather Srl

**Address** : Via Muncipio 6
S. Agata Irpina Solofra 83020

**Tel.** : +39 0825 583 805/534 213
**Fax** : +39 0825 583 795

**Email** : info@carstens.it
**Web** : http://www.carstens.it

Italy Footwear – lining leather, Footwear – upper leather, Garment leather,

| | | | | |
|---|---|---|---|---|
| **Email** | : | info@carstens.it | | Leathergoods leather, Split leather |
| **Web** | : | http://www.carstens.it | | |
| **Activity** | : | | | |
| **Products** | : | *Hides and Skins* : Chrome crust,<br><br>*Leather* : Footwear – upper leather, Leathergoods leather, Footwear – lining leather, Garment leather, Split leather, | | |

Centomo Conceria Srl

| | | | | |
|---|---|---|---|---|
| **Address** | : | Via Arzignano 5/D<br>Chiampo (VI)-36072<br>Italy | Italy | Footwear – lining leather, Footwear – upper leather, Garment leather, Leathergoods leather, Sole leather, Split leather, Upholstery leather |
| **Tel.** | : | +39 444 623 090 | | |
| **Fax** | : | +39 444 420 192 | | |
| **Email** | : | centomo.comm@tin.it | | |
| **Web** | : | http://www.centomo.it | | |
| **Activity** | : | Manufacturer | | |
| **Products** | : | *Hides and Skins* : Chrome crust,<br><br>*Leather* : Footwear – upper leather, Leathergoods leather, Footwear – lining leather, Sole leather, Upholstery leather, Garment leather, Split leather, | | |

Centrorettili SpA

| | | | | |
|---|---|---|---|---|
| **Address** | : | Via Lombardia 12<br>Santa Croce S/A (PI)-56029<br>Italy | Italy | Footwear – upper leather, Gloving leather, Leathergoods leather |
| **Tel.** | : | +39 571 366 682 | | |
| **Fax** | : | +39 571 366 684 | | |
| **Email** | : | centrorettili@leonet.it | | |
| **Web** | : | | | |
| **Activity** | : | Manufacturer | | |
| **Products** | : | *Hides and Skins* : Chrome crust, Vegetable crust,<br><br>*Leather* : Footwear – upper leather, Leathergoods leather, Gloving leather, | | |
| **Raw Materials** | : | Reptile, Other (lizard, ostrich, crocodile, python) | | |

Cinpel Srl

| | | | | |
|---|---|---|---|---|
| **Address** | : | Isola 7 N° 757/758 - CIS Nola | Italy | Split leather |
| **Tel.** | : | +39 81 510 9292 | | |

**Fax** : +39 81 510 9003

**Email** : cinpel@cinpel.it
**Web** : http://www.cinpel.it

**Activity** : Wholesaler

**Products** : *Hides and Skins* : Chrome crust, Vegetable crust,

*Leather* : Split leather,

**Raw Materials** : Pig, Other (horse, fish)

Co RI Pel SpA

**Address** : Via delle Confina 26/27
Fucecchio (FI)-50054
Italy

**Tel.** : +39 571 21061/22213
**Fax** : +39 571 21028

**Email** : coripel@coripel.it
**Web** : http://www.coripel.it

**Activity** : Manufacturer

**Products** : *Hides and Skins* : Chrome crust,

*Leather* : Footwear – upper leather, Leathergoods leather,

Italy Footwear – upper leather, Leathergoods leather

Cofipel Srl

**Address** : Via Tommaso 59/61
Santa Croce S/A (PI)-56029
Italy

**Tel.** : +39 571 30204
**Fax** : +39 571 30429

**Email** : nobel@nobel.it
**Web** :

**Activity** : Manufacturer

**Products** : *Hides and Skins* : Chrome crust,

*Leather* : Split leather,

**Raw Materials** : Goat

Italy Split leather

Coimbra Conceria Sas

**Address** : Via Mariotti 27

**Tel.** : +39 571 20912/21594

**Email** : info@coimbra.it

Italy Footwear – lining leather, Footwear – upper leather, Leathergoods leather

**Web** : http://www.coimbra.it

**Activity** : Manufacturer

**Products** : *Hides and Skins* : Chrome crust,

*Leather* : Footwear – upper leather, Leathergoods leather, Footwear – lining leather,

**Raw Materials** : Goat

Colmar Srl

**Address** : Via Friuli 12/B
Monte Urano (AP)-63015
Italy

Italy Footwear – lining leather, Leathergoods leather, Upholstery leather

**Tel.** : +39 734 840 608
**Fax** : +39 734 840 392

**Email** :
**Web** :

**Activity** : Manufacturer, Importer, Exporter

**Products** : *Hides and Skins* : Chrome crust,

*Leather* : Leathergoods leather, Footwear – lining leather, Upholstery leather,

**Raw Materials** : Sheep, Goat, Pig

Comes Srl

**Address** : Via Castelfidardo 42
Civitanova Marche (MC) 62012
Italy

Italy Footwear – lining leather, Footwear – upper leather, Leathergoods leather, Split leather

**Tel.** : +39 733 812 649
**Fax** : +39 733 812 649

**Email** : comes@comesleather.it
**Web** : http://www.comesleather.com

**Activity** : Manufacturer

**Products** : *Hides and Skins* : Chrome crust,

*Leather* : Footwear – upper leather, Leathergoods leather, Footwear – lining leather, Split leather,

Compel Sas

**Address** : Via 1 Maggio, 18 Fraz. Quarto Inf.
Granarolo dell' Emilia 40050

Italy Garment leather, Split leather

**Tel.** : +39 051 768 124
**Fax** : +39 051 768 480

**Tel.** : +39 051 768 124
**Fax** : +39 051 768 480

**Email** : info@compel-bo.com
**Web** : http://www.compel-bo.com

**Activity** : Manufacturer

**Products** : *Hides and Skins* : Chrome crust,

*Leather* : Garment leather, Split leather,

**Raw Materials** : Sheep, Goat, Other

Compel SpA

**Address** : Via Valchiampo 1
Montorso Vicentino. VI-36070
Italy

**Tel.** : +39 0444 01 11
**Fax** : +39 0444 68 62 40

**Email** : williamsmartini@compelgroup.it
**Web** :

**Activity** : Manufacturer

**Products** : *Leather* : Footwear – upper leather, Leathergoods leather, Footwear – lining leather, Upholstery leather,

Italy

Footwear – lining leather, Footwear – upper leather, Leathergoods leather, Upholstery leather

Con - Pel Srl

**Address** : Via Delle Confina 9
Fucecchio (FI)-50054
Italy

**Tel.** : +39 571 22250
**Fax** : +39 571 20316

**Email** :
**Web** :

**Activity** : Manufacturer

**Products** : *Hides and Skins* : Chrome crust,

*Leather* : Footwear – upper leather, Leathergoods leather,

Italy

Footwear – upper leather, Leathergoods leather

Conam Gruppo Conciario Srl

**Address** : Via Regina Margherita 31

**Tel.** : +39 825 535 335

**Email** : info@gruppoconam.com

**Activity** : Manufacturer

Italy

Footwear – lining leather, Footwear – upper leather, Garment leather, Leathergoods leather

**Activity** : Manufacturer

**Products** : *Hides and Skins* : Chrome crust, Vegetable crust,

*Leather* : Footwear – upper leather, Leathergoods leather, Footwear – lining leather, Garment leather,

**Raw Materials** : Sheep, Goat

Conc. Caciagli Adolfo SpA

**Contact** : Sandra Caciagli
Owner

We are producers of high quality vegetable tanned shoulders for insole and underfoot.

**Address** : Via Martin Luther King snc
Ponte a Egola-San Miniato-56024
Italy

**Tel.** : +39 571 497 990
**Fax** : +39 571 484 304
**Email** :
**Web** :

Italy Other - leather, Sole leather

**Activity** : Wholesaler, Manufacturer, Importer, Exporter

**Products** : *Leather* : Other - leather, Sole leather,

**Raw Materials** : Bovine

Conceria 2 G Srl

**Address** : Via Verdi 18
Santa Croce sull' Arno
Pisa-56029
Italy

**Tel.** : +39 571 360 796
**Fax** : +39 571 385 145
**Email** : contact@conceria2g.com
**Web** : http://www.conceria2g.com

Italy Footwear – lining leather, Footwear – upper leather

**Activity** : Manufacturer

**Products** : *Hides and Skins* : Chrome crust,

*Leather* : Footwear – upper leather, Footwear – lining leather

Conceria 800 Srl

**Address** : Via G. Amendola, 2
Ponte a Egola (PI)-56024
Italy

Italy Footwear – lining leather, Footwear – upper leather, Leathergoods leather

**Tel.** : +39 571 497 156
**Fax** : +39 571 497 156

**Email**
**Web**



**Activity** : Manufacturer

**Products** : *Hides and Skins* : Chrome crust, Vegetable crust,

*Leather* : Footwear – upper leather, Leathergoods leather, Footwear – lining leather,

Conceria Beschingino SpA

**Address** : Via Della Concia 20
Arzignano (VI)-
Italy

**Tel.** : +39 0444 671 888
**Fax** : +39 0444 450 874

**Email** :
**Web** : http://www.beschin.it

**Activity** : Wholesaler, Manufacturer

**Products** : *Hides and Skins* : Wet blue,

*Leather* : Footwear – upper leather, Leathergoods leather, Footwear – lining leather, Upholstery leather, Garment leather, Split leather,

**Raw Materials** : Bovine

Italy

Footwear – lining leather, Footwear – upper leather, Garment leather, Leathergoods leather, Split leather, Upholstery leather

Conceria Bruttomesso

**Address** : Via Ottava Strada 7
Z. I.
Arzignano (VI)-36071
Italy

**Tel.** : +39 0444 673 544
**Fax** : +39 0444 450 455

**Email** : info@conceriabruttomesso.com
**Web** : http://www.conceriabruttomesso.com

**Activity** : Manufacturer

**Products** : *Hides and Skins* : Chrome crust,

*Leather* : Footwear – upper leather, Leathergoods leather, Footwear – lining leather, Upholstery leather, Garment leather,

Italy

Footwear – lining leather, Footwear – upper leather, Garment leather, Leathergoods leather, Upholstery leather

Conceria Caravel Pelli Pregiate SpA

**Address** : Via Franco Sacchetti 2
Fucecchio (FI)-50054
Italy

**Tel.** : +39 0571 260 291
**Fax** : +39 0571 260 978

**Email** : info@caravelspa.com
**Web** :

**Activity** : Manufacturer

Italy

**Products** : *Hides and Skins* : Chrome crust, Vegetable crust,

| | | | | |
|---|---|---|---|---|
| **Products** | : | *Hides and Skins* : Chrome crust, Vegetable crust, | | |
| **Raw Materials** | : | Reptile | | |

Conceria Cerbiatto Srl

| | | | | |
|---|---|---|---|---|
| **Address** | : | Via Padre Greggio 12<br>Biella (BI)-13051<br>Italy | Italy | Footwear – lining leather, Footwear – upper leather, Garment leather, Gloving leather, Leathergoods leather |
| **Tel.** | : | +39 0158 48 04 11 | | |
| **Fax** | : | +39 0158 40 00 35 | | |
| **Email** | : | conchior@chiorinotannery.it | | |
| **Web** | : | http://www.chiorinotannery.it | | |
| **Activity** | : | Manufacturer | | |
| **Products** | : | *Hides and Skins* : Vegetable crust,<br>*Leather* : Footwear – upper leather, Leathergoods leather, Automotive leather, Footwear – lining leather, Upholstery leather, | | |
| **Raw Materials** | : | Pig | | |

Conceria Chiorino Srl

| | | | | |
|---|---|---|---|---|
| **Address** | : | Via Padre Greggio 12<br>Biella (BI)-13051<br>Italy | Italy | Automotive leather, Footwear – lining leather, Footwear – upper leather, Leathergoods leather, Upholstery leather |
| **Tel.** | : | +39 0158 48 04 11 | | |
| **Fax** | : | +39 0158 40 00 35 | | |
| **Email** | : | conchior@chiorinotannery.it | | |
| **Web** | : | http://www.chiorinotannery.it | | |
| **Activity** | : | Manufacturer | | |
| **Products** | : | *Hides and Skins* : Vegetable crust,<br>*Leather* : Footwear – upper leather, Leathergoods leather, Automotive leather, Footwear – lining leather, Upholstery leather, | | |
| **Raw Materials** | : | Pig | | |

Conceria CILP Snc

| | | | | | |
|---|---|---|---|---|---|
| **Contact** | : | Leopoldo Cione | Production and trade of letahers for footwear and leather goods. | Italy | Footwear – lining leather, Footwear – upper leather, Leathergoods leather, Split leather |
| **Address** | : | Via del Melaccio 21<br>Santa Croce Sull'Arno<br>Pisa-56029<br>Italy | | | |
| **Tel.** | : | +39 571 322 33 | | | |
| **Fax** | : | +39 571 302 23 | | | |
| **Email** | : | info@cilp.it | | | |
| **Web** | : | | | | |
| **Activity** | : | Manufacturer | | | |



Products : *Leather* : Footwear – upper leather

**Products** : *Leather* : Footwear – upper leather, Leathergoods leather, Footwear – lining leather, Split leather,

**Raw Materials** : Bovine

Conceria Dea Pel Srl

**Address** : Via Sardegna 9/11
Ponte a Cappiano (FI)-50050
Italy

**Tel.** : +39 0571 29 79 44
**Fax** : +39 0571 29 50 29
**Email** : info@deapel.it
**Web** : http://www.deapel.it
**Activity** : Manufacturer
**Products** : *Hides and Skins* : Chrome crust, Vegetable crust,

*Leather* : Footwear – upper leather, Leathergoods leather, Footwear – lining leather,

Italy Footwear – lining leather, Footwear – upper leather, Leathergoods leather

Conceria del Chienti SpA

**Address** : Via Willy Weber, 24
Tolentino (MC)-62029
Italy

**Tel.** : +39 733 971 916
**Fax** : +39 733 974 767
**Email** : ctc@ctc.it
**Web** : http://www.ctc.it
**Activity** : Manufacturer
**Products** : *Hides and Skins* : Chrome crust,

*Leather* : Footwear – upper leather, Leathergoods leather, Other - leather, Footwear – lining leather,

*Footwear* : Women's shoes,

**Raw Materials** : Sheep, Goat

Italy Footwear – lining leather, Footwear – upper leather, Leathergoods leather, Other - leather

Conceria Di Urgnano Srl

**Address** : Loc. Battaina
**Tel.** : +39 35 893 005
**Email** : sales@skiver.it
**Activity** : Manufacturer

Italy Footwear – lining leather, Footwear – upper leather, Garment leather, Leathergoods leather

**Activity** : Manufacturer

**Products** : *Hides and Skins* : Chrome crust, Vegetable crust,

*Leather* : Footwear – upper leather, Leathergoods leather, Footwear – lining leather, Garment leather,

**Raw Materials** : Sheep, Goat

Conceria Duma SantaCroce Srl

**Address** : Via Toscana 34 E-F
Santa Croce sull' Arno
Pisa-56029
Italy

**Tel.** : +39 571 33354
**Fax** : +39 571 366 839

**Email** : info@dumasantacroce.it
**Web** : http://www.dumasantacroce.it

**Activity** : Manufacturer

**Products** : *Hides and Skins* : Chrome crust,

*Leather* : Footwear – upper leather, Leathergoods leather, Footwear – lining leather, Garment leather,

Italy Footwear – lining leather, Footwear – upper leather, Garment leather, Leathergoods leather

Conceria Dusini Pio Srl

**Address** : Via del Commercio 37
Trento (TN)-38100
Italy

**Tel.** : +39 461 421 280
**Fax** : +39 461 422 266

**Email** : nidusini@tin.it
**Web** :

**Activity** : Manufacturer

**Products** : *Hides and Skins* : Vegetable crust,

*Leather* : Footwear – upper leather, Sole leather,

Italy Footwear – upper leather, Sole leather

Conceria F.LLI Nazzi Snc

**Address** : Via G. Sozzi, 32
Santa Croce sull' Arno
Pisa-56029
Italy

**Tel.** : +39 571 30412
**Fax** : +39 57132327

Italy Leathergoods leather, Upholstery leather

**Email** : f.llinazzi@libero.it
**Web** :



**Activity** : Manufacturer

**Products** : *Hides and Skins* : Vegetable crust,

*Leather* : Leathergoods leather, Upholstery leather

**Products** : *Hides and Skins* : Vegetable crust,

*Leather* : Leathergoods leather, Upholstery leather,

Conceria F.Lli Pellizzari SpA

**Address** : Via Pieve Bassa N° 49
Chiampo (VI)-36072
Italy

**Tel.** : +39 0444 62 34 99
**Fax** : +39 0444 42 02 66

**Email** :
**Web** :

**Activity** : Manufacturer

**Products** : *Leather* : Footwear – upper leather, Leathergoods leather, Footwear – lining leather, Upholstery leather, Garment leather,

Italy Footwear – lining leather, Footwear – upper leather, Garment leather, Leathergoods leather, Upholstery leather

Conceria Genesis 98 Srl

**Address** : Via E. Romagna, 13
Santa Croce sull'Arno PI-56029
Italy

**Tel.** : +39 0571 360 115
**Fax** : +39 0571 367 441

**Email** : info@conceriagenesis98.com
**Web** : http://www.conceriagenesis98.com

**Activity** : Manufacturer, Importer, Exporter

**Products** : *Hides and Skins* : Chrome crust, Vegetable crust,

*Leather* : Footwear – upper leather, Leathergoods leather,

**Raw Materials** : Bovine

Italy Footwear – upper leather, Leathergoods leather

Conceria Giamaica

**Address** : Via Lombardia 4

**Tel.** : +39 0571 311 78

**Email** : info@conceriagiamaica.com

**Activity** : Manufacturer, Exporter

**Products** : *Hides and Skins* : Chrome crust, Vegetable

Italy Footwear – upper leather, Leathergoods leather

**Raw Materials** : Bovine, Buffalo

Conceria Guidi Srl

**Address** : Via Stignanese 76
Ponte Buggianese (PT)-51019
Italy

**Tel.** : +39 572 930 211
**Fax** : +39 572 931 490

**Email** : succ@guidi.it
**Web** : http://www.guidi.it

**Activity** :

**Products** : *Hides and Skins* : Vegetable crust,

*Leather* : Footwear – upper leather, Leathergoods leather, Automotive leather, Footwear – lining leather, Sole leather, Garment leather,

Italy Automotive leather, Footwear – lining leather, Footwear – upper leather, Garment leather, Leathergoods leather, Sole leather

**Raw Materials** : Other (Horse)

Conceria Incas

**Address** : Via Enrico Mattei 11
Castelfranco di Sotto-PI-56022
Italy

**Tel.** : +39 0571 48 99 55
**Fax** : +39 0571 48 99 59

**Email** : incas@incas.it
**Web** : http://www.incas.it

**Activity** : Manufacturer

**Products** : *Leather* : Footwear – upper leather, Leathergoods leather, Footwear – lining leather,

Italy Footwear – lining leather, Footwear – upper leather, Leathergoods leather

Conceria Jaipur Srl

**Address** : Via Sardegna 4-6-8
Ponte a Cappiano (FI)-50050
Italy

Italy Footwear – lining leather, Footwear – upper leather, Garment leather, Leathergoods leather

**Tel.** : +39 0571 297 879
**Fax** : +39 0571 297 881

**Email** : info@jaipur.it
**Web** : http://www.jaipur.it

**Activity** : Manufacturer



**Products** : *Hides and Skins* : Vegetable crust,

**Products** : *Hides and Skins* : Vegetable crust,

*Leather* : Footwear – upper leather, Leathergoods leather, Footwear – lining leather, Garment leather,

**Raw Materials** : Bovine, Goat

## Conceria Leather Italia Srl

**Address** : Via Colombara 21 - G
Chiampo (VI)-36072
Italy

**Tel.** : +39 444 420 741
**Fax** : +39 444 420 154

**Email** : leaitalia@libero.it
**Web** : http://www.concerialeatheritalia.com

**Activity** : Manufacturer

**Products** : *Leather* : Footwear – upper leather, Footwear – lining leather, Upholstery leather, Garment leather,

Italy Footwear – lining leather, Footwear – upper leather, Garment leather, Upholstery leather

## Conceria Maiora SpA.

**Address** : Via dei Conciatori Nord 34/36
Ponte a Egola (PI)-56024
Italy

**Tel.** : +39 571 485 174
**Fax** : +39 571 498 588

**Email** : info@conceria-maiora.it
**Web** : http://www.conceria-maiora.it

**Activity** : Manufacturer

**Products** : *Hides and Skins* : Chrome crust,

*Leather* : Footwear – upper leather, Leathergoods leather, Footwear – lining leather,

**Raw Materials** : Bovine

Italy Footwear – lining leather, Footwear – upper leather, Leathergoods leather

## Conceria Montana Srl

**Address** : Via Gramsci 136
P.O. Box 107

**Tel.** : +39 0571 48 54 00
**Fax** : +39 0571 49 77 04

**Email** : montana@montana.it
**Web** : http://www.montana.it

**Activity** : Manufacturer

**Products** : *Leather* : Leathergoods leather,

Italy Leathergoods leather

**Products** : *Leather* : Leathergoods leather,

**Raw Materials** : Bovine

Conceria N.C.L Srl

**Address** : Localita' Carpisano
Zona Industriale
Solofra (AV)-83029
Italy

**Tel.** : +39 825 534 607
**Fax** : +39 825 534 608

**Email** : info@ncleather.com
**Web** : http://www.ncleather.com

**Activity** : Manufacturer

**Products** : *Hides and Skins* : Chrome crust, Vegetable crust, Other - hides and skins,

*Leather* : Footwear – upper leather, Leathergoods leather, Garment leather, Gloving leather,

**Raw Materials** : Sheep, Goat

Italy Footwear – upper leather, Garment leather, Gloving leather, Leathergoods leather

Conceria Nord SpA Italy Footwear – lining leather, Footwear – upper leather, Garment leather, Gloving leather, Leathergoods leather, Split leather

Conceria Nuvola Srl

**Address** : Via Montorso 14/d/e/f/g
Arzignano (VI)-36071
Italy

**Tel.** : +39 0444 673916
**Fax** : +39 0444 450709

**Email** : conceria.nuvola@keycomm.it
**Web** : http://www.tannerynuvola.com

**Activity** : Manufacturer

**Products** : *Leather* : Footwear – upper leather, Leathergoods leather, Footwear – lining leather, Garment leather,

Italy Footwear – lining leather, Footwear – upper leather, Garment leather, Leathergoods leather

Conceria Oregon Euro Srl Italy Footwear – lining leather.

**Address** : Via E. Fermi 35
P.O. Box 97
Santa Croce S/A (PI)-56029
Italy

Footwear – upper leather, Garment leather, Leathergoods leather, Upholstery leather

**Tel.** : +39 571 31297/31648
**Fax** : +39 571 32617
**Email** : conceriaoregoneuro@libero.it
**Web** :
**Activity** : Manufacturer
**Products** : *Leather* : Footwear – upper leather, Leathergoods leather, Footwear – lining leather, Upholstery leather, Garment leather,

Conceria Peretti SpA

**Address** : Via Industria 101
Arzignano (VI)-36701
Italy

Italy Automotive leather, Leathergoods leather, Upholstery leather

**Tel.** : +39 0444 670 832/676 944
**Fax** : +39 0444 676 944
**Email** : conceriaperettispa@tin.it
**Web** :
**Activity** : Manufacturer
**Products** : *Hides and Skins* : Chrome crust,

*Leather* : Leathergoods leather, Automotive leather, Upholstery leather,

Conceria Priante SpA

**Address** : Via Quinta Strada 1
Zona Industriale
Arzignano (VI)-36071
Italy

Italy Upholstery leather

**Tel.** : +39 0444 451 514
**Fax** : +39 0444 450 435
**Email** : cipria@conceriapriante.com
**Web** : http://www.conceriapriante.com
**Activity** : Manufacturer, Exporter
**Products** : *Hides and Skins* : Chrome crust,

*Leather* : Upholstery leather,

Conceria R.C.M. Srl

Italy Footwear – lining leather, Footwear – upper leather.

**Address** : Via del Collettore, 4/10
Ponte a Cappiano (FI)-50050
**Tel.** : +39 0571 29 70 39
**Fax** : +39 0571 29 72 25

**Tel.** : +39 0571 29 70 39
**Fax** : +39 0571 29 72 25

Leathergoods leather

**Email** : info@conceriarcm.it
**Web** : http://www.conceriarcm.it

**Activity** : Manufacturer

**Products** : *Leather* : Footwear – upper leather, Leathergoods leather, Footwear – lining leather,

Conceria Romano Nicola & Michele Snc

**Address** : Via Celentane 29
Solofra (AV)-83029
Italy

**Tel.** : +39 825 532 171
**Fax** : +39 825 583 513

**Email** : info@conceriaromano.com
**Web** : http://www.conceriaromano.com

Italy

Garment leather

**Activity** : Manufacturer

**Products** : *Hides and Skins* : Chrome crust,

*Leather* : Garment leather,

**Raw Materials** : Sheep, Goat

Conceria Sabrina SpA

**Address** : Via Lungochiampo, 3
Zermeghedo (VI) 36050
Italy

**Tel.** : +39 0444 476 100
**Fax** : +39 0444 476 181

Italy

**Email** : info@conceriasabrina.com
**Web** : http://www.conceriasabrina.com

**Activity** : Manufacturer

Conceria Samanta SpA

**Address** : Via dei Conciatori 24-28
Ponte a Egola (PI)-56024
Italy

**Tel.** : +39 0571 485 71
**Fax** : +39 0571 498 818

Italy

**Email** : info@samanta.com
**Web** : http://www.samanta.com

**Activity** : Manufacturer

**Products** : *Leather Goods* : Small leather goods, Large leather goods,

Conceria San Firenze Srl

| | | | | |
|---|---|---|---|---|
| **Address** | : | Via Puglie 1<br>Santa Croce S/A (PI)-56029<br>Italy | | |
| **Tel.**<br>**Fax** | :<br>: | +39 571 31363/33214<br>+39 571 34273 | Italy | Footwear – lining leather, Footwear – upper leather, Leathergoods leather |
| **Email**<br>**Web** | :<br>: | sanfirenzesrl@virgilio.it | | |
| **Activity** | : | Manufacturer | | |
| **Products** | : | *Leather* : Footwear – upper leather, Leathergoods leather, Footwear – lining leather, | | |
| **Raw Materials** | : | Goat | | |

Conceria Thule Srl

| | | | | |
|---|---|---|---|---|
| **Address** | : | Via A. Grandi 9-15<br>Santa Croce s/Arno (PI)-56029<br>Italy | | |
| **Tel.**<br>**Fax** | :<br>: | +39 0571 32 831<br>+39 0571 30 134 | Italy | Footwear – upper leather, Leathergoods leather |
| **Email**<br>**Web** | :<br>: | info@thuleconceria.it<br>http://www.thuleconceria.it | | |
| **Activity** | : | Manufacturer, Exporter | | |
| **Products** | : | *Leather* : Footwear – upper leather, Leathergoods leather, | | |
| **Raw Materials** | : | Bovine | | |

Conceria Tirrena SpA

| | | | | |
|---|---|---|---|---|
| **Address** | : | Via Sonnino 39/41/41A<br>Civitanova Marche (MC)-62012<br>Italy | | |
| **Tel.**<br>**Fax** | :<br>: | +39 0733 825 511<br>+39 0733 825 532 / 3 | Italy | Footwear – lining leather, Footwear – upper leather, Garment leather, Leathergoods leather |
| **Email**<br>**Web** | :<br>: | info@conceriatirrena.com<br>http://www.conceriatirrena.com | | |
| **Activity** | : | Manufacturer, Exporter | | |
| **Products** | : | *Leather* : Footwear – upper leather, Leathergoods leather, Footwear – lining leather, Garment leather, | | |
| **Raw Materials** | : | Bovine, Sheep, Goat, Pig | | |

Conceria Toska Srl — Italy — Footwear – lining leather, Footwear –

**Address** : Via Copernico 48/50
Trezzano S/Naviglio (MI)-20090
Italy

**Tel.** : +39 2 4846 4018
**Fax** : +39 2 4846 4018

**Email** : info@conceriatoska.com
**Web** : http://www.toskaleather.com

**Activity** : Manufacturer

**Products** : *Hides and Skins* : Vegetable crust,

*Leather* : Footwear – upper leather, Leathergoods leather, Footwear – lining leather, Upholstery leather, Garment leather,

upper leather, Garment leather, Leathergoods leather, Upholstery leather

## Conceria Val Cismon Srl

**Address** : Via Latifondi 6
Cismon del Grappa (VI)-36020
Italy

**Tel.** : +39 424 92138
**Fax** : +39 424 92429

**Email** : conceria.valcismon@keycomm.it
**Web** : http://www.conceriavalcismon.com

**Activity** : Manufacturer

**Products** : *Leather* : Footwear – upper leather, Footwear – lining leather, Garment leather,

**Raw Materials** : Other (Deer)

Italy

Footwear – lining leather, Footwear – upper leather, Garment leather

## Conceria Vecchia Toscana SpA

**Address** : Via Sicilia 1
Ponte a Cappiano (FI)-50050
Italy

**Tel.** : +39 0571 29 72 52
**Fax** : +39 0571 29 71 44

**Email** : vecchiatoscana@leonet.it
**Web** :

**Activity** : Manufacturer

Italy

## Conceria Vicar Srl

**Address** : Via Del Cuoio 19

**Tel.** : +39 571 497 114

**Email** : vicar@vicar.it

**Activity** : Manufacturer

Italy

Footwear – lining leather, Footwear – upper leather, Garment leather

**Activity** : Manufacturer

**Products** : *Hides and Skins* : Chrome crust,

*Leather* : Footwear – upper leather, Footwear – lining leather, Garment leather,

**Raw Materials** : Sheep, Goat

Conceria Vicenza Pelli Srl

**Address** : Via Arzignano 158/A
Chiampo (VI)-36072
Italy

**Tel.** : +39 444 420 456
**Fax** : +39 444 420 458

**Email** : vicpelli@tin.it
**Web** : http://www.vicenzapelli.com

**Activity** : Manufacturer

**Products** : *Hides and Skins* : Chrome crust,

*Leather* : Footwear – upper leather, Leathergoods leather, Footwear – lining leather, Upholstery leather, Garment leather,

**Raw Materials** : Bovine, Other (Horse)

Italy Footwear – lining leather, Footwear – upper leather, Garment leather, Leathergoods leather, Upholstery leather

Conceria Vignola Nobile

**Address** : Via Selvapiana 18
Solofra (AV)-83029
Italy

**Tel.** : +39 0825 581 208/9
**Fax** : +39 0825 532 655

**Email** : conceriavignolanobile@tin.it
**Web** :

**Activity** : Manufacturer

**Products** : *Leather* : Garment leather,

Italy Garment leather

Conceria Zini SpA

**Address** : Via Valdichiampo, 8
Zermeghedo (VI)-36050
Italy

**Tel.** : +39 0444 472 900
**Fax** : +39 0444 686 095

**Email** : zini@zini.it
**Web** : http://www.zini.it

**Activity** : Manufacturer, Exporter

Italy Automotive leather, Footwear – lining leather, Footwear – upper leather, Garment leather, Leathergoods leather, Other - leather, Saddlery and



**Products** : *Leather* : Footwear – upper leather, Leathergoods leather, Automotive leather, Other - leather, Footwear – lining leather, Upholstery leather, Garment leather, Saddlery

Other - leather, Footwear – lining leather, Upholstery leather, Garment leather, Saddlery and harness leather,

harness leather, Upholstery leather

**Raw Materials** : Bovine

## Concerie Riunite GB SpA

**Contact** : Dino Guerrini
President

**Address** : Via Romaiano 20
Ponte a Egola (PI)-56024
Italy

**Tel.** : +39 571 41511
**Fax** : +39 571 485444

**Email** : concerieriunitegb@gbcuoio.it
**Web** : http://www.gbcuoio.com

**Activity** : Manufacturer

**Products** : *Hides and Skins* : Vegetable crust,

*Leather* : Leathergoods leather, Sole leather, Upholstery leather, Saddlery and harness leather,

Italy

Leathergoods leather, Saddlery and harness leather, Sole leather, Upholstery leather

## Conciaria Adriatica SpA

**Address** : Via Quinta Strada
Arzignano (VI)-36071
Italy

**Tel.** : +39 0444 473 711
**Fax** : +39 0444 473 722

**Email** : info@gcveneto.com
**Web** : http://www.gcveneto.com

**Activity** : Manufacturer

**Products** : *Hides and Skins* : Chrome crust,

*Leather* : Footwear – upper leather, Leathergoods leather, Automotive leather, Footwear – lining leather, Upholstery leather,

Italy

Automotive leather, Footwear – lining leather, Footwear – upper leather, Leathergoods leather, Upholstery leather

## Conciaria Bonaudo SpA

**Address** : Corso Galileo Ferraris 154
Chivasso (TO)-10034
Italy

**Tel.** : +39 11 910 1470
**Fax** : +39 11 910 2801

**Email** : bonaudo@nevib.it
**Web** :

**Activity** : Manufacturer

**Products** : *Hides and Skins* : Chrome crust,

Italy

Footwear – lining leather, Footwear – upper leather, Garment leather, Gloving leather, Leathergoods leather

Leathergoods leather, Footwear – lining leather, Garment leather, Gloving leather,

**Raw Materials** : Sheep, Goat, Other (Kangaroo)

## Conti Conceria SpA

**Address** : Via Michelangelo 3
Urgnano (BG)-24059
Italy

**Tel.** : +39 35 891 012
**Fax** : +39 35 892 316

**Email** : conceria.conti@tiscalinet.it
**Web** :

**Activity** : Manufacturer

**Products** : *Hides and Skins* : Chrome crust, Vegetable crust,

*Leather* : Split leather,

Italy Split leather

## Cora Trade SpA

**Address** : Via Francesca Sud 404
Monsummano Terme (PT)-51015
Italy

**Tel.** : +39 572 53667/8
**Fax** : +39 572 53557

**Email** : info@coratrade.it
**Web** : http://www.coratrade.it

**Activity** : Agent

**Products** : *Hides and Skins* : Chrome crust,

*Leather* : Footwear – upper leather, Leathergoods leather, Footwear – lining leather,

**Raw Materials** : Bovine, Sheep, Goat, Pig, Other (horse, deer)

Italy Footwear – lining leather, Footwear – upper leather, Leathergoods leather

## Corapel SAS.

**Address** : Piazza Marconi 23
Stra (VE)-30039
Italy

**Tel.** : +39 49 503 677
**Fax** : +39 49 980 0005

**Email** : info@corapel.com
**Web** : http://www.corapel.com

**Activity** : Manufacturer

**Products** : *Hides and Skins* : Chrome crust,

*Leather* : Footwear – upper leather

Italy Footwear – lining leather, Footwear – upper leather, Garment leather, Leathergoods leather

Leathergoods leather, Footwear – lining leather, Garment leather,

**Raw Materials** : Bovine, Sheep, Goat, Pig, Other (horse)

Corinna Conceria Srl

**Address** : Via 1Y Settembre 2
Santa Croce S/A (PI)-56029
Italy

**Tel.** : +39 571 31109
**Fax** : +39 571 381 708
**Email** :
**Web** :
**Activity** : Manufacturer
**Products** : *Hides and Skins* : Chrome crust,

*Leather* : Footwear – upper leather, Footwear – lining leather,

Italy Footwear – lining leather, Footwear – upper leather

Cormorano Conceria SpA

**Address** : Via del Bosco, 105
Santa Croce S/A (PI)-56029
Italy

**Tel.** : +39 571 366 845
**Fax** : +39 571 366 849
**Email** : cormorano@cormoranoconceria.it
**Web** :
**Activity** : Manufacturer
**Products** : *Hides and Skins* : Chrome crust, Vegetable crust,

*Leather* : Footwear – upper leather, Leathergoods leather, Footwear – lining leather,

Italy Footwear – lining leather, Footwear – upper leather, Leathergoods leather

Cristina Conceria SpA

**Address** : Via della Concia 140
Arzignano (VI)-36071
Italy

**Tel.** : +39 0444 644 111
**Fax** : +39 0444 648 835
**Email** : commerciale@gruppoperetti.com
**Web** : http://www.gruppoperetti.com
**Activity** : Manufacturer
**Products** : *Hides and Skins* : Chrome crust,

*Leather* : Footwear – upper leather, Leathergoods leather, Automotive leather, Footwear – lining leather, Garment leather,

Italy Automotive leather, Footwear – lining leather, Footwear – upper leather, Garment leather, Leathergoods leather

Cuoieria Artigiana Srl

**Address** : Piazza G. Rossa 27
Ponte a Egola (PI)-56024
Italy

**Tel.** : +39 571 499 222
**Fax** : +39 571 497 241
**Email** : cuoieriaartigiana@volpi.it
**Web** :
**Activity** : Manufacturer
**Products** : *Hides and Skins* : Vegetable crust,

*Leather* : Footwear – upper leather, Leathergoods leather, Footwear – lining leather, Saddlery and harness leather,

Italy

Footwear – lining leather, Footwear – upper leather, Leathergoods leather, Saddlery and harness leather

Cuoificio Duranti

**Contact** : Roberto Duranti
Owner

**Address** : Via S. Tommaso, 105
P.O. Box 24
Santa Croce sull'Arno PI-56029
Italy

**Tel.** : +39 0571 302 10
**Fax** : +39 0571 309 04
**Email** : info@cuoificioduranti.it
**Web** :
**Activity** : Manufacturer
**Products** : *Hides and Skins* : Vegetable crust,

*Leather* : Footwear – upper leather, Leathergoods leather, Other - leather, Sole leather, Saddlery and harness leather, Industrial leather,

**Raw Materials** : Bovine

Italy

Footwear – upper leather, Industrial leather, Leathergoods leather, Other - leather, Saddlery and harness leather, Sole leather

Cuoificio La Querce Srl

**Address** : Via Della Spira 13
Ponte a Egola (PI)-56024
Italy

**Tel.** : +39 571 49652
**Fax** : +39 571 485 517
**Email** :
**Web** :
**Activity** : Manufacturer
**Products** : *Hides and Skins* : Vegetable crust,

*Leather* : Sole leather,

Italy

Sole leather

Cuoificio Macchi & Salvadori Snc

Italy

Sole leather

**Address** : Via Vicolo Abruzzi 18
Santa Croce S/A (PI)-56029
Italy

**Tel.** : +39 571 30474
**Fax** : +39 571 35097

**Email** : info@macchi-salvadori.it
**Web** : http://www.macchi-salvadori.it

**Activity** :

**Products** : *Hides and Skins* : Vegetable crust,

*Leather* : Sole leather,

Curtiba Industria Conciaria SpA

**Address** : Via E. Fermi 8
Santa Croce S/A (PI)-56029
Italy

**Tel.** : +39 571 366 251
**Fax** : +39 571 35647

**Email** : info@curtiba.it
**Web** : http://www.curtiba.it

**Activity** : Manufacturer

**Products** : *Hides and Skins* : Vegetable crust,

*Leather* : Footwear – upper leather, Leathergoods leather, Footwear – lining leather, Split leather,

Italy Footwear – lining leather, Footwear – upper leather, Leathergoods leather, Split leather

D. & Co Consorzio

**Address** : Via Lombardia, 4
P.O. Box 79
Santa Croce sull'Arno. PI-56029
Italy

**Tel.** : +39 0571 47249
**Fax** : +39 0571 480145

**Email** : upimar@leonet.it
**Web** :

**Activity** : Manufacturer

**Products** : *Leather* : Footwear – upper leather, Leathergoods leather, Garment leather, Gloving leather,

Italy Footwear – upper leather, Garment leather, Gloving leather, Leathergoods leather

**Raw Materials** : Bovine

D.R.P. Srl

**Address** : Via Elpidiense Sud, 199
Montegranaro (AP) 63014

Italy Sole leather

**Tel.** : +39 0734 890 931
**Fax** : +39 0734 890 942

| | | | | |
|---|---|---|---|---|
| **Tel.** | : | +39 0734 890 931 | | |
| **Fax** | : | +39 0734 890 942 | | |
| **Email** | : | info@drpsoles.com | | |
| **Web** | : | http://www.drpsoles.com | | |
| **Activity** | : | Manufacturer | | |
| **Products** | : | *Leather* : Sole leather | | |

DA. MI. Srl

| | | | | |
|---|---|---|---|---|
| **Address** | : | Via Montunarese, 1462<br>S. Elpidio a Mare (AP)-63019<br>Italy | | |
| **Tel.** | : | +39 0734 810 207 | Italy | Sole leather |
| **Fax** | : | +39 0734 819 469 | | |
| **Email** | : | dami@dami.it | | |
| **Web** | : | http://www.dami.it | | |
| **Activity** | : | Manufacturer | | |
| **Products** | : | *Leather* : Sole leather, | | |

Dal Maso Callisto Spa Conceria

| | | | | |
|---|---|---|---|---|
| **Address** | : | Via Quinta Strada 20<br>Z.I.<br>Arzignano (VI)-36071<br>Italy | | |
| **Tel.** | : | +39 0444 474400 | | |
| **Fax** | : | +39 0444 474433 | | |
| **Email** | : | sales@dalmasocallisto.com | Italy | Footwear – upper leather, Garment leather, Upholstery leather |
| **Web** | : | | | |
| **Activity** | : | Manufacturer | | |
| **Products** | : | *Leather* : Footwear – upper leather, Upholstery leather, Garment leather, | | |
| **Raw Materials** | : | Bovine | | |

D'Alessio Galliano Srl

| | | | | |
|---|---|---|---|---|
| **Address** | : | Via Clelia, 16 | | |
| **Tel.** | : | +39 06 7806 891 | | |
| **Email** | : | info@dalessiogalliano.com | | |
| **Activity** | : | Manufacturer | | |
| **Products** | : | *Hides and Skins* : Chrome crust, Vegetable | Italy | Footwear – upper leather, Leathergoods leather |
| **Raw Materials** | : | Bovine, Sheep, Goat | | |

**Raw Materials** : Bovine, Sheep, Goat

Dalla Benetta Luigi Spa

**Address** : Via Monte Rosa, 22/B
Chiampo (VI)-36072
Italy

**Tel.** : +39 0444 623 349
**Fax** : +39 0444 420 929

**Email** : info@dallabenetta.com
**Web** : http://www.dallabenetta.com

**Activity** : Manufacturer, Exporter

**Products** : *Leather* : Footwear – upper leather, Leathergoods leather, Footwear – lining leather, Garment leather,

**Raw Materials** : Bovine, Pig

Italy Footwear – lining leather, Footwear – upper leather, Garment leather, Leathergoods leather

Dallas FG 92 Spa Indtria Conciari

**Address** : Via del Puntone, 24-26
Ponte a Cappiano-50050
Italy

**Tel.** : +39 0571 295 051/2/3
**Fax** : +39 0571 297 125

**Email** : dallasfg92@leonet.it
**Web** :

**Activity** : Manufacturer

**Products** : *Hides and Skins* : Chrome crust,

*Leather* : Footwear – upper leather, Leathergoods leather,

**Raw Materials** : Bovine

Italy Footwear – upper leather, Leathergoods leather

Dani Leather Group

**Contact** : Giuseppe Lucente
Director Automotive Sales Manager

**Address** : Via 4° Strada 20
Z.I.
Arzignano (VI)-36071
Italy

**Tel.** : +39 0444 471 211
**Fax** : +39 0444 450 839

**Email** : giuseppe_lucente@danileather.it
**Web** : http://www.danileather.it

**Activity** : Manufacturer

**Products** : *Leather* : Automotive leather, Footwear – lining leather, Upholstery leather, Split leather,

**Raw Materials** : Bovine

Italy Automotive leather, Footwear – lining leather, Split leather, Upholstery leather

David International Spa Conceria

**Address** : Via S. Tommaso, 111/113
S. Croce S/A-
Italy

**Tel.** : +39 0571 31265
**Fax** : +39 0571 34557

**Email** : info@davidinternational.it
**Web** : http://www.davidinternational.it

**Activity** : Manufacturer, Exporter

**Products** : *Hides and Skins* : Chrome crust, Vegetable crust,

*Leather* : Footwear – upper leather, Leathergoods leather,

**Raw Materials** : Bovine (Buffalo)

Italy Footwear – upper leather, Leathergoods leather

DB LEATHER di Diego Boldrini

**Contact** : Diego Boldrini
Owner

**Address** : Via Tosco Romagnola Est, 536
San Miniato Basso (PI)-56028
Italy

**Tel.** : +39 348 605 6834
**Fax** :

**Email** : diego@dbleather.it
**Web** : http://www.dbleather.it

**Activity** : Exporter, Agent

**Products** : *Leather* : Footwear – upper leather, Leathergoods leather, Automotive leather, Split leather,

DB Leather di Diego Boldrini is an italian firm representing several Italian tanneries, we can offer You a very large range of products like: COW SHOULDERS - FRONTS - SIDES - BELLIES classic Italian Vacchetta style, pure Veg., fatten, mat or shiny, for Leathergoods and Shoe-upper. CALF SIDES - COW/BULL BELLIES chrome tanned and nubuck with many different finishings for . FULL COW SKINS chrome tanned for furnishing and automotive. SPLIT LEATHER in different finishing from suede to embossed. REAL PYTON/OSTRICH/LIZARD SKINS with many different finishings for Leathergoods and Shoe-upper. PATENT LEATHER from the official supplier of Tod's BONDED LEATHER for soles, belts and leathergoods.

Italy Automotive leather, Footwear – upper leather, Leathergoods leather, Split leather

**Raw Materials** : Bovine, Reptile

Dean Spa Industria Conciaria Pelli

**Address** : Corso S. D'Amato 96
Arzano (NA)-80022
Italy

**Tel.** : +39 081 5734 850
**Fax** : +39 081 7315 966

**Email** : deanspa@tiscalinet.it
**Web** : http://www.deanspa.it

Italy Footwear – upper leather, Garment leather, Gloving leather, Leathergoods leather

**Activity** : Manufacturer

**Products** : *Hides and Skins* : Chrome crust,

*Leather* : Footwear – upper leather, Leathergoods leather, Garment leather, Gloving leather,

**Raw Materials** : Sheep, Goat

Dea-Pel Conceria Srl

**Address** : Via Lombardia, 19
Ponte a Cappiano (PI)-50050
Italy

**Tel.** : +39 0571 297 944/5
**Fax** : +39 0571 295 029

**Email** : info@deapel.it
**Web** : http://www.deapel.it

**Activity** : Manufacturer

**Products** : *Hides and Skins* : Chrome crust, Vegetable crust,

*Leather* : Footwear – upper leather, Leathergoods leather,

**Raw Materials** : Bovine

Italy Footwear – upper leather, Leathergoods leather

Del Vacchio Leather Diffusion SAS

**Address** : Via Carpisano, 1
Solofra (AV)-83029
Italy

**Tel.** : +39 0825 581 480
**Fax** : +39 0825 534 781

**Email** : leatherdiffusion@libero.it
**Web** : http://www.delvacchioleather.it

**Activity** : Manufacturer

**Products** : *Leather* : Garment leather,

**Raw Materials** : Other (Chamois)

Italy Garment leather

Delhi Conceria Spa

**Address** : Via del Puntone, 2-4

**Tel.** : +39 0571 295 085

**Email** :

**Activity** : Manufacturer

Italy Footwear – upper leather

**Activity** : Manufacturer

**Products** : *Leather* : Footwear – upper leather,

Delta Suole Srl

**Address** : Zona Industriale II Strada Nr. 1
Fosso' (VE)-30030
Italy

**Tel.** : +39 041 466 588
**Fax** : +39 041 466 236

Italy Sole leather

**Email** : info@deltasuole.com
**Web** : http://www.deltasuole.com

**Activity** : Manufacturer

**Products** : *Leather* : Sole leather,

Dettagli Srl Bordificio

**Address** : Via Bernardo Rossi, 2
Montegranaro (AP)-63014
Italy

**Tel.** : +39 0734 8909 09
**Fax** : +39 0734 8908 98

Italy Footwear – upper leather, Leathergoods leather

**Email** : dettaglisrl@tiscalinet.it
**Web** : http://www.dettaglisrl.it

**Activity** : Manufacturer

**Products** : *Leather* : Footwear – upper leather,
Leathergoods leather,

Diamfondi Srl

**Address** : Via della Costituzione, 8
Monte Vidon Corrado (AP)-63020
Italy

**Tel.** : +39 0734 760872
**Fax** : +39 0734 760513

Italy Sole leather

**Email** : diamfondi@migamma.it
**Web** : http://www.diamfondi.com

**Activity** : Manufacturer

**Products** : *Leather* : Sole leather,

Dick Suolificio Srl

**Address** : Via Ponte di Monsummano, 87
Pieve a Nievole (PT)-51018
Italy

Italy Sole leather

**Tel.** : +39 0572 82963
**Fax** : +39 0572 82964

**Activity** : Manufacturer

**Products** : *Leather* : Sole leather,

Dimar Spa Conceria

**Address** : Via Valchiampo, 28
Montorso (VI)-36050
Italy

**Tel.** : +39 0444 685442/264
**Fax** : +39 0444 686138

**Email** : dimar@dimar.com
**Web** : http://www.dimar.com

**Activity** : Manufacturer

**Products** : *Leather* : Footwear – upper leather, Leathergoods leather, Automotive leather, Footwear – lining leather, Upholstery leather, Garment leather, Gloving leather,

**Raw Materials** : Bovine

Italy

Automotive leather, Footwear – lining leather, Footwear – upper leather, Garment leather, Gloving leather, Leathergoods leather, Upholstery leather

Dingo Conceria Snc

**Address** : Via G. Sozzi, 16
Santa Croce sull'Arno PI-56029
Italy

**Tel.** : +39 057130586
**Fax** : +39 0571 35287

**Email** : dingo@leonet.it
**Web** : http://www.leathernet.it/dingo

**Activity** : Manufacturer

**Products** : *Leather* : Footwear – upper leather, Leathergoods leather, Automotive leather, Footwear – lining leather, Upholstery leather, Industrial leather,

**Raw Materials** : Bovine

Italy

Automotive leather, Footwear – lining leather, Footwear – upper leather, Industrial leather, Leathergoods leather, Upholstery

Ditta Viterbo & C. di Gustavo & Luciano Viterbo

**Contact** : Gustavo Viterbo

**Address** : Piazza Vittorio Veneto n° 14
P.O. Box 63
Turin-10123
Italy

**Tel.** : +39 011 8122 223
**Fax** : +39 011 8351 85

**Email** : guluvit@libero.it
**Web** :

**Activity** : Agent

Italy

Footwear – lining leather, Garment leather

**Products** : *Hides and Skins* : Wet salted, Dry salted, Air/Frame dried, Pickled, Wet blue, Chrome crust, Vegetable crust,

*Leather* : Footwear – lining leather, Garment leather,

**Raw Materials** : Bovine, Sheep, Goat, Reptile, Other

Dmd Solofra Spa Industria Conciaria

**Address** : Via Celentane, 9
Solofra (AV)-83029
Italy

**Tel.** : +39 0825 532 201/582 742
**Fax** : +39 0825 582 850

**Email** : info@dmdsolofra.it
**Web** : http://www.dmdsolofra.it

**Activity** : Exporter

**Products** : *Leather* : Footwear – upper leather, Leathergoods leather, Footwear – lining leather, Sole leather, Garment leather, Gloving leather, Industrial leather,

**Raw Materials** : Sheep, Goat

Italy Footwear – lining leather, Footwear – upper leather, Garment leather, Gloving leather, Industrial leather, Leathergoods leather, Sole leather

Dolmen Spa

**Address** : Via del Bosco, 73
Santa Croce s/Arno (PI)-56029
Italy

**Tel.** : +39 0571 38 35
**Fax** : +39 0571 36 60 97

**Email** : info@dolmenspa.com
**Web** : http://www.dolmenspa.com

**Activity** : Manufacturer

**Products** :

**Raw Materials** : Bovine. Reptile, Other

Italy

Domenico Finco Concerie Srl

**Address** : Via SS Fortunato e Lazzaro 91
Bassano del Grappa. VI-36061
Italy

**Tel.** : +39 0424 56 67 78
**Fax** : +39 0424 56 67 84

**Email** : domfin@tin.it
**Web** :

Italy Footwear – lining leather, Footwear – upper leather, Garment leather, Leathergoods leather



**Activity** : Manufacturer

**Products** : *Leather* : Footwear – upper leather, Leathergoods leather, Footwear – lining leather, Garment leather,

**Products** : *Leather* : Footwear – upper leather, Leathergoods leather, Footwear – lining leather, Garment leather,

**Raw Materials** : Bovine, Sheep, Goat

Donati. Luciano Srl

**Address** : Via Verdi, 18
S. Croce S/A (PI)-56029
Italy

**Tel.** : +39 0571 297 100
**Fax** : +39 0571 297 000

**Email** : info@conceriadonati.it
**Web** :

**Activity** : Manufacturer

**Products** : *Hides and Skins* : Chrome crust, Vegetable crust,

*Leather* : Footwear – upper leather, Leathergoods leather,

**Raw Materials** : Bovine

Italy Footwear – upper leather, Leathergoods leather

Duma Spa

**Address** : Via Della Tecnica 78
Z.I.
Arzignano (VI)-36071
Italy

**Tel.** : +39 0444 474600
**Fax** : +39 0444 474602

**Email** : m.graizzaro@dumaleather.com
**Web** : http://www.dumaleather.com

**Activity** : Manufacturer, Exporter

**Products** : *Leather* : Automotive leather, Upholstery leather, Garment leather,

**Raw Materials** : Bovine

Italy Automotive leather, Garment leather, Upholstery leather

Ecopell 2000 Srl

**Address** : Via 1Y Settembre 4
SantaCroce S/A (PI)-56029
Italy

**Tel.** : +39 571 366 168
**Fax** : +39 571 366 674

**Email** : ecopell@leonet.it
**Web** : http://www.ecopell.it

Italy Footwear – lining leather, Footwear – upper leather, Leathergoods leather

**Activity** : Manufacturer



**Products** : *Hides and Skins* : Vegetable crust,

*Leather* : Footwear – upper leather, Leathergoods leather, Footwear –

*Leather* : Footwear – upper leather, Leathergoods leather, Footwear – lining leather,

Effegi Conceria Srl

| | | | | |
|---|---|---|---|---|
| **Address** | : | Via W. Tobagi 16<br>Castelfranco di Sotto -PI-56022<br>Italy | Italy | Footwear – lining leather, Footwear – upper leather, Leathergoods leather |
| **Tel.** | : | +39 571 486 061 | | |
| **Fax** | : | +39 571 486 062 | | |
| **Email** | : | robertoconceriaeffegi@tin.it | | |
| **Web** | : | | | |
| **Activity** | : | Manufacturer | | |
| **Products** | : | *Hides and Skins* : Chrome crust, Vegetable crust,<br><br>*Leather* : Footwear – upper leather, Leathergoods leather, Footwear – lining leather, | | |
| **Raw Materials** | : | Sheep, Goat | | |

Ellegi Pellami SpA

| | | | | |
|---|---|---|---|---|
| **Address** | : | Piazza del Volontariato 7<br>Castelfranco di Sotto- PI-56022<br>Italy | Italy | |
| **Tel.** | : | +39 571 479 231 | | |
| **Fax** | : | +39 571 471 077 | | |
| **Email** | : | lg@ellegipellami.it | | |
| **Web** | : | http://www.ellegipellami.it | | |
| **Activity** | : | Manufacturer | | |
| **Products** | : | *Hides and Skins* : Chrome crust, Vegetable crust,<br><br>*Footwear* : Women's shoes,<br><br>*Leather Goods* : Small leather goods, Belts, | | |
| **Raw Materials** | : | Bovine | | |

Emmedue Conceria Snc

| | | | | |
|---|---|---|---|---|
| **Address** | : | Via Quinta Strada 12 | Italy | Footwear – lining leather, Footwear – upper leather, Garment leather, Leathergoods leather, Other - leather |
| **Tel.** | : | +39 0444 452 012/674 683 | | |
| **Email** | : | conceria_emmedue@inwind.it | | |

**Web** : http://www.conceriaemmedue.com

**Activity** : Manufacturer

**Products** : *Hides and Skins* : Chrome crust,

*Leather* : Footwear – upper leather, Leathergoods leather, Other - leather, Footwear – lining leather, Garment leather,

Enterprise Srl

**Address** : Via San Tommaso 181
Santa Croce S/A (PI)-56029
Italy

**Tel.** : +39 0571 32004
**Fax** : +39 0571 34500

**Email** : pellami.enterprise@libero.it
**Web** :

**Activity** : Manufacturer

**Products** : *Leather* : Footwear – upper leather, Leathergoods leather, Footwear – lining leather,

**Raw Materials** : Bovine, Sheep, Goat, Others

Italy Footwear – lining leather, Footwear – upper leather, Leathergoods leather

Erreci Snc

**Address** : Via II Strada 21
Arzignano (VI)-36071
Italy

**Tel.** : +39 0444 673 514
**Fax** : +39 0444 675 972

**Email** : info@errepi-sas.com
**Web** : http://www.errepi-sas.com

**Activity** : Manufacturer

**Products** : *Hides and Skins* : Chrome crust,

*Leather* : Footwear – upper leather, Leathergoods leather, Upholstery leather,

**Raw Materials** : Goat

Italy Footwear – lining leather, Footwear – upper leather, Garment leather, Gloving leather, Leathergoods leather, Upholstery leather

Errepi Snc

**Address** : Via II Strada 21

**Tel.** : +39 0444 673 514

**Email** : info@errepi-sas.com

Italy Footwear – upper leather, Leathergoods leather, Upholstery leather

| | | | | |
|---|---|---|---|---|
| **Web** | : | http://www.errepi-sas.com | | |
| **Activity** | : | Manufacturer | | |
| **Products** | : | *Hides and Skins* : Chrome crust,<br><br>*Leather* : Footwear – upper leather, Leathergoods leather, Upholstery leather, | | |
| **Raw Materials** | : | Goat | | |

Esapel Spa

| | | | | |
|---|---|---|---|---|
| **Address** | : | Via Bioli, 18<br>Chiampo (VI)-<br>Italy | Italy | Automotive leather, Footwear – lining leather, Footwear – upper leather, Gloving leather, Leathergoods leather, Split leather, Upholstery leather |
| **Tel.** | : | +39 444 674 188 | | |
| **Fax** | : | +39 444 675 123 | | |
| **Email** | : | info@esapel.com | | |
| **Web** | : | | | |
| **Activity** | : | Manufacturer | | |
| **Products** | : | *Hides and Skins* : Wet blue, Chrome crust,<br><br>*Leather* : Footwear – upper leather, Leathergoods leather, Automotive leather, Footwear – lining leather, Upholstery leather, Gloving leather, Split leather, | | |
| **Raw Materials** | : | Bovine | | |

Esotica Srl

| | | | | |
|---|---|---|---|---|
| **Address** | : | Via Rossini 5<br>Bodio Lomnago (VA)-21020<br>Italy | Italy | Footwear – upper leather, Garment leather, Leathergoods leather, Upholstery leather |
| **Tel.** | : | +39 0332 948 871 | | |
| **Fax** | : | +39 0332 948 657 | | |
| **Email** | : | esotica@esoticasrl.com | | |
| **Web** | : | http://www.esoticasrl.com | | |
| **Activity** | : | Manufacturer | | |
| **Products** | : | *Hides and Skins* : Chrome crust, Vegetable crust,<br><br>*Leather* : Footwear – upper leather, Leathergoods leather, Upholstery leather, Garment leather, | | |
| **Raw Materials** | : | Reptile, Other (Ostrich) | | |

Eugenia Conceria Srl — Italy — Footwear – lining leather. Footwear –

**Address** : Via Lombardia 3-5-7
Ponte a Cappiano (FI)-50050
Italy

upper leather, Sole leather

**Tel.** : +39 0571 297 021/297 219
**Fax** : +39 0571 297 798
**Email** : info@conceriaeugenia.it
**Web** : http://www.conceriaeugenia.it
**Activity** : Manufacturer
**Products** : *Hides and Skins* : Chrome crust,

*Leather* : Footwear – upper leather, Footwear – lining leather, Sole leather,

**Raw Materials** : Bovine

Euroleather Srl

**Contact** : Troisi Gallucci
Manager
**Address** : Via S. Lucia, 87
Solofra-83029
Italy
**Tel.** : +39 0825 534 895 / 535 935
**Fax** : +39 0825 535 928 / 582 716
**Email** : leader.sas@libero.it
**Web** :
**Activity** : Importer, Agent
**Products** : *Hides and Skins* : Dry salted, Pickled, Wet blue, Chrome crust,

*Leather* : Footwear – upper leather, Other - leather, Footwear – lining leather, Garment leather, Gloving leather,

We wish to introduce our company and our system of work and our organisation: We have a warehouse of 2000 metres in free-zone where our supplying ones send the goods to us, give us the possibility to show the skins to our customers, facilitate us the sales. Ours is a representation company that operates on the Italian Market from 14 Years introduced in the best Italian factories guaranteeing to our customers the quality and the regular selection, for this reason we are to search of serious suppliers for being able to have one collaboration that hard in the time. We are interested to having one collaboration with you in Pickle, wet-blue and crust Sheep and Goat Skins.

Italy

Footwear – lining leather, Footwear – upper leather, Garment leather, Gloving leather, Other - leather

**Raw Materials** : Bovine, Sheep, Goat

Eurorettil Srl

**Address** : Zona Industriale Ponticelli
Santa Maria a Monte (PT) 56020

Italy Other - leather

**Tel.** : +39 0587 709 120
**Fax** : +39 0587 705 222

**Tel.** : +39 0587 709 120
**Fax** : +39 0587 705 222

**Email** :
**Web** :

**Activity** : Manufacturer

**Products** : *Leather* : Other - leather,

Eurostal Srl Conceria

**Address** : Via della Robinia 13
Castelfranco di Sotto -PI-56022
Italy

**Tel.** : +39 0571 478 206
**Fax** : +39 0571 489 027

**Email** : eurostal@tin.it
**Web** : http://www.paginegialle.it/eurostal

**Activity** : Wholesaler, Manufacturer

**Products** : *Hides and Skins* : Vegetable crust,

*Leather* : Footwear – upper leather, Leathergoods leather, Sole leather

Italy Footwear – upper leather, Leathergoods leather, Sole leather

Everest Srl

**Address** : Via del Trebbio 50
Santa Croce S/A (PI)-56029
Italy

**Tel.** : +39 0571 366 808
**Fax** : +39 0571 366 813

**Email** :
**Web** :

**Activity** : Manufacturer

**Products** : *Hides and Skins* : Chrome crust, Vegetable crust,

*Leather* : Footwear – upper leather, Footwear – lining leather,

Italy Footwear – lining leather, Footwear – upper leather

Exopelli Srl

**Address** : Via Paolo Maspero, 16/1
Milano (MI) 20137

**Tel.** : +39 02 5519 5595
**Fax** : +39 02 5519 5653

**Email** :
**Web** :

**Activity** : Manufacturer

**Products** : *Leather* : Footwear – upper leather, Leathergoods leather, Footwear –

Italy Footwear – lining leather, Footwear – upper leather, Leathergoods leather

lining leather,

**Raw Materials** : Reptile, Other

## F.P.V. Skins Srl

**Contact** : Clara Foppa Pedretti
Import/Export

**Address** : Via A. Binda 5
Milano-20143
Italy

**Tel.** : +39 02 891 222 20
**Fax** : +39 02 891 223 27

**Email** : fpvskins@tin.it
**Web** :

**Activity** : Wholesaler, Importer, Exporter

**Products** : *Hides and Skins* : Chrome crust, Vegetable crust,

*Leather* : Footwear – upper leather, Leathergoods leather,

Flancs de caiman, Peaux de alligator/crocodiles, Autruches, Lézards, Galichat, Phoques, Requin, Différentes peaux exotiques. Caiman Flanks, Alligator/crocodile skins, Ostrich, Lizard, Galuchat, Seal Skins, Different exotic leather, Shark. Faldas de Caiman, Pieles de alligator/crocodilo, Avestruz, Lagartia, Galuchat, Foca, Tiburón, Differentes pieles exoticas.

Italy Footwear – upper leather, Leathergoods leather

**Raw Materials** : Reptile

## Faeda Conceria Srl

**Address** : Largo O. Mazzocco, 4
P.O. Box 53
Chiampo (VI)-36072
Italy

**Tel.** : +39 0444 422 000
**Fax** : +39 0444 420 222

**Email** : info@faeda.com
**Web** : http://www.faeda.com

**Activity** : Manufacturer, Exporter

**Products** : *Leather* : Footwear – upper leather, Leathergoods leather, Upholstery leather,

Italy Footwear – upper leather, Leathergoods leather, Upholstery leather

**Raw Materials** : Bovine

## Felice Ferrara SAS

**Address** : Via Melito 6
Solofra (AV) 83029

**Tel.** : +39 0825 582 849
**Fax** : +39 0825 583 825

**Email** : feliceferrarasas@libero.it
**Web** :

**Activity** : Manufacturer

**Products** : *Leather* : Garment leather,

Italy Garment leather

| | | | |
|---|---|---|---|
| **Products** | : *Leather* : Garment leather, | | |
| **Raw Materials** | : Bovine, Sheep, Goat | | |

Ferrero Conceria SpA

| | | | |
|---|---|---|---|
| **Address** | : Stradale Torino, 9<br>Castagneto Po (TO)-10090<br>Italy | | |
| **Tel.** | : +39 011 917 0848 / 0768 | Italy | Footwear – upper leather, Leathergoods leather |
| **Fax** | : +39 011 917 0800 | | |
| **Email** | : info@conceriaferrero.com | | |
| **Web** | : http://www.conceriaferrero.com | | |
| **Activity** | : Manufacturer | | |
| **Products** | : *Leather* : Footwear – upper leather, Leathergoods leather, | | |
| **Raw Materials** | : Bovine, Pig | | |

Fiesole Industria Conciaria Srl

| | | | |
|---|---|---|---|
| **Address** | : Via del Bosco, 312/AB<br>S. Croce sull Arno (PI)-56029<br>Italy | | |
| **Tel.** | : +39 0571 484 91 | Italy | Footwear – upper leather, Leathergoods leather |
| **Fax** | : +39 0571 499 104 | | |
| **Email** | : iperpellami@iperpellami.it | | |
| **Web** | : http://www.iperpellami.it | | |
| **Activity** | : Manufacturer | | |
| **Products** | : *Leather* : Footwear – upper leather, Leathergoods leather, | | |
| **Raw Materials** | : Bovine, Goat | | |

Foder Point Srl

| | | | |
|---|---|---|---|
| **Address** | : Via Borgo Nuovo 128<br>Monte Urano (AP)-63015<br>Italy | | |
| **Tel.** | : +39 0734 842 305 | Italy | Footwear – lining leather |
| **Fax** | : +39 0734 841 014 | | |
| **Email** | : info@foderpoint.net | | |
| **Web** | : http://www.foderpoint.net | | |
| **Activity** | : Importer, Exporter | | |
| **Products** | : *Leather* : Footwear – lining leather, | | |
| **Raw Materials** | : Pig | | |

Fraschini Conceria SpA

**Address** : Via Sottosasso 2
Brenta (VA)-21030
Italy

**Tel.** : +39 0332 601 600
**Fax** : +39 0332 604 440
**Email** : info@conceriafraschini.com
**Web** : http://www.conceriafraschini.com
**Activity** : Manufacturer, Exporter
**Products** : *Leather* : Footwear – upper leather, Leathergoods leather, Footwear – lining leather, Sole leather,

Italy — Footwear – lining leather, Footwear – upper leather, Leathergoods leather, Sole leather

**Raw Materials** : Bovine, Other

Frontoni Gabriele Industriale Srl

**Address** : Viale Leopardi 17
Montappone (AP)-63020
Italy

**Tel.** : +39 0734 760 396
**Fax** : +39 0734 760 417
**Email** : info@frontoniindustriale.com
**Web** : http://www.frontoniindustriale.com
**Activity** : Manufacturer
**Products** : *Leather* : Footwear – upper leather, Leathergoods leather,

Italy — Footwear – upper leather, Leathergoods leather

G.B. Leathers Srl

**Address** : Via Dei Conciatori 8/10
Ponte a Egola (PI)-56024
Italy

**Tel.** : +39 0571 415 299
**Fax** : +39 0571 485 271
**Email** : gbleathers@gbcuoio.it
**Web** : http://www.gbcuoio.it
**Activity** : Manufacturer, Exporter
**Products** : *Hides and Skins* : Vegetable crust,

*Leather* : Leathergoods leather, Sole leather, Upholstery leather, Saddlery and harness leather,

Italy — Leathergoods leather, Saddlery and harness leather, Sole leather, Upholstery leather

G.T.

**Contact** : Gentilin
**Address** : Mazzini, 31
Vicenza-36076
Italy

Italy — Split leather, Upholstery leather

**Tel.** : +39 347 887 4799 / +39 0445 963 334
**Fax** : +39 0445 963 334
**Email** : gentilin.tomas@libero.it
**Web** :
**Activity** : Importer, Exporter, Agent
**Products** : *Hides and Skins* : Wet salted, Dry salted, Air/Frame dried, Limed, Wet blue, Chrome crust,

*Leather* : Upholstery leather, Split leather,

**Raw Materials** : Bovine, Sheep, Goat, Reptile

Gaiera Giovanni Conceria SpA

**Address** : Via Manzoni 21/23
Robecchetto (MI)-20020
Italy

**Tel.** : +39 0331 87 55 22
**Fax** : +39 0331 87 59 77
**Email** : gaiera@gaiera.it
**Web** : http://www.gaiera.it
**Activity** : Manufacturer
**Products** :
**Raw Materials** : Sheep, Goat

Italy

Ghepardo Conceria SpA

**Address** : Via De'Carrai 8
Castelfranco di Sotto, PI-56022
Italy

**Tel.** : +39 0571 478 084
**Fax** : +39 0571 480 795
**Email** : info@ghepardo.it
**Web** : http://www.ghepardo.it
**Activity** : Manufacturer, Exporter
**Products** : *Hides and Skins* : Vegetable crust,

*Leather* : Footwear – upper leather, Leathergoods leather, Upholstery leather,

**Raw Materials** : Bovine

Italy Footwear – upper leather, Leathergoods leather, Upholstery leather

Giglio Rosso Snc

**Address** : Via della Spira 2/4
Ponte a Egola (PI) 56024

**Tel.** : +39 0571 492 50
**Fax** : +39 0571 481 82
**Email** : info@gigliorosso.it
**Web** : http://www.gigliorosso.it

Italy Sole leather

**Email** : info@gigliorosso.it
**Web** : http://www.gigliorosso.it

**Activity** : Manufacturer, Importer, Exporter

**Products** : *Leather* : Sole leather,

**Raw Materials** : Bovine

Il Veliero SpA Tannery

**Address** : Via del Bosco 112
P.O. Box 81
Santa Croce sull'Arno, PI-56029
Italy

**Tel.** : +39 0571 366 477
**Fax** : +39 0571 32253

**Email** : info@ilveliero.it
**Web** : http://www.ilveliero.it

**Activity** : Manufacturer

**Products** : *Leather* : Footwear – upper leather, Leathergoods leather, Footwear – lining leather,

Italy Footwear – lining leather, Footwear – upper leather, Leathergoods leather

Industria Conciaria Europa SpA

**Contact** : Jan Barrasso
Area Manager

**Address** : Viale Brenta 117
Tezze sul Brenta (VI)-36056
Italy

**Tel.** : +39 0424 539 150
**Fax** : +39 0424 539 156
**Email** : jan@industriaconciariaeuropa.it
**Web** : http://www.industriaconciariaeuropa.it
**Activity** : Manufacturer, Exporter
**Products** : *Hides and Skins* : Wet blue,

*Leather* : Footwear – upper leather, Leathergoods leather, Footwear – lining leather, Upholstery leather, Saddlery and harness leather, Industrial leather,

*Machinery* : Pollution control,

*Footwear* : Men's shoes, Women's shoes, Children shoes, Sandals, Boots, Sport,

*Leather Goods* : Small leather goods, Large leather goods, Saddlery and harness, Furniture, Car components,

**Raw Materials** : Bovine

Italy Footwear – lining leather, Footwear – upper leather, Industrial leather, Leathergoods leather, Saddlery and harness leather, Upholstery leather

Industrie Pellami Srl Italy Garment leather.

| | | | |
|---|---|---|---|
| **Address** | : Via Giuntini 66/68<br>Empoli, FI-50053<br>Italy | | Leathergoods leather |
| **Tel.** | : +39 0571 599 101 | | |
| **Fax** | : +39 0571 591 663 | | |
| **Email** | : info@industriepellami.com | | |
| **Web** | : http://www.industriepellami.com | | |
| **Activity** | : Manufacturer | | |
| **Products** | : *Leather* : Leathergoods leather, Garment leather, | | |
| **Raw Materials** | : Bovine, Sheep, Goat, Pig | | |

Italpelli Srl

| | | | | |
|---|---|---|---|---|
| **Contact** | : Fulvio Lazzari<br>General Manager | ITALPELLI works in the international trade of grain leathers and splits in wet blue and crust for furniture, car interiors, shoes and leather goods. ITALPELLI distinguishes itself thanks to the professionalism of its staff and for the seriousness it manages relations with customers. ITALPELLI proposes: * WET BLUE AND SEMIFINISHED HIDES - Full thickness - Split * WET BLUE AND SEMIFINISHED SPLITS - Whole hide split or trimmed - Splitted and shaved hide split * WET BLUE SPLITS (by-products) - Bottom splits (flesh part of the split hide) - Shoulders - Bellies The target is to give the customers what they are looking for! A precise way to think and communicate is asserting itself: ITALPELLI's style. | Italy | Automotive leather, Footwear – lining leather, Footwear – upper leather, Gloving leather, Industrial leather, Leathergoods leather, Split leather, Upholstery leather |
| **Address** | : Via del Lavoro 93<br>Arzgnano - VI-36071<br>Italy | | | |
| **Tel.** | : +39 0444 451 020 | | | |
| **Fax** | : +39 0444 451 025 | | | |
| **Email** | : info@italpelli.com | | | |
| **Web** | : http://www.italpelli.com | | | |
| **Activity** | : Exporter | | | |
| **Products** | : *Hides and Skins* : Wet blue, Chrome crust,<br><br>*Leather* : Footwear – upper leather, Leathergoods leather, Automotive leather, Footwear – lining leather, Upholstery leather, Gloving leather, Industrial leather, Split leather, | | | |
| **Raw Materials** | : Bovine | | | |

Ivan Belloni Hides & Skins

| | | | |
|---|---|---|---|
| **Contact** | : Ivan Belloni | Italy | Automotive leather, Footwear – lining leather, Footwear – upper leather, Garment leather, Gloving leather, Industrial leather, Leathergoods |
| **Address** | : Viale Matteotti 53<br>Parabiago (MI)-20155 | | |
| | : +39 335 604 93 68 / 0331 551596 | | |
| | : +39 0331 555167 / 334 510 44 16 | | |

**Tel.** : +39 335 604 93 68 / 0331 551596
**Fax** : +39 0331 555167 / 334 510 44 16
**Email** : ibello@tin.it
**Web** :
**Activity** : Retailer, Importer, Exporter, Agent
**Products** : *Hides and Skins* : Wet salted, Dry salted, Air/Frame dried, Limed, Pickled, Wet blue, Chrome crust, Vegetable crust,

*Leather* : Footwear – upper leather, Leathergoods leather, Automotive leather, Footwear – lining leather, Sole leather, Upholstery leather, Garment leather, Gloving leather, Saddlery and harness leather, Industrial leather, Split leather,

*Chemicals* : Pretanning, Tanning, Retanning, Dyeing,

*Footwear* : Men's shoes, Women's shoes, Children shoes, Sandals, Safety, Sport,

*Garments and Gloves* : Motorcycling,

*Leather Goods* : Small leather goods, Large leather goods, Belts, Saddlery and harness,

**Raw Materials** : Bovine, Sheep, Goat, Pig, Reptile, Other

are always interested in develop business with serious Companies with mutual benefits.

leather, Saddlery and harness leather, Sole leather, Split leather, Upholstery leather

Kara Centro Pelli Stampate Srl

**Address** : Via Mario Pagano 58 - 60
Trezzano San Naviglio-20090
Italy

**Tel.** : +39 2 4840 1913
**Fax** : +39 2 4840 1999
**Email** : info@conceriakara.com
**Web** : http://www.conceriakara.com
**Activity** : Manufacturer
**Products** : *Hides and Skins* : Wet blue, Chrome crust, Vegetable crust,

*Leather* : Footwear – upper leather, Leathergoods leather, Footwear – lining leather, Upholstery leather, Garment leather,

**Raw Materials** : Bovine, Sheep, Goat

Italy

Footwear – lining leather, Footwear – upper leather, Garment leather, Leathergoods leather, Upholstery leather

Legnotan SpA

| | | | | |
|---|---|---|---|---|
| **Address** | : | Via A.Diaz 105<br>Ponte a Egola, PI-56024<br>Italy | | |
| **Tel.** | : | +39 0571 498 408 | Italy | Sole leather |
| **Fax** | : | +39 0571 499 425 | | |
| **Email** | : | info@legnotan.com | | |
| **Web** | : | http://www.legnotan.com | | |
| **Activity** | : | Manufacturer | | |
| **Products** | : | *Hides and Skins* : Wet salted, Wet blue,<br><br>*Leather* : Sole leather, | | |
| **Raw Materials** | : | Bovine, Reptile | | |

Mangusta Industria Conciaria SpA

| | | | | |
|---|---|---|---|---|
| **Address** | : | Via Liguria<br>Santa Croce s/Arno (PI)-56029<br>Italy | | |
| **Tel.** | : | +39 0571 33436 | Italy | Footwear – upper leather, Leathergoods leather |
| **Fax** | : | +39 0571 33436 | | |
| **Email** | : | info@tecnologiemangusta.com | | |
| **Web** | : | http://www.tecnologiemangusta.com | | |
| **Activity** | : | Manufacturer, Exporter | | |
| **Products** | : | *Leather* : Footwear – upper leather, Leathergoods leather, | | |
| **Raw Materials** | : | Bovine | | |

Martucci Teresa Srl

| | | | | |
|---|---|---|---|---|
| **Address** | : | Via Consolazione, 11<br>Solofra (AV)-83029<br>Italy | | |
| **Tel.** | : | +39 0825 581 731 | Italy | Footwear – upper leather, Garment leather |
| **Fax** | : | +39 0825 581 263 | | |
| **Email** | : | martucci@martuccitannery.com | | |
| **Web** | : | http://www.martuccitannery.com | | |
| **Activity** | : | Manufacturer, Exporter | | |
| **Products** | : | *Leather* : Footwear – upper leather, Garment leather, | | |

Masini Conceria Snc

| | | | | |
|---|---|---|---|---|
| **Address** | : | Via Lombardia 27<br>Santa Croce sull' Arno<br>Pisa-56029<br>Italy | Italy | Footwear – lining leather, Footwear – upper leather, Leathergoods leather |

**Tel.** : +39 571 30841/366 155
**Fax** : +39 571 366 075

**Email** : conc.masini@libero.it
**Web** :

**Activity** : Manufacturer

**Products** : *Hides and Skins* : Chrome crust, Vegetable crust,

*Leather* : Footwear – upper leather, Leathergoods leather, Footwear – lining leather,

## Mastrotto Italia SpA

**Address** : Via Quinta Strada 55
Z.I.
Arzignano (VI)-36071
Italy

**Tel.** : +39 0444 473 301
**Fax** : +39 0444 473 302

**Email** : salit@mastrotto.com
**Web** : http://www.mastrotto.com

**Activity** : Manufacturer, Exporter

**Products** : *Leather* : Automotive leather, Upholstery leather, Garment leather,

Italy — Automotive leather, Garment leather, Upholstery leather

## Matrix Srl

**Address** : Via A. Giannattasio, 41
Solofra (AV)-83029
Italy

**Tel.** : +39 0825 535 593 / +39 340 626 2238
**Fax** : +39 0825 536 445

**Email** : matrix.srl2002@libero.it
**Web** :

**Activity** : Wholesaler, Manufacturer, Importer, Exporter

**Products** : *Hides and Skins* : Wet blue,

*Leather* : Footwear – lining leather, Garment leather,

**Raw Materials** : Sheep, Goat

Italy — Footwear – lining leather, Garment leather

## Mengoni Srl

**Contact** : Rita .

**Address** : Via carducci, 40
Morrovalle Scalo (MC)-62015

**Tel.** : +39 0733 564132
**Fax** : +39 0733 564132

: info@mengonisrl.com
: http://www.mengonisrl.com

Italy — Footwear – lining leather, Footwear – upper leather, Sole leather, Split leather

**Email** : info@mengonisrl.com
**Web** : http://www.mengonisrl.com
**Activity** : Wholesaler, Importer, Exporter
**Products** : *Leather* : Footwear – upper leather, Footwear – lining leather, Sole leather, Split leather,

hesitate to contact us but also if you have good stock of leather send us your offer.

Morena Srl

**Contact** : Mario Zuffellato
**Address** : Via dell' Industria 15
Arzignano
Vicenza-36071
Italy
**Tel.** : +39 444 453267
**Fax** : +93 444 453263
**Email** : morena@morenasrl.com
**Web** : http://morenasrl.com
**Activity** : Wholesaler, Exporter, Agent
**Products** : *Hides and Skins* : Wet blue,

*Leather* : Footwear – upper leather, Upholstery leather, Industrial leather,

**Raw Materials** : Bovine

Italy

Footwear – upper leather, Industrial leather, Upholstery leather

Motta Alfredo SpA

**Contact** : Andrea Motta
**Address** : Via Luciano Manara, 3
Cinisello Balsamo (MI)-20092
Italy
**Tel.** : +39 02 660 495 41
**Fax** : +39 02 612 900 57
**Email** : an.motta@mottaalfredo.com
**Web** : http://www.mottaalfredo.com
**Activity** : Manufacturer, Exporter
**Products** : *Leather* : Garment leather,

**Raw Materials** : Sheep, Goat, Pig

We are a tannery for leather garments and we have been working lamb and goat skins since 1912. We are producing goat suede, full and semi aniline nappa, shearlings, printings embossing and we can give you the best italian contractors.

Italy

Garment leather

Nuova Osba SpA Conceria

**Address** : Via delle Confina, 11
Fucecchio (FI)-50054
**Tel.** : +39 0571 22393/4/5
**Fax** : +39 0571 23382
**Email** : info@nuovaosba.it
**Web** : http://www.nuovaosba.it
**Activity** : Manufacturer

**Products** : *Leather* : Footwear – upper leather, Leathergoods leather, Footwear –

Italy

Footwear – lining leather, Footwear – upper leather, Leathergoods leather

Leathergoods leather, Footwear – lining leather,

Overgroup Consorzio

**Address** : Via Roma, 28
Santa Croce s/Arno (PI)-56029
Italy

**Tel.** : +39 0571 366 235
**Fax** : +39 0571 366 236
**Email** : info@overgroup.it
**Web** : http://www.overgroup.it
**Activity** : Manufacturer, Exporter
**Products** : *Hides and Skins* : Chrome crust, Vegetable crust,

*Leather* : Footwear – upper leather, Leathergoods leather, Other - leather, Garment leather,

Italy

Footwear – upper leather, Garment leather, Leathergoods leather, Other - leather

Pellami Macchini

**Contact** : Enrico Macchini
Managing Director

**Address** : Via Della Repubblica 136
Pieve A Nievole Via Francesca 109
Monsummano Terme Pistoia-51015
Italy

**Tel.** : +39 0572 950 888 / 335 688 1820
**Fax** : +39 0572 950 142 / 950 753
**Email** : pellamimacchini@tiscali.it
**Web** :
**Activity** : Wholesaler, Manufacturer, Importer, Exporter, Agent
**Products** : *Hides and Skins* : Vegetable crust,

*Leather* : Footwear – upper leather, Garment leather, Gloving leather,

**Raw Materials** : Bovine, Sheep, Goat

We are working in finished leather sector since many years exporting all over the word all type of kids, goat suede sheep lamb for shoes and garment, free crome calf and goat.

Italy

Footwear – upper leather, Garment leather, Gloving leather

Pelleteria "Dantesca"

**Contact** : Marco

**Address** : Via S. Margherita 13/r
P.O. Box 50123

: +39 33 325 19179
:

Italy

Leathergoods leather

**Tel.** : +39 33 325 19179
**Fax** :
**Email** : floris72@virgilio.it
**Web** :
**Activity** : Manufacturer, Exporter
**Products** : *Leather* : Leathergoods leather,

*Leather Goods* : Small leather goods, Belts, Other - leather goods,

**Raw Materials** : Bovine

bags, wallets, belts, bookmarks, lipstckcases and triangular change pouches.

Pellimpex Srl

**Contact** : Edo Trape
Manager
**Address** : Via G.Galilei, 230
P.O. Box 21
Sant' Elpidio a Mare-63019
Italy
**Tel.** : +39 734 871 825
**Fax** : +39 734 871 926
**Email** : info@pellimpex.com
**Web** : http://www.pellimpex.com
**Activity** : Manufacturer, Importer, Exporter
**Products** : *Hides and Skins* : Wet blue, Chrome crust,

*Leather* : Footwear – lining leather, Garment leather, Split leather,

**Raw Materials** : Bovine, Sheep, Goat, Pig

- Leather for shoe linings and leatherwear - Peaux pour doublures de chaussures, peaux pour habillement.

Italy

Footwear – lining leather, Garment leather, Split leather

Renato Marianelli Srl Hides & Skins

**Contact** : Renato Marianelli
**Address** : Via Viviani, 4
**Tel.** : +39 0571 382 640 / 367 511
**Email** : info@renatomarianelli.it
**Activity** : Wholesaler, Retailer,
**Products** : *Hides and Skins* : Wet salted,
**Raw Materials** : Bovine, Pig, Other

Italy

Other - leather, Sole leather

**Raw Materials** : Bovine, Pig, Other

## Roma Tannery - Conceria Roma

**Contact** : Lawrence De Leo
International Operation Manager

**Address** : Via Sambuco 10/12
Solofra-83029
Italy

**Tel.** : +39 0825 535 297 / 3381 514 846
**Fax** : +39 0825 581 854
**Email** : news@conceriaroma.it
**Web** : http://www.conceriaroma.it
**Activity** : Wholesaler, Manufacturer, Importer, Exporter
**Products** : *Hides and Skins* : Wet salted, Dry salted, Limed, Pickled, Wet blue, Chrome crust, Vegetable crust, Other - hides and skins,

*Leather* : Footwear – upper leather, Leathergoods leather, Automotive leather, Footwear – lining leather, Sole leather, Garment leather, Gloving leather, Saddlery and harness leather, Split leather,

Your leather for garments, bags and shoes. Export house for all type of leather, exposure to the international Market; we are second to none in quality and still very much competitive price wise. We have good opportunity (stocks) in ours storehouses and you can receive every week an e-mail about ours stocks. Contact us for any of your requirements of leather and you will get an immediate response alongwith samples as per your specification and most competitive prices plus schedule of timely shipments, with some card colours. If you need a colour that there isn't in our card colours we can prepare it, just we need a little reference you can send to ours offices; generally articles and leathers we produce are: South Africa, Middle east, North Africa (Siria), New Zealand and more...

Italy

Automotive leather, Footwear – lining leather, Footwear – upper leather, Garment leather, Gloving leather, Leathergoods leather, Saddlery and harness leather, Sole leather, Split leather

## Rossetti Leather Group SpA

**Contact** : Ferdinando Rossetti
President

25 years of experience in the leather businnes from raw to finished, cow-bufalo-pig. Enquire welcome!

Italy

Automotive leather, Footwear – lining leather, Footwear – upper leather, Garment leather, Gloving leather, Industrial leather, Leathergoods leather, Split leather, Upholstery leather

**Address** : Via Industria 48
P.O. Box 63
Arzignano (VI)-36071
Italy

**Tel.** : +39 0444 673 608
**Fax** : +39 0444 675 666

**Products** : *Hides and Skins* : Wet salted, Dry salted, Wet blue, Chrome crust, Other - hides and skins,

*Leather* : Footwear – upper leather, Leathergoods leather, Automotive leather, Footwear – lining leather, Upholstery leather, Garment leather, Gloving leather, Industrial leather, Split leather,

**Raw Materials** : Bovine, Pig, Other

## Ruggeri Pellami Sas

**Contact** : Roberto Ruggeri
General Manager

**Address** : Via Della Pace 15/F
San Giuliano Milanese-20098
Italy

**Tel.** : +39 02 9840 711
**Fax** : +39 02 9845 611

**Email** : info@ruggeripellami.com
**Web** : http://www.ruggeripellami.com

**Activity** : Exporter, Agent

**Products** : *Leather* : Leathergoods leather, Split leather,

We deal in leather for the production of belts, bags and leathergoods. Our production range is very wide, from pu split to high quality calves.

Italy Leathergoods leather, Split leather

## Schroeder Italia Srl

**Address** : Via Lodovico Ariosto, 8
Reggio Emilia (RE)-42100
Italy

**Tel.** : +39 522 453 845
**Fax** : +39 522 454 931

**Email** : infofootwear@sadesa.com
**Web** : http://www.sadesa.com

**Activity** : Manufacturer, Importer, Exporter

**Products** : *Hides and Skins* : Wet blue, Chrome crust, Vegetable crust,

*Leather* : Footwear – upper leather, Leathergoods leather, Footwear – lining leather, Sole leather, Gloving leather, Saddlery and harness leather,

**Raw Materials** : Bovine

Italy Footwear – lining leather, Footwear – upper leather, Gloving leather, Leathergoods leather, Saddlery and harness leather, Sole leather

## Somali Hides and Skins

**Contact** : Mohamed Dalmar
Director

Italy Upholstery leather

**Address** : Via Volturno 21
Roma-
Italy

**Tel.** : +39 06 474 37 83
**Fax** : +39 06 474 37 83
**Email** : dalmar35@yahoo.co.uk
**Web** :
**Activity** : Manufacturer, Exporter
**Products** : *Hides and Skins* : Dry salted, Wet blue, Other - hides and skins,

*Leather* : Upholstery leather,

*Footwear* : Men's shoes, Other - footwear,

*Garments and Gloves* : Jacket, coats, Industrial gloves, Other - garments,

*Leather Goods* : Other - leather goods,

**Raw Materials** : Bovine, Sheep, Goat

Studio Franca Leonardi Srl

**Contact** : Franca Leonardi
Owner
**Address** : Vl. Papiniano 36
Milano-20123
Italy

**Tel.** : +39 02 49 876 43
**Fax** : +39 02 49 866 44
**Email** : info@francaleonardi.it
**Web** : http://www.francaleonardi.it
**Activity** : Manufacturer, Exporter
**Products** : *Leather* : Leathergoods leather,

*Leather Goods* : Small leather goods, Large leather goods,

**Raw Materials** : Bovine, Sheep, Goat, Pig

Italy Leathergoods leather

Suolificio Tuttocuoio Srl

**Contact** : Giuseppe Di Domenico

**Address** : Via Paolo Borsellino 6/8/10
Ponte a Egola-San Miniato-
**Tel.** : +39 571 484 248
**Fax** : +39 571 484 116
: info@tuttocuoio.it
: http://www.tuttocuoio.it

Italy Sole leather

**Email** : info@tuttocuoio.it
**Web** : http://www.tuttocuoio.it
**Activity** : Manufacturer
**Products** : *Leather* : Sole leather,

*Footwear* : Shoe components,

and machinery, an exemplary service and punctuality in delivery, a know-how in buying with years of experience, all make Suolificio Tuttocuoio, the ideal partner for shoe factories who are in search of supply of the best quality ready-made men and women's soles.

Tannery Motta Alfredo S.p.a.

**Address** : Via Luciano Manara, 3
P.O. Box 94
Cinisello Balsamo - Milan-20092
Italy

**Tel.** : +39 02 66 04 95 41
**Fax** : +39 02 61 29 00 57
**Email** : tannery@mottaalfredo.com
**Web** : http://www.mottaalfredo.com
**Activity** : Manufacturer, Exporter
**Products** : *Leather* : Leathergoods leather, Other - leather, Garment leather, Gloving leather,

**Raw Materials** : Sheep, Goat

Italy — Garment leather, Gloving leather, Leathergoods leather, Other - leather

Tari Srl

**Address** : Via Calabria 16-18-20
Napoli (NA)-80142
Italy

**Tel.** : +39 081 734 99 88
**Fax** : +39 081 734 06 05
**Email** : infotari@tin.it
**Web** :
**Activity** : Manufacturer
**Products** : *Leather* : Footwear – upper leather, Leathergoods leather, Garment leather, Gloving leather,

**Raw Materials** : Bovine, Sheep, Goat

Italy — Footwear – upper leather, Garment leather, Gloving leather, Leathergoods leather

Ti Emme Srl

**Address** : Via Toscana 25
S. Elpidio A Mare (AP)-63019

**Tel.** : +39 0734 810 310
**Fax** : +39 0734 810 428
**Email** : tiemmesrl@tin.it
**Web** : http://www.tiemmesrl.com

Italy — Footwear – lining leather, Leathergoods leather

**Email** : tiemmesrl@tin.it
**Web** : http://www.tiemmesrl.com

**Activity** : Manufacturer, Exporter

**Products** : *Leather* : Leathergoods leather, Footwear – lining leather,

**Raw Materials** : Goat

## Tigre Conceria Srl

**Address** : Via Risorgimento 96
San Pietro Mussolino (VI)-36070
Italy

**Tel.** : +39 0444 488 800
**Fax** : +39 0444 487 501

**Email** : commerciale@conceriatigre.com
**Web** : http://www.conceriatigre.com

**Activity** : Manufacturer

**Products** : *Leather* : Footwear – upper leather, Upholstery leather,

**Raw Materials** : Bovine

Italy Footwear – upper leather, Upholstery leather

## Tolio Conceria SpA

**Address** : Via Arzignano 146
Chiampo (VI)-36072
Italy

**Tel.** : +39 0444 420 800
**Fax** : +39 0444 420 793

**Email** : info@conceriatolio.com
**Web** : http://www.conceriatolio.com

**Activity** : Manufacturer, Exporter

**Products** : *Leather* : Footwear – upper leather, Leathergoods leather, Upholstery leather,

**Raw Materials** : Bovine

Italy Footwear – upper leather, Leathergoods leather, Upholstery leather

## Toscana Leather Srl

**Address** : Via S. Tommaso 161
**Tel.** : +39 571 30 005
**Email** : info@toscanaleather.it
**Activity** : Manufacturer, Exporter

Italy Footwear – lining leather, Footwear – upper leather, Split leather

**Activity** : Manufacturer, Exporter

**Products** : *Hides and Skins* : Chrome crust,

*Leather* : Footwear – upper leather, Footwear – lining leather, Split leather,

**Raw Materials** : Bovine

## Tre Gazzelle SpA

**Address** : Via dell 'industria, 8/10
P.O. Box 139
Castelfranco Di Sotto-PI-56022
Italy

**Tel.** : +39 0571 471 297
**Fax** : +39 0571 471 311

**Email** : info@tregazzelle.it
**Web** : http://www.tregazzelle.com

**Activity** : Manufacturer, Exporter

**Products** : *Leather* : Leathergoods leather, Upholstery leather, Saddlery and harness leather,

Italy | Leathergoods leather, Saddlery and harness leather, Upholstery leather

## Tris (Conceria) SpA

**Address** : Via Rio Camparolo 5
Lonigo (VI)-36045
Italy

**Tel.** : +39 0444 436 433
**Fax** : +39 0444 436 394

**Email** : info@conceriatris.it
**Web** : http://www.conceriatris.it

**Activity** : Manufacturer, Exporter

**Products** : *Leather* : Footwear – upper leather, Leathergoods leather, Other - leather, Upholstery leather, Garment leather,

Italy | Footwear – upper leather, Garment leather, Leathergoods leather, Other - leather, Upholstery leather

**Raw Materials** : Bovine, Other (Equine)

## Tuscania Industria Conciaria Srl

**Address** : Via Delle Confina 15-18
Fucecchio (FI)-50054
Italy

**Tel.** : +39 0571 204 48
**Fax** : +39 0571 261 782

**Email** : tuscania@leonet.it
**Web** :

**Activity** : Manufacturer

Italy | Footwear – upper leather, Garment leather, Leathergoods leather, Upholstery leather

**Products** : *Leather* : Footwear – upper leather, Leathergoods leather, Upholstery leather, Garment leather

Leathergoods leather, Upholstery leather, Garment leather,

**Raw Materials** : Bovine, Goat

## Valle Esina SpA

**Contact** : Magnatti Mauro
Export Manager

**Address** : Loc. Campocuiano 119
Esanatoglia-62023
Italy

**Tel.** : +39 0737 881274
**Fax** : +39 0737 889137

**Email** : valleesina@libero.it
**Web** : http://www.valle-esina.com

**Activity** : Manufacturer, Exporter

**Products** : *Leather* : Other - leather,

Valle Esina manufactures reprocessed leatherboards and fibreboard for use in the shoe, accessory, handbag, leather goods and furnishing sectors.

Italy Other - leather

## Valpel Srl

**Address** : Via G. Sozzi 9
Santa Croce s/Arno (PI)-56029
Italy

**Tel.** : +39 0571 360 404
**Fax** : +39 0571 352 72

**Email** : info@valpel.com
**Web** : http://www.valpel.com

**Activity** : Manufacturer, Importer, Exporter

**Products** : *Leather* : Leathergoods leather,

Italy Leathergoods leather

## Valter Cecconi

**Contact** : Valter Cecconi
Titolare

I am a wholesaler, I sell and buy the leather at stock.

Italy Automotive leather, Footwear – lining leather, Footwear – upper leather, Garment leather, Gloving leather, Industrial leather, Leathergoods leather, Other - leather, Saddlery and harness leather, Sole leather, Split leather, Upholstery leather

**Address** : Via Andrea Costa 2
S. Corce Sull'Arno-56029
Italy

**Tel.** : +39 0571 366 311
**Fax** : +39 0571 366 311

**Products** : *Leather* : Footwear – upper leather, Leathergoods leather, Automotive leather, Other - leather, Footwear – lining leather, Sole leather, Upholstery leather, Garment leather, Gloving leather, Saddlery and harness leather, Industrial leather, Split leather,

**Raw Materials** : Bovine, Sheep, Goat, Pig, Reptile, Other

## Veneta Conciaria Valle Agno SpA

**Address** : Via Stazione
Trissino (VI)-36070
Italy

**Tel.** : +39 0445 428 711
**Fax** : +39 0445 428 733
**Email** : info@gcveneto.com
**Web** : http://www.gcveneto.com
**Activity** : Manufacturer, Exporter
**Products** : *Hides and Skins* : Chrome crust, Vegetable crust,

*Leather* : Footwear – upper leather, Leathergoods leather,

Italy

Footwear – upper leather, Leathergoods leather

## Vergolani Gianantonio

**Contact** : Gianantonio Vergolani

Our company is a brokerage agency, is active in several market sectors: - sale of covering leathers for forniture adn paddings - sale of italian leather forniture to foreign markets - sale leather crust - sale leather wet blue - sale leather salted

Italy

Automotive leather, Footwear – lining leather, Footwear – upper leather, Garment leather, Industrial leather, Other - leather, Upholstery leather

**Products** : *Hides and Skins* : Wet salted, Wet blue, Chrome crust, Other - hides and skins,

*Leather* : Footwear – upper leather, Automotive leather, Other - leather, Footwear – lining leather, Upholstery leather, Garment leather, Industrial leather,

*Chemicals* : Preservation, Other - chemicals, Tanning, Shoe finishing,

*Machinery* : Quality control,

*Leather Goods* : Furniture, Car components, Other - leather goods,

**Raw Materials** : Bovine, Goat

Victoria Srl

**Address** : Via Del Bosco 111
Santa Croce s/Arno (PI)-56029
Italy

Italy — Footwear – upper leather, Leathergoods leather

**Tel.** : +39 0571 337 86
**Fax** : +39 0571 356 03

**Email** : info@conceriavictoria.it
**Web** : http://www.conceriavictoria.it

**Activity** : Manufacturer, Importer, Exporter

**Products** : *Leather* : Footwear – upper leather, Leathergoods leather,

Volpi Giuseppe SpA

**Address** : Via della Tecnica 44/46
Ponte a Egola (PI)-56024
Italy

Italy — Footwear – upper leather, Leathergoods leather, Saddlery and harness leather, Sole leather

**Tel.** : +39 0571 499 81
**Fax** : +39 0571 498 805

**Email** : volpi@volpi.it
**Web** :

**Activity** : Manufacturer

**Products** : *Leather* : Footwear – upper leather, Leathergoods leather, Sole leather, Saddlery and harness leather,

Walpier Conceria Snc — Italy — Leathergoods leather

**Address** : Via A. Gramsci 158
Ponte a Egola (PI)-56024
Italy

**Tel.** : +39 0571 497 883
**Fax** : +39 0571 497 738

**Email** : walpier@libero.it
**Web** :

**Activity** : Manufacturer, Exporter

**Products** : *Leather* : Leathergoods leather,

Wipelli Srl

**Contact** : Alexander Hill
Sales Director

**Address** : Via Antonio Salieri n°9
Zermeghedo, Vicenza-36050
Italy

**Tel.** : +39 0444 686 171
**Fax** : +39 0444 686 199

**Email** : alexander@wipelli.com
**Web** : http://www.wipelli.com

**Activity** : Manufacturer, Exporter, Agent

**Products** : *Hides and Skins* : Wet salted, Dry salted, Wet blue, Chrome crust, Vegetable crust, Other - hides and skins,

*Leather* : Footwear – upper leather, Leathergoods leather, Automotive leather, Other - leather, Footwear – lining leather, Sole leather, Upholstery leather, Garment leather, Gloving leather, Saddlery and harness leather, Industrial leather, Split leather,

Wipelli with more than 30 years experience in the leather industry is situated approximately one hour from Venice, in the heart of the tanning district of Arzignano. Being internationally based we are able to insure that our products are always on a high standard, in line with customer demands and trends. Our range of products is very wide and varies from Furniture leather Automotive leather Shoe leather Wet Blue Crust leather Cut & sew Programs Hair on Hides For the furniture upholstery industry we can offer not only the leather but also just in time delivery out of our leather programs from several of our warehouses around the world. Looking forward to do business with your company. Best regards Wipelli Srl.

Italy

Automotive leather, Footwear – lining leather, Footwear – upper leather, Garment leather, Gloving leather, Industrial leather, Leathergoods leather, Other - leather, Saddlery and harness leather, Sole leather, Split leather, Upholstery leather

**Raw Materials** : Bovine

Zabri Conceria SpA

**Address** : Viale C. Colombo 204/206
Ponte A Cappiano
Fucecchio (FI)-50050
Italy

**Tel.** : +39 0571 297 744
**Fax** : +39 0571 297 470

Italy

Footwear – upper leather, Garment leather, Leathergoods leather, Upholstery leather

**Email** : info@zabri.it
**Web** : http://www.zabri.it



**Activity** : Manufacturer, Exporter

**Products** : *Leather* : Footwear – upper leather, Leathergoods leather, Upholstery leather, Garment leather,

**Products** : *Leather* : Footwear – upper leather, Leathergoods leather, Upholstery leather, Garment leather,

**Raw Materials** : Bovine

Zani Marcello Srl

**Address** : Viale C. Colombo, 86/88
Fucecchio (FI)-50054
Italy

**Tel.** : +39 0571 214 07
**Fax** : +39 0571 244 058
**Email** : m.zani@marcellozani.it
**Web** : http://www.marcellozani.it
**Activity** : Importer, Exporter
**Products** : *Leather* : Footwear – upper leather, Leathergoods leather, Footwear – lining leather, Sole leather, Garment leather,

Italy Footwear – lining leather, Footwear – upper leather, Garment leather, Leathergoods leather, Sole leather

**Raw Materials** : Bovine

Zetapelli Srl

**Address** : Via Vasco de Gama 58
Bassano del Grappa (VI)-36061
Italy

**Tel.** : +39 0424 567 724
**Fax** : +39 0424 567 725
**Email** : info@zetapelli.it
**Web** : http://www.zetapelli.it
**Activity** : Manufacturer, Exporter
**Products** : *Leather* : Footwear – upper leather, Leathergoods leather, Upholstery leather, Garment leather, Gloving leather, Saddlery and harness leather,

Italy Footwear – upper leather, Garment leather, Gloving leather, Leathergoods leather, Saddlery and harness leather, Upholstery leather

**Raw Materials** : Bovine, Other

# LITHUANIA

JSC "Siauliu Stumbras" Tannery

**Contact** : Antanas Malinauskas

**Address** : Tilzes Street 225
Siauliai - LT-76200

: +370 41 500 550 / +370 686 13555
: +370 41 500 555 / 515

Lithuania Footwear – lining leather, Footwear – upper leather

**Tel.** : +370 41 500 550 / +370 686 13555
**Fax** : +370 41 500 555 / 515

of the oldest

| | | |
|---|---|---|
| **Products** | : *Hides and Skins* : Wet salted, Wet blue, Chrome crust,<br><br>*Leather* : Footwear – upper leather, Footwear – lining leather, | established in 1898. Tannery "SIAULIU STUMBRAS" is processing w/s cattle hides into wet blue, crust and finished leather, mainly shoe uppers chrome tanned. Practically, the leather of all types and characteristics for shoe-upper is being produced: - with natural grain and corrected; - smooth and printed of various size and design; - milled and smooth; - with full, partial and oily finishing; - for military, working and civil purpose; - with hydrophobic and regular properties, using scotchgard, goretex, etc. We want to build a strong and lasting business relationship with organizations which have interest in leather for shoe-upper or may offer raw materials for production. Also we can offer Lithuanian origin wet salted hides and W/B. |

**Raw Materials** : Bovine

Uab Odos Gaminiai and Co.

**Contact** : Aleksandras Rostovskis
Director

**Address** : Aerouosto 11
Shiauliai-5400
Lithuania

**Tel.** : +370 699 48185/370 41 503 010
**Fax** : +370 415 03008

**Email** : arostovskis@takas.lt
**Web** : http://www.og.lt

**Activity** : Manufacturer, Exporter

**Products** : *Hides and Skins* : Wet salted, Wet blue,

*Leather* : Footwear – upper leather, Leathergoods leather,

**Raw Materials** : Bovine

Lithuanian, Latvian cattle hides, calves, tannery for W/B 17+ kg, w/s cows 20-30 kg. Quality and constant production.

Lithuania

Footwear – upper leather, Leathergoods leather

## NETHERLANDS

C.J. Maas Leder/Lefa Medical Leather

**Contact** : G.A.P.C. Maas
Director

**Address** : Zanddonkweg 6
Waalwijk-5144 NX
Netherlands

**Tel.** : +31 416 379 902
**Fax** : +31 416 375 602

**Email** : gert.maas@medical-leather.nl
**Web** : http://www.medical-leather.nl

**Activity** : Wholesaler, Agent

**Products** : *Hides and Skins* : Vegetable crust,

*Leather* : Footwear – upper leather, Leathergoods leather, Footwear – lining leather, Sole leather, Saddlery and harness leather, Split leather,

**Raw Materials** : Bovine, Sheep, Goat

Special company for high quality leathers.

Netherlands

Footwear – lining leather, Footwear – upper leather, Leathergoods leather, Saddlery and harness leather, Sole leather, Split leather

Chroomlederfabriek Brabant BV

Netherlands

Industrial leather

**Contact** : Jan Vromans
Director

**Address** : Hogesteenweg 62
Loon op Zand-5175 AD
Netherlands

**Tel.** : +31 416 361 325
**Fax** : +31 416 361 974
**Email** : schoenklomp@hetnet.nl
**Web** :
**Activity** : Manufacturer
**Products** : *Leather* : Industrial leather,

*Footwear* : Other - footwear, Safety,

*Leather Goods* : Other - leather goods,

We are a producer of clogs and safety clogs, and industrial leather goods.

Jan de Ruijter Waalwijk B.V.

**Contact** : Frans Pulles
Sales Manager

**Address** : Prof. Lorentzweg 16
Waalwijk-5144 NP
Netherlands

**Tel.** : +31 416 332 992
**Fax** : +31 416 340 283
**Email** : info@jrwleather.com
**Web** : http://www.jrwleather.com
**Activity** : Wholesaler, Manufacturer, Importer, Exporter
**Products** : *Hides and Skins* : Chrome crust, Vegetable crust,

*Leather* : Footwear – upper leather, Leathergoods leather, Other - leather, Footwear – lining leather, Gloving leather, Industrial leather, Split leather,

Jan de Ruijter Waalwijk is an international operating company commercializing all kinds of leather. With branches in Hong Kong, Spain and Brazil we have a global coverage. We keep close contact with our customers in order to able to act quickly on the ever changing demands of the leather using industries.

Netherlands

Footwear – lining leather, Footwear – upper leather, Gloving leather, Industrial leather, Leathergoods leather, Other - leather, Split leather

Lederfabriek Ploem BV

**Address** : Vierhuunderswea 15

**Tel.** : +31 162 318 640

Netherlands

Footwear – upper leather, Leathergoods leather, Upholstery leather

**Fax** : +31 162 321 348
**Email** : info@ploem.nl
**Web** :
**Activity** : Manufacturer
**Products** : *Leather* : Footwear – upper leather, Leathergoods leather, Upholstery leather,

**Raw Materials** : Bovine

Max Moser Ledermaatschappij BV

**Contact** : F. R. Moser
Director

**Address** : .
P.O. Box 4391
Tilburg-5004 JJ
Netherlands

**Tel.** : +31 13 534 87 36
**Fax** : +31 13 534 64 39
**Email** : sales@maxmoser.nl
**Web** : http://www.maxmoser.nl
**Activity** : Importer, Exporter
**Products** : *Leather* : Footwear – upper leather, Leathergoods leather, Other - leather, Footwear – lining leather, Upholstery leather, Split leather,

Netherlands

Footwear – lining leather, Footwear – upper leather, Leathergoods leather, Other - leather, Split leather, Upholstery leather

Rompa Leather BV

**Contact** : J. M. Rompa
Director

Producer of upholstery, leathergoods, and shoe leather; raw material: European hides

Netherlands

Automotive leather, Footwear – upper leather, Leathergoods leather, Saddlery and harness leather, Upholstery leather

**Address** : Provincienbaan 19
P.O. Box 9
Rijen-
Netherlands

**Tel.** : +31 161 223 025
**Fax** : +31 161 227 785



**Email** : jm.rompa@rompaleather.com
**Web** : http://www.rompaleather.com

**Products** : *Hides and Skins* : Wet blue,

*Leather* : Footwear – upper leather, Leathergoods leather, Automotive leather, Upholstery leather, Saddlery and harness leather,

**Raw Materials** : Bovine

Unico Leather BV

**Address** : Vierbundersweg, 1
Dongen-5107 NL
Netherlands

**Tel.** : +31 162 322 717
**Fax** : +31 162 315 678

**Email** : mia@unicoleather.com
**Web** : http://www.unicoleather.com

**Activity** : Manufacturer, Exporter

**Products** : *Leather* : Footwear – upper leather, Leathergoods leather, Automotive leather, Upholstery leather,

**Raw Materials** : Bovine

Netherlands

Automotive leather, Footwear – upper leather, Leathergoods leather, Upholstery leather

Van Hoorn Trading

**Contact** : W. Van Hoorn
Director

Van Hoorn Trading B.V., worldwide importer of pigskin leather for the shoe . At Van Hoorn we only sell high

Netherlands

Footwear – lining leather, Leathergoods leather, Other - leather, Split leather

**Address** : Tuinstraat 28
P.O. Box 76
Waalwijk-5144NT
Netherlands

**Tel.** : +31 416 333 831
**Fax** : +31 416 332 445



**Email** : info@van-hoorn.com
**Web** : http://www.pigskin-lining.com

**Products** : *Hides and Skins* : Wet blue, Chrome crust, Other - hides and skins,

*Leather* : Leathergoods leather, Other - leather, Footwear – lining leather, Split leather,

**Raw Materials** : Pig

## NORWAY

Aarenes Lærfabrikk A/S

| | | |
|---|---|---|
| **Contact** | : | Andreas Möller |
| **Address** | : | Drangeid 54<br>Flekkefjord-4400<br>Norway |
| **Tel.** | : | +47 383 26 700 |
| **Fax** | : | +47 383 26 701 |
| **Email** | : | aarenes@aarenes.no |
| **Web** | : | |
| **Activity** | : | Manufacturer, Exporter |
| **Products** | : | *Hides and Skins* : Wet blue,<br><br>*Leather* : Footwear – upper leather, Other - leather, |
| **Raw Materials** | : | Bovine |

Norway Footwear – upper leather, Other - leather

## POLAND

| | | |
|---|---|---|
| Tanled Ltd. | Poland | Automotive leather, Footwear – upper leather, Industrial leather, Leathergoods leather, Other - leather, Split leather, Upholstery leather |
| TCH Services | Poland | Footwear – lining leather, Footwear – upper leather, Split leather, Upholstery leather |

## PORTUGAL

Antonio Nuñes de Carvalho SA

| | | | | |
|---|---|---|---|---|
| **Address** | : | Gouxaria<br>P.O. Box 5<br>Alcanena-2380<br>Portugal | | |
| **Tel.** | : | +351 249 891 729 | Portugal | Footwear – lining leather, Footwear – upper leather, Garment leather, Leathergoods leather |
| **Fax** | : | +351 249 881 451 | | |
| **Email** | : | export@ancarvalho.pt | | |
| **Web** | : | | | |
| **Activity** | : | Manufacturer | | |
| **Products** | : | *Hides and Skins* : Chrome crust,<br><br>*Leather* : Footwear – upper leather, Leathergoods leather, Footwear – lining leather, Garment leather, | | |
| **Raw Materials** | : | Sheep, Goat | | |

Couro Azul SA

| | | | | |
|---|---|---|---|---|
| **Address** | : | Gouxaria/ Ponte do Peral<br>P.O. Box 70<br>Alcanena-2380<br>Portugal | | |
| **Tel.** | : | +351 249 889 050 | Portugal | Automotive leather, Footwear – lining leather, Footwear – upper leather, Leathergoods leather, Upholstery leather |
| **Fax** | : | +351 249 889 069/8 | | |
| **Email** | : | export@ancarvalho.pt | | |
| **Web** | : | | | |
| **Activity** | : | Manufacturer | | |
| **Products** | : | *Hides and Skins* : Chrome crust, Other - hides and skins,<br><br>*Leather* : Footwear – upper leather, Leathergoods leather, Automotive leather, Footwear – lining leather, Upholstery leather, | | |
| **Raw Materials** | : | Bovine | | |

Curtumes Fabricio Lda.

| | | | | |
|---|---|---|---|---|
| **Contact** | : | José Pedro Santos | Portugal | Footwear – lining leather, Footwear – upper leather. |

**Address** : Apartado 805, Vila Verde
Paranhosda Da Beira-
6270907
Portugal

Garment leather, Leathergoods leather

**Tel.** : +351 238 97 90 10
**Fax** : +351 238 97 90 19
**Email** : fabricios@mail.telepac.pt
**Web** : http://www.fabricios.pt
**Activity** : Manufacturer
**Products** : *Leather* : Footwear – upper leather, Leathergoods leather, Footwear – lining leather, Garment leather,

**Raw Materials** : Sheep, Goat

Curtumes Raminho-Joaquim Coutinho Cadete & Filhos, Lda

**Contact** : Miguel Cadete
Manager

**Address** : Rua da Loureira, 7
P.O. Box 4
Alcanena-2384-909
Portugal

**Tel.** : +351 249 887070 / 919 395173
**Fax** : +351 249 887079 / 249 887079
**Email** : jccadete@mail.telepac.pt
**Web** : http://www.guianet.pt/curtumesraminho
**Activity** : Manufacturer, Exporter
**Products** : *Hides and Skins* : Vegetable crust,

*Leather* : Sole leather, Saddlery and harness leather, Industrial leather,

*Leather Goods* : Belts, Saddlery and harness, Furniture, Other - leather goods,

**Raw Materials** : Bovine

Sole leather, shoulders - High quality, 70 years of experience in vegetable tanning. Every Thickness. Contact us.

Portugal

Industrial leather, Saddlery and harness leather, Sole leather

Dias Ruivo - Curtumes e Produtos Industriais Lda

**Contact** : Pedro Silva

Portuguese Leathers company.

Portugal

Footwear – upper leather, Garment leather, Industrial leather, Leathergoods leather, Other - leather, Split leather, Upholstery leather

**Address** : Rua Central de Campos, 720
P.O. Box 4431-801
Villa Nova de Gaia-
Portugal

**Tel.** : +351 227 82 02 68
**Fax** : +351 22 7[illegible]



**Email** : info@diasruivo.com

**Products** : *Leather* : Footwear – upper leather, Leathergoods leather, Other - leather, Upholstery leather, Garment leather, Industrial leather, Split leather,

*Leather Goods* : Other - leather goods,

Inducol SA Industria de Peleteria Cruz Costa

**Address** : Amiais de Cima
P.O. Box 13
Amiais de Baixo-2025-998
Portugal

**Tel.** : +351 249 87 70 00
**Fax** : +351 249 87 06 34

**Email** : inducol@mail.telepac.pt
**Web** :

**Activity** : Manufacturer

**Products** : *Leather* : Footwear – upper leather, Leathergoods leather, Other - leather, Garment leather, Gloving leather,

Portugal

Footwear – upper leather, Garment leather, Gloving leather, Leathergoods leather, Other - leather

Joaquim Francisco Inácio, Sucrs Lda

**Contact** : Joaquim Marquez Ferreira Inácio

**Address** : Fonte Velha
Alcanena-2384 909
Portugal

Specialists: - chrome free tannage - vegetable tannage For shoes, saddlery abd harness leather, leathergoods.

**Tel.** : +351 249 88 90 92
**Fax** : +351 249 88 90 99
**Email** :
**Web** :

**Activity** : Manufacturer, Importer, Exporter

**Products** : *Hides and Skins* : Wet salted, Vegetable crust,

*Leather* : Footwear – upper leather, Leathergoods leather, Saddlery and harness leather, Industrial leather,

**Raw Materials** : Bovine

Portugal

Footwear – upper leather, Industrial leather, Leathergoods leather, Saddlery and harness leather

MC - Couroquimica

**Contact** : Costa

**Address** : Rua General Trindade 132-1° B
Mira de Aire-2485 - 135

: +351 244 440 464
: +351 244 440 464

Portugal

Garment leather, Split leather, Upholstery leather

**Tel.** : +351 244 440 464
**Fax** : +351 244 440 464
**Email** : mc_couroquimica@hotmail.com
**Web** :
**Activity** : Wholesaler, Consultant, Agent
**Products** : *Hides and Skins* : Wet salted, Dry salted, Air/Frame dried, Pickled, Wet blue, Chrome crust, Vegetable crust,

*Leather* : Upholstery leather, Garment leather, Split leather,

*Chemicals* : Tanning, Dyeing, Effluent treatment, Shoe finishing,

*Machinery* : Wet working, Finishing, Pollution control, Quality control,

*Footwear* : Other - footwear, Shoe components,

*Leather Goods* : Small leather goods, Car components,

chemicalien. As consultant, specially for Beauhouse we work worldwide with preference for Africa because our director is from Mozambique.

Monteiro Ribas - Rubber Division

**Contact** : Germano Moura
Commercial Director
**Address** : Est. Da Circunvalaçao, 9020
EC Amial
P.O. Box 52511
Porto-4202-351
Portugal
**Tel.** : +351 22 832 31 51
**Fax** : +351 22 832 40 94
**Email** : leather@mri.pt
**Web** : http://www.mri.pt
**Activity** : Manufacturer, Exporter
**Products** : *Leather* : Footwear – upper leather, Leathergoods leather, Automotive leather, Sole leather, Upholstery leather,

Portugal

Automotive leather, Footwear – upper leather, Leathergoods leather, Sole leather, Upholstery leather

Peltea lda

**Contact** : Jorge Rodrigues
Export Manager

Portuguese company of leather handbags (classic and fashion) is looking for agents worldwide. All interested parts please

Portugal

Leathergoods leather

**Address** : Porto da Pedra
Turquel-2460-814
Portugal

**Tel.** : +351 262 919856
**Fax** : +351 262 919152



**Email** : peltea@peltea.com
**Web** : http://www.peltea.com

**Products** : *Leather* : Leathergoods leather,

*Leather Goods* : Large leather goods,

**Raw Materials** : Bovine, Goat

União Distribuidora De Curtidos Do Alviela Lda

**Address** : Vila Moreira
Alcanena-2380
Portugal

**Tel.** : +35 149890539
**Fax** : +35 149890713

Portugal

**Email** :
**Web** :

**Activity** : Manufacturer

# ROMANIA

Pielorex SA

**Contact** : Acsinte Dorel
General Manager

**Address** : Prelungirea Sos Giurgiului 33A
Jilava-Ilfov-
Romania

**Tel.** : +40 21 420 75 60/450 25 21
**Fax** : +40 21 470 75 60/450 25 21
**Email** : pielorexsa@yahoo.com
**Web** :

**Activity** : Manufacturer

**Products** : *Hides and Skins* : Wet blue, Chrome crust,

*Leather* : Footwear – upper leather, Leathergoods leather, Upholstery leather, Split leather,

**Raw Materials** : Bovine

Founded 42 years ago, S.C. Pielorex S.A. continues to manufacture wet blue, crust, split, finished leather for shoe uppers, furniture and goods. We work over 1000 bovine hides every year. Try us!...it's the moment.

Romania

Footwear – upper leather, Leathergoods leather, Split leather, Upholstery leather

S.C. Medimpact SA

**Contact** : Lorincz Eduard
Commercial Manager

Romania

Footwear – upper leather, Saddlery and harness leather

**Address** : I. C. Bratianu street, n°
20-26
Medias-3125
Romania

**Tel.** : +4 0269 841 740/834 391
**Fax** : +4 0269 845 045
**Email** : office@medimpact.ro
**Web** : http://www.medimpact.ro
**Activity** : Manufacturer
**Products** : *Leather* : Footwear – upper leather, Saddlery and harness leather,

*Footwear* : Men's shoes, Women's shoes, Children shoes, Safety, Military,

*Leather Goods* : Saddlery and harness,

**Raw Materials** : Bovine

# RUSSIA

Andrefish

**Address** : Moscow area, Mytichi
Moscow-141008
Russian Federation

**Tel.** : +7 795 5100902
**Fax** :
**Email** : andrefish@mail.ru
**Web** : http://www.andrefish.com
**Activity** : Manufacturer
**Products** : *Hides and Skins* : Other - hides and skins,
*Leather* : Footwear – upper leather,

Russian Federation

Footwear – upper leather

# SLOVENIA

IUV Industrija Usnja Vrhnika, d.d.

**Contact** : Vesna Dabo
Marketing

**Address** : Trzaska 31
Vrhnika-1360
Slovenia

Slovenia

Footwear – lining leather, Footwear – upper leather, Garment leather, Leathergoods leather, Split leather, Upholstery leather

| | | |
|---|---|---|
| **Address** | : | Trzaska 31<br>Vrhnika-1360<br>Slovenia |
| **Tel.** | : | +386 1 755 8700 |
| **Fax** | : | +386 1 755 8880 |
| **Email** | : | vesna.dabo@iuv.si |
| **Web** | : | http://www.iuv.si |
| **Activity** | : | Retailer,<br>Manufacturer,<br>Exporter |
| **Products** | : | *Leather* : Footwear – upper leather, Leathergoods leather, Footwear – lining leather, Upholstery leather, Garment leather, Split leather,<br><br>*Garments and Gloves* : Jacket, coats, Trousers, Skirts,<br><br>*Leather Goods* : Small leather goods, Car components, |
| **Raw Materials** | : | Pig |

# SPAIN

## Acabados del Valles SA

| | | | | |
|---|---|---|---|---|
| **Address** | : | Pol. Ind. Congost<br>Av. Ramón Ciurans Parcela 8<br>La Garriga - Barcelona-08530<br>Spain | | |
| **Tel.** | : | +34 93 871 8161 | | |
| **Fax** | : | +34 93 871 8272 | | |
| **Email** | : | acabados@acabadosvalles.com | Spain | Garment leather |
| **Web** | : | http://www.acabadosvalles.com | | |
| **Activity** | : | Manufacturer, Importer, Exporter | | |
| **Products** | : | *Hides and Skins* : Chrome crust,<br>*Leather* : Garment leather, | | |
| **Raw Materials** | : | Sheep, Goat | | |

## Alfa Tenerias SA

| | | | | |
|---|---|---|---|---|
| **Address** | : | Poligono Industrial Juncaril, 227<br>Albolote-18220<br>Spain | | |
| **Tel.** | : | +34 958 466 536 | | |
| **Fax** | : | +34 958 466 554 | | |
| **Email** | : | t.alfa@lederval.es | Spain | Footwear – lining leather, Footwear – upper leather, Garment leather, Leathergoods leather |
| **Web** | : | | | |
| **Activity** | : | Manufacturer | | |
| **Products** | : | *Leather* : Footwear – upper leather, Leathergoods leather, Footwear – lining leather, Garment leather, | | |
| **Raw Materials** | : | Sheep, Goat | | |

## Andres Bresca SA

| | | | | | |
|---|---|---|---|---|---|
| **Contact** | : | Juan Ignacio Fernández Parugues<br>Gerente | Empresa registrada en el sistema EMAS II, y certificada según ISO 14001. Pieles ecológicas, certificadas con eco-etiquetas OKO-TEX (según standard 100, clase II) y Distintivo de Calidad Medioambiental (Generalitat de Catalunya). Pieles | Spain | Footwear – upper leather, Leathergoods leather, Other - leather, Saddlery and harness leather, Upholstery leather |
| **Address** | : | c/ Hospital 104-108 bajos<br>Barcelona.-08001<br>Spain | | | |
| **Tel.** | : | +34 93 4414 718/712 | | | |
| **Fax** | : | +34 93 4414 721 | | | |
| **Email** | : | bresca@bresca.com | | | |
| **Web** | : | http://www.bresca.com | | | |
| **Activity** | : | Wholesaler, Manufacturer | | | |

**Products** : *Leather* : Footwear – upper leather, Leathergoods leather, Other - leather, Upholstery leather, Saddlery and harness leather,

**Raw Materials** : Bovine, Sheep

Arepiel S.C.V.L

**Contact** : Enrique Gonzalez Presidente

**Address** : Ctra Madrid-Valencia Km 274
P.O. Box 59
Requena (Valencia)-46340
Spain

**Tel.** : +34 96 230 10 51/232 30 59
**Fax** : +34 96 230 20 02

**Email** : arepiel@arepiel.com
**Web** : http://www.arepiel.com

**Activity** : Manufacturer

**Products** : *Hides and Skins* : Wet blue, Chrome crust, Vegetable crust,

*Leather* : Leathergoods leather, Footwear – lining leather, Upholstery leather, Split leather,

*Chemicals* : Preservation, Pretanning, Retanning, Dyeing, Fatliquoring, Waterproofing, Effluent treatment, Shoe finishing,

*Machinery* : Wet working, Drying, Softening, Finishing, Pollution control, Quality control,

*Footwear* : Men's shoes, Women's shoes, Children shoes, Sandals, Boots, Sport,

*Leather Goods* : Small leather goods, Large leather goods, Belts, Furniture, Car components,

**Raw Materials** : Bovine, Goat, Pig

Empresa fundada en 1983 con una superficie de 20.000 m2, de los cuales 12.000 m2 están destinados a planta de producción, con instalaciones de última tecnología. Elabora cueros con destino a los sectores de calzado, marroquinería y automoción.

Spain — Footwear – lining leather, Leathergoods leather, Split leather, Upholstery leather

Argent Tenerias SA — Spain — Footwear – upper leather. Garment

**Address** : Riba San Antonio
Canals (Valencia)-46650
Spain

leather

**Tel.** : +34 96 224 0400
**Fax** : +34 96 224 2154

**Email** : targent@lederval.es
**Web** :

**Activity** : Manufacturer

**Products** : *Leather* : Footwear – upper leather, Garment leather,

**Raw Materials** : Goat

Bartomeu SA

**Contact** : Bartolome Tortella Segui
Administrador

**Address** : Juan de Austria 126
P.O. Box 64
Inca (Mallorca) Baleares-07300
Spain

**Tel.** : +34 71501262
**Fax** : +34 71504165

**Email** :
**Web** :

**Activity** : Wholesaler/retailer/trader, Importer, Exporter, Agent

**Products** : *Leather* : Leathergoods leather, Other - leather, Footwear – lining leather, Sole leather, Upholstery leather, Garment leather, Saddlery and harness leather, Split leather,

**Raw Materials** : Bovine, Sheep, Goat, Pig

Importación, exportación y venta, así como representación y depósitos de PIELES CURTIDAS Y ACABADAS, para las industrias de calzado, marroquinería, confección, tapicería. Otro departamento: representación y venta de artículos para decoración.

Spain

Footwear – lining leather, Garment leather, Leathergoods leather, Other - leather, Saddlery and harness leather, Sole leather, Split leather, Upholstery leather

Carlos Capella Arto SL

**Contact** : Carlos Capella
Administrador

Spain

Footwear – lining leather, Footwear – upper leather, Gloving leather, Industrial leather, Leathergoods leather, Other - leather, Saddlery and harness leather, Split leather

**Address** : Miguel Ricoma. 162
Granollers - Barcelona-08400
Spain



**Tel.** : +34 93 879 6229
**Fax** : +34 93 879 5102

**Products** : *Hides and Skins* : Wet salted, Dry salted, Air/Frame dried, Limed, Pickled, Wet blue, Chrome crust, Vegetable crust, Other - hides and skins,

*Leather* : Footwear – upper leather, Leathergoods leather, Other - leather, Footwear – lining leather, Gloving leather, Saddlery and harness leather, Industrial leather, Split leather,

**Raw Materials** : Bovine, Pig, Other

Coimpex S.L.

**Contact** : Joan Font
Owner

**Address** : Ctra. de Roda, 57
Vic-08500
Spain

Established in 1985, we have a large experience sourcing the Spanish market and providing the right products to customers all over the world. We come from the tanning business being well known and valued skin dealers. Domestically, we do an abundance of "Contract Tanning" of various leathers including cowhide, rabbit, lambskin, sheepskin and hairsheep. In many cases we act as selling office for tanneries that do not want or can not handle export communications and procedures. The main articles are rabbit, lamb, goat, hairsheep, sheep, and cattle in crust and finished stages.

Spain

Footwear – upper leather, Garment leather, Gloving leather, Leathergoods leather

Colomer Munmany SA

**Address** : Carretera de Roda 70
VIC Barcelona-08500
Spain

**Tel.** : +34 93 881 4040
**Fax** : +34 93 881 4640

**Email** : cymsa@colomer.es
**Web** : http://www.colomer.es

**Activity** : Manufacturer, Exporter

**Products** : *Leather* : Footwear – upper leather, Leathergoods leather, Footwear – lining leather, Garment leather, Gloving leather,

**Raw Materials** : Sheep, Pig

Spain

Footwear – lining leather, Footwear – upper leather, Garment leather, Gloving leather, Leathergoods leather

Combalia SA

**Address** : Sant Antoni Baix 56 - 58
Igualada (Barcelona) 08700

**Tel.** : +34 93 803 1887
**Fax** : +34 93 805 1854

**Email** : combalia@maptel.es
**Web** :

Spain

Footwear – lining leather, Footwear – upper leather, Leathergoods leather

**Email** : combalia@maptel.es
**Web** :

**Activity** : Manufacturer

**Products** : *Hides and Skins* : Chrome crust, Vegetable crust,

*Leather* : Footwear – upper leather, Leathergoods leather, Footwear – lining leather,

## Cueros Importados SL

**Contact** : Pedro Laguia Martinez
Gerente

**Address** : Avda. Algudor Poligono Ind. 34 C/9
P.O. Box 46460
Silla-
Spain

Suministramos cuero origen pais, wet blue y crust, y cualquier clase de cuero terminado en vacuno.

**Tel.** : +34 96 120 1772
**Fax** :

**Email** : cimportsl@hotmail.com
**Web** :

**Activity** : Manufacturer, Importer, Exporter

**Products** : *Hides and Skins* : Wet salted, Dry salted, Wet blue, Chrome crust, Vegetable crust,

*Leather* : Footwear – upper leather, Footwear – lining leather, Split leather,

*Footwear* : Men's shoes, Women's shoes, Children shoes, Sandals, Boots, Safety, Sport, Military,

**Raw Materials** : Bovine

Spain

Footwear – lining leather, Footwear – upper leather, Split leather

## Curtidos Badia SA

**Address** : C/ Sol, 52

**Tel.** : +34 938 054 250

**Email** : curtidosbadia@curtidosbadia.com

**Activity** : Manufacturer

**Products** : *Leather* : Footwear – upper

Spain

Footwear – lining leather, Footwear – upper leather, Leathergoods leather, Saddlery and harness leather

**Raw Materials** : Bovine

Curtidos Codina SA

**Address** : Sant Jaume, 37
VIC - Barcelona-08500
Spain

**Tel.** : +34 93 883 3161
**Fax** : +34 93 883 2161

**Email** : codina@curtidoscodina.com
**Web** :

**Activity** : Manufacturer

**Products** : *Hides and Skins* : Vegetable crust,

*Leather* : Footwear – upper leather, Leathergoods leather, Footwear – lining leather,

**Raw Materials** : Sheep, Goat

Spain

Footwear – lining leather, Footwear – upper leather, Leathergoods leather

Curtidos Gil Bujeque SA

**Contact** : Fulgencio Gil Jodar
Gerente

**Address** : Ctra. del Pantano de Puentes, 139
P.O. Box 103
Lorca-30800
Spain

**Tel.** : +34 968 468 462/468 466
**Fax** : +34 968 464 745

**Email** : info@gilbujeque.com
**Web** : http://www.gilbujeque.com

**Activity** : Manufacturer

**Products** : *Hides and Skins* : Wet blue, Chrome crust,

*Leather* : Footwear – upper leather, Leathergoods leather, Footwear – lining leather,

Tenería del Sureste español con producción diaria de 50.000 p2 especializada en napas naturales, anilinas, box calf, artículos transparentes, Nubuck, Pull up, grabados, bombeados, imitación de reptiles y artículos de seguridad hidrofugados y normalitados UNE-EN-ISO.

Spain

Footwear – lining leather, Footwear – upper leather, Leathergoods leather

**Raw Materials** : Bovine

Curtidos Gregori SA

**Contact** : Joaquim Gregori Font

**Address** : Via de Ronda S/N Pol.Ind.
La Borda

**Tel.** : +34 938 65 43 53
**Fax** : +34 938 65 46 67

: admin@gregori.biz
:

Spain

Footwear – lining leather, Garment leather, Other - leather, Sole leather

**Email** : admin@gregori.biz
**Web** :
**Activity** : Manufacturer, Exporter
**Products** : *Leather* : Other - leather, Footwear – lining leather, Sole leather, Garment leather,

marroquinería de alta calidad. Adicionalmente existe une segunda linea sobre piel de oveja. En multitud de acabados y grabados. Destinada a los mercados que requieren artículos de calidad y moda a precios competitivos.

Curtidos Jacobo Gomez y Asociados S.L

**Address** : Diputacion Rio
Complejo Industrial de Serrata
Lorca - Murcia-30800
Spain
**Tel.** : +34 968 444 711
**Fax** : +34 968 444 568
**Email** : jacobocu@arrakis.es
**Web** :
**Activity** : Manufacturer
**Products** : *Leather* : Footwear – upper leather, Leathergoods leather, Footwear – lining leather,
**Raw Materials** : Bovine

Spain

Footwear – lining leather, Footwear – upper leather, Leathergoods leather

Curtidos Jomar, S.L.

**Contact** : Jose Martinez Garcia
Gerente
**Address** : Autovia Madrid-Alicante. km. 356,1
P.O. Box 216
Villena (Alicante)-03400
Spain
**Tel.** : +34 96 534 63 41
**Fax** : +34 96 580 61 58
**Email** : curjomar@alc.es
**Web** :
**Activity** : Importer, Exporter, Agent
**Products** : *Leather* : Leathergoods leather, Footwear – lining leather, Garment leather, Gloving leather, Split leather,
**Raw Materials** : Bovine, Sheep, Goat, Pig

Spain

Footwear – lining leather, Garment leather, Gloving leather, Leathergoods leather, Split leather

Curtidos Julbe SA

**Address** : Cami Terri, 45
Porqueres (Girona) 17834
**Tel.** : +34 972 581 375
**Fax** : +34 972 575 464
**Email** : julbe@julbe.com
**Web** : http://www.julbe.com

Spain

Footwear – lining leather, Footwear – upper leather, Garment leather, Leathergoods leather

**Email** : julbe@julbe.com
**Web** : http://www.julbe.com

**Activity** : Manufacturer, Exporter

**Products** : *Hides and Skins* : Chrome crust,

*Leather* : Footwear – upper leather, Leathergoods leather, Footwear – lining leather, Garment leather,

**Raw Materials** : Sheep, Goat

Curtidos Luprimo S.L.

**Contact** : Luis y Fernando Prieto
Gerentes

**Address** : Sacramento 1
Villarramiel (Palencia)-
34341
Spain

**Tel.** : +34 979 837 069
**Fax** : +34 979 837 069

**Email** : curtidos@luprimo.com
**Web** : http://www.luprimo.com

**Activity** : Manufacturer

**Products** : *Hides and Skins* : Wet salted, Dry salted, Pickled,

*Leather* : Leathergoods leather, Footwear – lining leather, Saddlery and harness leather, Split leather,

**Raw Materials** : Bovine

Spain

Footwear – lining leather, Leathergoods leather, Saddlery and harness leather, Split leather

Curtidos Mare Nostrum S.L.

**Contact** : Francisco Candía

**Address** : Ctra. Chilches, s/n.

**Tel.** : +34 964 69 79 40

**Email** : ventas@curtidosmarenostrum.com

**Activity** : Manufacturer, Exporter

**Products** : *Hides and Skins* : Wet blue,

**Raw Materials** : Bovine

Spain

Footwear – lining leather, Leathergoods leather

**Raw Materials** : Bovine

Curtidos Martinez Leal S.L.

| | | | | |
|---|---|---|---|---|
| **Contact** : José Ramon Martinez Pardo<br>Gerente<br>**Address** : Polígono Industrial de Lorca<br>Parcela J-3<br>P.O. Box 444<br>Lorca - Murcia-30800<br>Spain<br>**Tel.** : +34 968 476 012<br>**Fax** : +34 968 466 312<br>**Email** : cmartinezleal@terra.es<br>**Web** :<br>**Activity** : Manufacturer<br>**Products** : *Leather* : Footwear – upper leather, Split leather, | Fabricantes de cueros en flor y serrajes de cueros vacunos, para su empleo en la fabricación de calzados, tales como NOBUCK, NAPAS, TAN-CALF, SERRAJES HIDROFUGADOS AFELPADOS Y ENGRASADOS, ARTICULOS CON EFECTO PULL, GRABADOS, etc. | Spain | Footwear – upper leather, Split leather |

**Raw Materials** : Bovine

Curtidos Monserrat SA

| | | | |
|---|---|---|---|
| **Contact** : Marti Montserrat Quadrada<br>Director de Ventas<br>**Address** : Foneria 33, Poligono Industrial<br>Mata-Rocafonda<br>Mataro-08304<br>Spain<br>**Tel.** : +93 74 104 78<br>**Fax** : +93 79 077 93<br>**Email** :<br>**Web** :<br>**Activity** : Manufacturer<br>**Products** : *Leather* : Leathergoods leather, | Nuestra pequeña empresa se dedica a la fabricación o curtición de piel vacuna. Nuestros artículos están destinados principalmente para la marroquinería. | Spain | Leathergoods leather |

**Raw Materials** : Bovine

Curtidos Nules SA

| | | | |
|---|---|---|---|
| **Contact** : Carlos Garcia<br>Export Manager<br>**Address** : Camino Aseit s/n<br>Nules - Castellon-12520<br>Spain<br>**Tel.** : +34 64 673 462<br>**Fax** : +34 64 671 050<br>**Email** : curtinules@nexo.es<br>**Web** : | | Spain | Footwear – lining leather, Footwear – upper leather, Leathergoods leather, Split leather |

**Products** : *Leather* : Footwear – upper leather, Leathergoods leather, Footwear – lining leather, Split leather,

**Raw Materials** : Bovine

Curtidos Parera SA

**Address** : Calle Juan Ramon Jimenez, 40
Valencia-46026
Spain

**Tel.** : +34 96 333 8900
**Fax** : +34 96 373 2431

**Email** : parera@ono.com
**Web** : http://www.curtidosparera.com

Spain

**Activity** : Manufacturer, Importer, Exporter

**Products** : *Hides and Skins* : Chrome crust, Vegetable crust,

**Raw Materials** : Reptile, Other

Curtidos Prats SL

**Contact** : Francisco Guillen
Gerente

**Address** : C/. Celada 35
P.O. Box 314
VIllena (Alicante)-03400
Spain

**Tel.** : +34 96 5 801976/802369
**Fax** : +34 96 5 802369

**Email** : curtidosprats@wanadoo.es
**Web** :

**Activity** : Wholesaler, Importer, Agent

**Products** : *Leather* : Footwear – upper leather, Leathergoods leather, Footwear – lining leather, Sole leather, Split leather,

*Footwear* : Men's shoes, Women's shoes, Children shoes, Sandals, Boots, Sport, Shoe components,

*Leather Goods* : Small leather goods, Large leather goods, Belts,

Curtidos Prats S.L esta situado en Villena, en pleno eje industrial del calzado. Tenemos una larga experiencia en la comercialización y distribución de pleles. Nos esforzamos continuamente en buscar nuevos y mejores artículos que esten en la vanguardia de la moda. Poseemos gran variedad de artículos, entre los que destacan: las faldas de vacuno entodas sus variedades, nuestra ampla gama de charoles y sobre todo nuestra anilinas y napas plena flor, asi como nuestra sección especial para marroquinería.

Spain

Footwear – lining leather, Footwear – upper leather, Leathergoods leather, Sole leather, Split leather

**Raw Materials** : Bovine, Pig

Curtidos Riba Guixa SA

**Contact** : Carlos Riba
General Manager

**Address** : Paseo del Remedio 2
Caldes de Montbui
Barcelona-08140
Spain

**Tel.** : +34 93 865 42 00
**Fax** : +34 93 865 30 42

**Email** : ribaguixa@ribaguixa.com
**Web** : http://www.ribaguixa.com

**Activity** : Manufacturer, Exporter

**Products** : *Leather* : Garment leather, Gloving leather,

**Raw Materials** : Sheep, Goat

Spain

Garment leather, Gloving leather

Curtidos Salat SA - Curdesa

**Address** : Travesia Baja San Antonio, 4
P.O. Box 206
Igualada - Barcelona-08700
Spain

**Tel.** : +34 93 803 1097
**Fax** : +34 93 805 5328

**Email** : curdesa@inescop.es
**Web** :

**Activity** : Manufacturer

**Products** : *Hides and Skins* : Vegetable crust,

*Leather* : Leathergoods leather, Sole leather,

Spain

Leathergoods leather, Sole leather

Curtidos Salles SA

**Address** : Raval Cortines, 44
VIC - Barcelona-08500
Spain

**Tel.** : +34 93 886 2611
**Fax** : +34 93 889 1532

**Email** : salles@inescop.es
**Web** : http://www.inescop.es/SALLES/

**Activity** : Manufacturer

**Products** : *Hides and Skins* : Chrome crust,

*Leather* : Footwear – upper leather, Footwear – lining leather,

**Raw Materials** : Sheep, Goat

Spain

Footwear – lining leather, Footwear – upper leather

Curtidos Sanchez Y Carrillo S.L.

Spain

Footwear – lining leather. Footwear –

| | | | | |
|---|---|---|---|---|
| **Contact** | : Francisco Javier Carrillo Devesa<br>Gerente | | | upper leather, Garment leather, Upholstery leather |
| **Address** | : Garrido Lestache 56<br>Elda (Alicante)-03600<br>Spain | | | |
| **Tel.** | : +34 96 538 01 84 | | | |
| **Fax** | : +34 96 539 04 90 | | | |
| **Email** | : sanchezcarrillo@teleline.es | | | |
| **Web** | : | | | |
| **Activity** | : Agent | | | |
| **Products** | : *Hides and Skins* : Wet blue, Chrome crust,<br><br>*Leather* : Footwear – upper leather, Footwear – lining leather, Upholstery leather, Garment leather, | | | |
| **Raw Materials** | : Bovine, Sheep, Goat | | | |

Curtidos Sierras SA

| | | | |
|---|---|---|---|
| **Address** | : Don Quijote, 15<br>Elda (Alicante)-03600<br>Spain | | |
| **Tel.** | : +34 96 538 6540 | | |
| **Fax** | : +34 96 538 6022 | Spain | Footwear – lining leather, Leathergoods leather |
| **Email** | : sierras@inescop.es | | |
| **Web** | : | | |
| **Activity** | : Manufacturer | | |
| **Products** | : *Leather* : Leathergoods leather, Footwear – lining leather, | | |
| **Raw Materials** | : Sheep, Goat, Pig | | |

Curtidos Viguer SA

| | | | |
|---|---|---|---|
| **Contact** | : Amparo Viguer | | |
| | | Spain | Footwear – lining leather, Footwear – upper leather, Leathergoods leather, Split leather |
| **Address** | : Crta. Quart a Domeño, Km. 17<br>Villamarchante<br>Valencia-46191<br>Spain | | |
| **Tel.** | : +34 96 271 0000 | | |
| **Fax** | : +34 96 271 0001 | | |
| **Email** | : curvisa@infonegocio.com | | |
| **Web** | : http://www.curvisa.com | | |

**Products** : *Hides and Skins* : Chrome crust,

*Leather* : Footwear – upper leather, Leathergoods leather, Footwear – lining leather, Split leather,

Danvila S.L.

**Address** : C/ Cuidad de Sevilla, 66/A
Paterna. Valencia-46988
Spain

**Tel.** : +34 96 1320 228
**Fax** : +34 96 1341 127
**Email** : danvila@danvila.com
**Web** :
**Activity** : Manufacturer
**Products** : *Leather* : Footwear – upper leather, Leathergoods leather,

**Raw Materials** : Reptile

Spain

Footwear – upper leather, Leathergoods leather

Dercosa - Grupo Lederval

**Address** : Poligono Industrial Castilla
P.O. Box 13
Cheste (Valencia)-46380
Spain

**Tel.** : +34 96 251 2270
**Fax** : +34 96 251 2850
**Email** : dercosa@lederval.es
**Web** : http://www.lederval.es
**Activity** : Manufacturer, Exporter
**Products** : *Leather* : Footwear – upper leather, Leathergoods leather, Footwear – lining leather, Sole leather, Garment leather, Split leather,

Spain

Footwear – lining leather, Footwear – upper leather, Garment leather, Leathergoods leather, Sole leather, Split leather

Despell SA

**Contact** : Pere Tomàs Riba
Administrador

Despell SA es una fábrica de curtidos especializada en la fabricación de cuero vacuno

**Address** : Calle Molí de l' Abadia 28
P.O. Box 227
Igualada-Barcelona-08700
Spain

**Tel.** : +34 93 805 0000
**Fax** : +34 93 805 1470

Spain

Footwear – upper leather, Leathergoods leather, Saddlery and harness leather, Split leather



**Email** : admin@despell.es
**Web** : http://www.despell.es

**Products** : *Leather* : Footwear – upper leather, Leathergoods leather, Saddlery and harness leather, Split leather,

**Raw Materials** : Bovine

Exportpiel SA

**Contact** : Emilio Soto Ferrer
Gerente

**Address** : Calle Aldaya, 16
P.O. Box 32
Quart de Poblet,
Valencia-46930
Spain

**Tel.** : +34 96 153 9460
**Fax** : +34 96 153 3144
**Email** : exportpiel@coingasa.com
**Web** :

Spain — Split leather

**Activity** : Importer, Exporter, Agent

**Products** : *Hides and Skins* : Wet salted, Dry salted, Air/Frame dried, Wet blue,

*Leather* : Split leather,

**Raw Materials** : Bovine

Font Palomas SA

**Contact** : Josep Font Bosque
Director

Especialidad en faldas y cuellos de vacuno para fabricantes de calzado, marroquinería y cinturones.

**Address** : San Antoni de Baix 62
P.O. Box 195
Igualada. Barcelona-08700
Spain

**Tel.** : +34 93 803 37 98
**Fax** : +34 93 805 32 08
**Email** : fontpalomas@fontpalomas.com
**Web** : http://www.fontpalomas.com

Spain — Footwear – lining leather, Industrial leather, Leathergoods leather

**Activity** : Manufacturer

**Products** : *Leather* : Leathergoods leather, Footwear – lining leather, Industrial leather,

**Raw Materials** : Bovine

Francopell S.L

**Contact** : Josep Franco Checa

**Address** : Pol. Industrial Halloles
c/san. 5-7

**Tel.** : +34 93 886 91 10
**Fax** : +34 93 886 91 13

Spain — Footwear – lining leather, Footwear – upper leather, Garment leather, Leathergoods leather, Split leather

**Tel.** : +34 93 886 91 10
**Fax** : +34 93 886 91 13
**Email** : francopell@worldonline.es
**Web** :
**Activity** : Importer, Exporter, Agent
**Products** : *Leather* : Footwear – upper leather, Leathergoods leather, Footwear – lining leather, Garment leather, Split leather,

*Garments and Gloves* : Jacket, coats, Trousers, Skirts,

**Raw Materials** : Bovine, Sheep, Goat

G. Estilo SA

**Contact** : Alexander Braun
**Address** : Ctra Hoyo de Mazanares Km. 3,500 Colmenar Viejo
Madrid-28770
Spain
**Tel.** : +34 91 845 47 63
**Fax** : +34 91 845 47 44
**Email** : paolo@gestilo.com
**Web** : http://www.gestilo.com
**Activity** : Manufacturer
**Products** : *Hides and Skins* : Chrome crust,

**Raw Materials** : Sheep

Spain

Genis Antel SA

**Address** : Prat d'en Galliners, 8
Vic - Barcelona-08500
Spain

**Tel.** : +34 93 889 27 00
**Fax** : +34 93 889 00 60
**Email** : ga@genisantel.com
**Web** : http://www.genisantel.com
**Activity** : Manufacturer
**Products** :
**Raw Materials** : Sheep

Spain

Grupo Ledexport SA

Spain

Footwear – lining leather, Footwear – upper

**Address** : Carretera de Roda 70
Vic - Barcelona-08500
Spain

leather, Garment leather, Gloving leather

**Tel.** : +34 93 881 46 46
**Fax** : +34 93 881 46 40

**Email** : ledexport@colomer.com
**Web** : http://www.colomer.com

**Activity** : Manufacturer

**Products** : *Hides and Skins* : Pickled, Wet blue, Chrome crust, Vegetable crust,

*Leather* : Footwear – upper leather, Footwear – lining leather, Garment leather, Gloving leather,

**Raw Materials** : Sheep, Goat

Hijos de Jose Bassols SA

**Contact** : Philip de Ros Wallace
Export Manager

Finished Goat Leather for shoe uppers and lining and leather goods. Hairsheep leather for shoe uppers Pigskin for lining Goat crust.

**Address** : Ronda Vall d'Uxo, Nave 5
Poligono Industrial Carrus
Elche-03206
Spain

**Tel.** : +34 966 660610
**Fax** : +34 965 431316

Spain Footwear – upper leather

**Email** : export@oscarbotella.com
**Web** : http://www.oscarbotella.com

**Activity** : Manufacturer

**Products** : *Hides and Skins* : Chrome crust,

*Leather* : Footwear – upper leather, Leathergoods leather, Footwear – lining leather,

**Raw Materials** : Sheep, Goat, Pig

Hijos de Juan Martinez SA

**Contact** : Manuel Martinez Leal
Gerente

Con más de 50 años de tradición curtidora, hijos de Juan Martnez S.A. abarca una gama de

Spain Footwear – lining leather, Footwear – upper leather, Leathergoods leather, Split leather

**Address** : Ctra. de Caravaca, Km. 3
P.O. Box 181
Lorca (Murcia)-30814
Spain

**Tel.** : +34 968 466 664
**Fax** : +34 968 466 801

**Email** : hijoma@arrakis.es
**Web** :



**Activity** : Manufacturer, Importer, Exporter

**Products** : *Leather* : Footwear – upper leather, Leathergoods leather, Footwear – lining leather, Split leather,

**Products** : *Leather* : Footwear – upper leather, Leathergoods leather, Footwear – lining leather, Split leather,

**Raw Materials** : Bovine

Hijos de Oscar Botella Sempere SL

**Contact** : Philip de Ros Wallace
Export Manager

**Address** : Ronda Vall d'Uxo, Nave 5
Poligono Industrial Carrus
Elche-03206
Spain

**Tel.** : +34 966 660610
**Fax** : +34 965 431316

**Email** : export@oscarbotella.com
**Web** : http://www.oscarbotella.com

**Activity** : Manufacturer

**Products** : *Hides and Skins* : Chrome crust,

*Leather* : Footwear – upper leather, Leathergoods leather, Footwear – lining leather,

**Raw Materials** : Sheep, Goat, Pig

Finished Goat Leather for shoe uppers and lining and leather goods. Hairsheep leather for shoe uppers Pigskin for lining Goat crust.

Spain

Footwear – lining leather, Footwear – upper leather, Leathergoods leather

Indasa

**Contact** : Daniel Medrano
Responsable de Eventos Internac.

**Address** : c/ Antonío García Martin s/n
P.O. Box 51
Burgos-09007
Spain

**Tel.** : +34 947 245 050
**Fax** : +34 947 224 237

**Email** : indasa@grupoindasa.com
**Web** :

**Activity** : Manufacturer, Exporter

**Products** : *Leather* : Footwear – upper leather, Leathergoods leather, Footwear – lining leather, Sole leather,

**Raw Materials** : Bovine

Empresa familiar fundada en 1965 en posesión del certificado ISO 9001, dedicada a la curtición, teñido y acabado de pieles vacunas mejores procedencías Europa Occidental, con destino a los fabricantes de zapatos, bolsos y marroquinería de todo el mundo. Alta tecnología, Ultima moda, Precios Competitivos. 30% de su producción dirigida a clientes europeos, norteamericanos y asiaticos.

Spain

Footwear – lining leather, Footwear – upper leather, Leathergoods leather, Sole leather

Industrial Igualadina SL

**Contact** : David Serasols Tort

**Address** : Avda Angel Guimerá, 37
P.O. Box 11

**Tel.** : +34 93 803 1256
**Fax** : +34 93 803 1258

**Email** : direccio@iisl.es
**Web** : http://www.iisl.es

Spain

Footwear – upper leather, Garment leather, Industrial leather, Sole leather, Split leather

**Email** : direccio@iisl.es
**Web** : http://www.iisl.es
**Activity** : Manufacturer, Agent
**Products** : *Hides and Skins* : Wet salted, Dry salted, Air/Frame dried, Limed, Pickled,

*Leather* : Footwear – upper leather, Sole leather, Garment leather, Industrial leather, Split leather,

**Raw Materials** : Bovine

Industrias del Curtido SA (Incusa)

**Contact** : Silvino Navarro Casanova
Director General
**Address** : Avda. Alicante, s/n
Silla - Valencia-46460
Spain
**Tel.** : +34 96 121 88 81
**Fax** : +34 96 121 2557
**Email** : comercial@incusa-lederval.es
**Web** : http://www.lederval.es
**Activity** : Manufacturer
**Products** : *Hides and Skins* : Wet salted, Wet blue,

*Leather* : Footwear – upper leather, Leathergoods leather, Split leather,

*Footwear* : Men's shoes, Women's shoes, Children shoes, Sandals, Boots, Safety, Military,

*Leather Goods* : Small leather goods, Large leather goods, Belts,

**Raw Materials** : Bovine

Fue fundada en 1952. Está especializada en la curtición y acabado de pieles de bovino, produciendo un millón de pies cuadrados al mes en una amplia y variada gama de productos tanto para calzado como marroquinería. Donde hay una perfecta conjunción entre nuevas tecnologías y moda. Está localizada en Silla (Valencia), su domocilio es Universidad 4 (Valencia).

Spain

Footwear – upper leather, Leathergoods leather, Split leather

Industrias del Curtido SA (Incusa)

**Contact** : Jorge Báguena
Compras Materia Prima

Grupo Lederval comprende 5 empresas. INCUSA fabricante de Vacuno plena flor, Nubuck y charol para calzado y marroquinería. ARGENT de Cabra: ante, tafilete abrillantado y napa, para calzado y confección. ALFA de Mestizo y Cordero para calzado y pequeña marroquinería. DERCOSA de Serrajes para calzafdo

Spain

Automotive leather, Footwear – lining leather, Footwear – upper leather, Garment leather, Industrial leather, Leathergoods leather, Saddlery and harness leather, Split

**Address** : Avda de Alicante s/n°
Silla - Valencia-46460
Spain



**Tel** : +34 96 12 124 58

**Products** : *Hides and Skins* : Wet salted, Dry salted, Air/Frame dried, Limed, Pickled, Wet blue, Chrome crust, Vegetable crust,

*Leather* : Footwear – upper leather, Leathergoods leather, Automotive leather, Footwear – lining leather, Upholstery leather, Garment leather, Saddlery and harness leather, Industrial leather, Split leather,

leather, Upholstery leather

**Raw Materials** : Bovine, Sheep, Goat

## Inpelsa Industrias Peleteras SA

**Contact** : Manuel Rios
Director General

**Address** : Ctra. Montesa S/N
P.O. Box 31
Canals-46650
Spain

**Tel.** : +34 96 224 1200
**Fax** : +34 96 224 2240

Spain Garment leather

**Email** : inpelsa@lederval.es
**Web** : http://www.lederval.es

**Activity** : Manufacturer, Exporter

**Products** : *Leather* : Garment leather,

**Raw Materials** : Sheep

## International Leather Systems

**Address** : Ave. Ragull 60 1° a
San Cugat del Valles-08190
Spain

**Tel.** : +34 93 589 51 61
**Fax** : +34 93 589 52 26

Spain

**Email** : badrinas.ils@terra.es
**Web** :

**Activity** : Manufacturer

## Interpel Ltd SL

**Contact** : Jordi Soler Roca
Director General

Spain Footwear – lining leather, Footwear – upper leather, Garment leather, Leathergoods leather, Sole leather

**Address** : Calle Cami Vell De Vic, 22,
Folgueroles - Barcelona-08519
Spain

**Tel.** : +34 93 888 81 28/81 13
**Fax** : +34 93 812 21 52

**Products** : *Hides and Skins* : Pickled, Wet blue, Chrome crust, Vegetable crust,

*Leather* : Footwear – upper leather, Leathergoods leather, Footwear – lining leather, Sole leather, Garment leather,

**Raw Materials** : Sheep, Goat

Interpiel R. Monzo

**Address** : Calle Almansa 119
Poligono Carrus
Elche-
Spain

**Tel.** : +34 96 666 1848
**Fax** :

**Products** : *Leather* : Garment leather, Gloving leather,

Spain | Garment leather, Gloving leather

Int'L Rodrigo Sancho SA

**Contact** : Norberto Ubeda
Director de las Ventas

**Address** : Avd. Les Moles s/n
Canáls, Valencia-46650
Spain

Pieles de caprino y bovino acabados, para el sector calzado y marroquinería. Nivel de calidad de producto, medio y alto.

**Tel.** : +34 96 224 53 84
**Fax** : +34 96 224 53 83
**Email** : irssa@rs-int.com
**Web** :
**Activity** : Manufacturer, Exporter
**Products** : *Leather* : Leathergoods leather, Footwear – lining leather,

**Raw Materials** : Bovine, Goat

Spain | Footwear – lining leather, Leathergoods leather

ITA-Europe

**Address** : Los almendros 55
**Tel.** : +34 91 886 68 60 / +54 223 451 9225
**Email** : elisabeth@ita-europe.com
**Activity** : Manufacturer, Importer, Exporter
**Products** : *Hides and Skins* : Wet blue, Vegetable crust, Other - hides
**Raw Materials** : Reptile, Other

Spain | Leathergoods leather

**Raw Materials** : Reptile, Other

J. Pomes Leather SL

**Contact** : Jep Pomés
Managing director

**Address** : St. Antoni de Baix 29
P.O. Box 391
Igualada-08700
Spain

**Tel.** : +34 93 803 0424
**Fax** : +34 93 803 0391

**Email** : info@jpomesleather.es
**Web** : http://www.jpomesleather.es

**Activity** : Wholesaler

**Products** : *Hides and Skins* : Wet blue, Vegetable crust,

*Leather* : Leathergoods leather, Garment leather, Saddlery and harness leather, Industrial leather,

**Raw Materials** : Bovine, Sheep, Goat

Tenemos en stock pieles para confección. Pieles vegetales de todos tipos. Tenemos un servicio propio de desarrollo de pieles a medida del cliente.

Spain

Garment leather, Industrial leather, Leathergoods leather, Saddlery and harness leather

JMT

**Contact** : Josep M. Torras Payerol

**Address** : Camelies, 9 - 1° 2a
Igualada-08700
Spain

**Tel.** : +34 93 80 52 653
**Fax** : +34 93 80 42 164

**Email** : josepmt@terra.es
**Web** :

**Activity** : Agent

**Products** : *Hides and Skins* : Wet salted, Dry salted, Pickled, Wet blue, Chrome crust, Vegetable crust,

*Leather* : Leathergoods leather, Footwear – lining leather, Sole leather, Upholstery leather, Garment leather, Gloving leather, Industrial leather, Split leather,

*Machinery* : Wet working, Drying, Softening, Finishing, Pollution control, Quality control,

**Raw Materials** : Bovine, Sheep, Goat

Intermediación en la compra de cueros, serrajes, pieles, stock lots: ovinos / caprinos / bovinos. Maquinaria nueva y usada

Spain

Footwear – lining leather, Garment leather, Gloving leather, Industrial leather, Leathergoods leather, Sole leather, Split leather, Upholstery leather

Juan Alonso e Hijos SA

**Contact** : Mikel San Juan
Sales

**Address** : Avenida del Zadorra, 130
P.O. Box 01013
Vitoria-
Spain

Spain

Automotive leather, Footwear – upper leather, Gloving

**Address** : Avenida del Zadorra, 130
P.O. Box 01013
Vitoria-
Spain

**Tel.** : +34 945 265 144
**Fax** : +34 945 265 763
**Email** : msanjuan@juan-alonso.com
**Web** : http://www.juan-alonso.com
**Activity** : Exporter
**Products** : *Hides and Skins* : Wet salted, Dry salted, Air/Frame dried, Pickled, Wet blue,

*Leather* : Footwear – upper leather, Leathergoods leather, Automotive leather, Upholstery leather, Gloving leather,

**Raw Materials** : Bovine, Sheep, Goat

leather, Leathergoods leather, Upholstery leather

## Juan Valles Soriano

**Contact** : Juan Valles Soriano
Gerente

**Address** : Ctra Can Macià, Km 1
08711 Odena
P.O. Box 180
Igualada-08700
Spain

**Tel.** : +34 93 803 77 11
**Fax** : +34 93 805 06 03
**Email** : vallesoriano@yahoo.es
**Web** :
**Activity** : Wholesaler, Exporter
**Products** : *Hides and Skins* : Wet salted, Wet blue, Chrome crust,

*Leather* : Leathergoods leather, Footwear – lining leather, Sole leather, Upholstery leather, Garment leather, Gloving leather, Split leather,

**Raw Materials** : Bovine, Sheep, Goat, Pig

We would like to introduce ourselves as exporters and traders of all kind of leather scraps, from garment, furniture, leather fine goods, shoes, etc.

Spain

Footwear – lining leather, Garment leather, Gloving leather, Leathergoods leather, Sole leather, Split leather, Upholstery leather

## La Doma SA

**Address** : Mas Els Casals s/n
Centelles - Barcelona 08190

**Tel.** : +34 93 881 12 16
**Fax** : +34 93 881 13 90
**Email** : ladoma@ladoma.com
**Web** : http://www.ladoma.com
**Activity** : Manufacturer, Exporter
**Products** : *Hides and Skins* : Chrome crust, Vegetable crust

Spain

crust,

**Raw Materials** : Sheep

## Mapiel SA

**Contact** : Elena Sanchey Otero
Responsable Administración

**Address** : Calle Pico Del Aguila 43
Pol. Los Linares
Humanes, Madrid-28970
Spain

**Tel.** : +34 91 604 94 09
**Fax** : +34 91 604 92 21

**Email** : mapielsa@infonegocio.com
**Web** : http://www.infonegocio.com/mapiel

**Activity** : Manufacturer, Exporter

**Products** : *Leather* : Garment leather,

**Raw Materials** : Sheep

Lamb fur skins for garments. Spanish Merino Double Face.

Spain

Garment leather

## Maximo Mor SA

**Contact** : Maximo Mor Gonzalez
Dirección

**Address** : Primero de Mayo 21
Montmeló, Barcelona-08160
Spain

**Tel.** : +34 93 572 1004
**Fax** : +34 93 572 0049

**Email** : ventas@maximomor.com
**Web** : http://www.maximomor.com

**Activity** : Manufacturer, Exporter

**Products** : *Hides and Skins* : Pickled, Wet blue, Chrome crust, Vegetable crust,

*Leather* : Footwear – upper leather, Leathergoods leather, Footwear – lining leather, Sole leather, Upholstery leather, Garment leather, Gloving leather,

**Raw Materials** : Sheep, Goat, Other

Spain

Footwear – lining leather, Footwear – upper leather, Garment leather, Gloving leather, Leathergoods leather, Sole leather, Upholstery leather

## Miguel Farres Rojas, SA

**Contact** : Dolores Farrés Llansana

**Address** : Calle Sant Antoni de Baix 46.48
Igualada, Barcelona-08700

**Tel.** : +34 93 803 78 11
**Fax** : +34 93 804 47 36

**Email** : farres@splenda.es
**Web** : http://www.splenda.es

Spain

Leathergoods leather, Saddlery and harness leather, Sole leather

**Email** : farres@splenda.es
**Web** : http://www.splenda.es
**Activity** : Manufacturer, Importer, Exporter
**Products** : *Hides and Skins* : Wet salted, Dry salted, Air/Frame dried,

*Leather* : Leathergoods leather, Sole leather, Saddlery and harness leather,

**Raw Materials** : Bovine

Morera Pell SL

**Contact** : Antoni Morera Dalmau
Administración
**Address** : Sol, 30
Igualada-Barcelona-08700
Spain

**Tel.** : +34 93 803 2703
**Fax** : +34 93 804 0312
**Email** : morerapell@morerapell.com
**Web** :
**Activity** : Manufacturer
**Products** : *Hides and Skins* : Wet blue,

*Leather* : Footwear – upper leather, Leathergoods leather, Split leather,

**Raw Materials** : Bovine

Spain

Footwear – upper leather, Leathergoods leather, Split leather

Mundi Cuir, S.L.

**Contact** : Josep Salat Morera
**Address** : C. de Sant Antoni Ma. Claret, 63
Igualada, Barcelona-08700
**Tel.** : +34 93 803 08 02
**Fax** : +34 93 804 38 69
**Email** : info@mundi-cuir.com
**Web** : http://www.mundi-cuir.com
**Activity** : Manufacturer, Exporter, Agent
**Products** : *Leather* : Footwear – upper leather, Leathergoods leather, Footwear –
**Raw Materials** : Bovine, Sheep, Goat, Reptile, Pig. Other

Spain

Footwear – lining leather, Footwear – upper leather, Garment leather, Leathergoods leather, Saddlery and harness leather, Upholstery leather

**Raw Materials** : Bovine, Sheep, Goat, Reptile, Pig. Other

## Palomares Piel S.L.

**Contact** : Juan Carlos Palomares Perez
Director Comercio Internacional

**Address** : Virgen de la Salud 10
P.O. Box 295
Elda (Alicante)-03600
Spain

**Tel.** : +34 96 538 2450/2742
**Fax** : +34 96 539 1783

**Email** : palomares@hpalomares.com
**Web** : http://www.hpalomares.com

**Activity** : Wholesaler/retailer/trader, Importer, Exporter, Agent

**Products** : *Hides and Skins* : Wet blue, Chrome crust,

*Leather* : Footwear – upper leather, Leathergoods leather, Footwear – lining leather, Split leather,

**Raw Materials** : Bovine, Sheep, Goat, Pig

Almacen de pieles de vacuno, caprino, porcino para la fabricación de calzado y marroquinería.

Spain

Footwear – lining leather, Footwear – upper leather, Leathergoods leather, Split leather

## Rodrigo Sancho SA

**Contact** : José Maria Sancho Navarro
Director General

**Address** : Paseo Industria, s/n
Canals (Valencia)-46650
Spain

**Tel.** : +34 96 22 40 200
**Fax** : +34 96 22 41 134

**Email** : rsancho@rodrigosancho.com
**Web** : http://www.rodrigosancho.com

**Activity** : Manufacturer

**Products** : *Hides and Skins* : Pickled, Wet blue, Chrome crust,

*Leather* : Footwear – upper leather, Footwear – lining leather,

*Chemicals* : Preservation, Pretanning, Tanning, Retanning, Dyeing, Fatliquoring, Waterproofing,

**Raw Materials** : Sheep, Goat

- Fabricante de pieles de cabra y cordero para calzado de señora y caballero. - Fabricante a terceros de corderos hasta piquel y wet blue. - Venta de productos químicos para la fabricación del cuero.

Spain

Footwear – lining leather, Footwear – upper leather

## Soler Garcia SA

**Contact** : Antonio Soler García

**Address** : Pol. Ind.
P.O. Box 166

**Tel.** : +34 96 534 33 67
**Fax** : +34 96 534 06 01

Spain

Footwear – lining leather, Upholstery leather

**Tel.** : +34 96 534 33 67
**Fax** : +34 96 534 06 01
**Email** : solergarcia@solergarcia.com
**Web** : http://www.solergarcia.com
**Activity** : Wholesaler, Importer, Exporter, Agent
**Products** : *Hides and Skins* : Pickled, Wet blue, Chrome crust,

*Leather* : Footwear – lining leather, Upholstery leather,

**Raw Materials** : Bovine, Goat, Pig

Spain Interproducts Sl

Spain

Footwear – lining leather, Footwear – upper leather, Gloving leather

**Contact** : Jaime Hugas
Managing Director
**Address** : Villa 29-31
Sant Cugat del Vallés-08173
Spain
**Tel.** : +34 93 590 8071 / +34 69 647 2395
**Fax** : +34 93 590 8072
**Email** : hugas@telefonica.net
**Web** :
**Activity** : Agent
**Products** : *Hides and Skins* : Wet salted, Dry salted, Air/Frame dried, Limed, Pickled, Wet blue, Chrome crust,

*Leather* : Footwear – upper leather, Footwear – lining leather, Gloving leather,

**Raw Materials** : Bovine, Sheep, Goat, Pig

Sucesores de Manuel Hernandez SL

Spain

Footwear – upper leather, Garment leather, Other - leather

**Contact** : Conchi Hernandez
Gerente
**Address** : Carretera Castellnovo s/n
P.O. Box 70
Segorbe (Castellón)-12400
Spain
**Tel.** : +34 964 710 116
**Fax** : +34 964 713 976
**Email** : mhernandez@gamuzaspiel.com
**Web** :
**Activity** : Manufacturer, Importer, Exporter
**Products** : *Hides and Skins* : Pickled,

*Leather* : Footwear – upper leather, Other - leather, Garment leather,

*Footwear* : Children shoes, Shoe components,

**Raw Materials** : Sheep

Suñe Curtidos SA

Spain

**Address** : Tanger 91
Barcelona-08018
Spain

**Tel.** : +34 93 300 9901
**Fax** : +34 93 485 0202

Teneria Industrial Valenciana S A

**Contact** : Jose Antonio Capo Camps

**Address** : Poligono Industrial de Picassent
C/6 s/n
P.O. Box 66
Picassent-46220
Spain

**Tel.** : +34 96 124 01 19
**Fax** : +34 96 124 10 38
**Email** : tivsa@inescop.es
**Web** :

**Activity** : Manufacturer, Importer, Exporter

**Products** : *Hides and Skins* : Wet salted, Wet blue, Chrome crust,

*Leather* : Footwear – upper leather, Footwear – lining leather, Split leather,

**Raw Materials** : Bovine, Reptile

Fabrica de curtidos especializada en pieles de vacuno (cuellos encogido natural) y pieles de reptiles (serpientes y lagartos), con 55 años de antiguedad. Exporta a USA, Mexico, todos los paises de Europa, Hong Kong, China, Japon. Asiste a las mayores ferias internacionales del sector.

Spain

Footwear – lining leather, Footwear – upper leather, Split leather

Tenerias Homs SL

**Address** : Poligono Ind. Moli Del Llobet, 25
Vic - Barcelona-08500
Spain

**Tel.** : +34 93 889 3099
**Fax** : +34 93 889 2974

**Email** : teneriashoms@terra.es
**Web** : http://www.teneriashoms.net

**Activity** : Manufacturer, Exporter

**Products** : *Hides and Skins* : Chrome crust, Vegetable crust,

*Leather* : Footwear – upper leather, Leathergoods leather, Footwear – lining leather,

**Raw Materials** : Sheep, Goat

Spain

Footwear – lining leather, Footwear – upper leather, Leathergoods leather

Tenerias Omega SA

**Contact** : Marta Mauleón
Responsable Exportación

**Address** : Ctra. Estella-Tafalla KM. 2,3
Villatuerta (Navarra)-31132
Spain

Spain

Leathergoods leather, Sole leather, Upholstery leather

**Address** : Ctra. Estella-Tafalla KM. 2,3
Villatuerta (Navarra)-31132
Spain

**Tel.** : +34 948 54 60 51
**Fax** : +34 948 54 61 44
**Email** : t.omega@lederval.es
**Web** : http://www.lederval.es
**Activity** : Manufacturer, Exporter
**Products** : *Leather* : Leathergoods leather, Sole leather, Upholstery leather,

**Raw Materials** : Bovine

## Vicpel SA

**Address** : Entenza 15
Mollet del Valles
Barcelona-08100
Spain

**Tel.** : +34 93 57 05 734
**Fax** : +34 93 57 02 183

Spain

**Email** : victor@vicpel.com
**Web** : http://www.vicpel.com
**Activity** : Manufacturer, Exporter

## Vidal Bosch SA

**Contact** : Susana Vidal
Marketing

**Address** : Baja San Antonio 75
P.O. Box 80
Igualada, Barcelona-08700
Spain

**Tel.** : +34 93 803 2100
**Fax** : +34 93 803 6960
**Email** : info@vidalbosch.com
**Web** : http://www.vidalbosch.com
**Activity** : Manufacturer, Exporter
**Products** : *Leather* : Automotive leather, Industrial leather, Split leather,

Spain Automotive leather, Industrial leather, Split leather

## Vivapel SA

**Address** : Carrera Del Rec, 16
Igualada (Barcelona) 08700

**Tel.** : +34 93 803 5511
**Fax** : +34 93 805 1995
**Email** : info@vivapel.com
**Web** : http://www.vivapel.com
**Activity** : Manufacturer, Exporter
**Products** : *Leather* : Footwear – upper leather, Leathergoods leather, Upholstery leather

Spain Footwear – upper leather, Leathergoods leather, Upholstery leather

| | |
|---|---|
| | Leathergoods leather, Upholstery leather, |
| **Raw Materials** | : Bovine, Sheep |

## SWITZERLAND

| | | |
|---|---|---|
| Eduard Gallusser AG | Switzerland | Footwear – lining leather, Footwear – upper leather, Industrial leather, Leathergoods leather, Saddlery and harness leather, Split leather |
| Emag AG | Switzerland | Footwear – upper leather, Garment leather, Upholstery leather |
| Ernesto Moos SA | Switzerland | Automotive leather, Footwear – lining leather, Footwear – upper leather, Garment leather, Gloving leather, Sole leather, Split leather, Upholstery leather |
| Felix Berger AG | Switzerland | Footwear – upper leather, Leathergoods leather, Upholstery leather |
| Gimmel Max AG Gerberei | Switzerland | Automotive leather, Footwear – upper leather, Garment leather, Leathergoods leather, Saddlery and harness leather, Upholstery leather |
| KT Trading AG | Switzerland | Footwear – lining leather |
| Küpfer Cuirs en Gros Genève | Switzerland | Footwear – upper leather, Garment leather, Industrial leather, Leathergoods leather, Other - leather, Upholstery leather |
| Novalpina AG | Switzerland | Footwear – upper leather, Garment leather, Leathergoods leather, Other - leather |
| O. Frey | Switzerland | Footwear – upper leather, Leathergoods leather |
| Schneider Leder AG | Switzerland | Automotive leather, Other - leather |
| Teleconsa Ag | Switzerland | Footwear – upper leather, Garment leather, Upholstery leather |
| Tradevcogen SA | Switzerland | Garment leather |

## UKRAINE

| | | |
|---|---|---|
| JSC Vozko<br>**Contact** : Andrey Shevchenko<br>**Address** : 287, October Revolution Street<br>**Tel.** : +38 0512 500 044<br>**Fax** : +38 0512 500 043<br>: andrey@vozko.com<br>: http://www.vozko.com | Ukraine | Footwear – lining leather, Footwear – upper leather, Garment leather, Gloving leather, Industrial leather, Leathergoods leather, Split leather, Upholstery leather |

**Email** : andrey@vozko.com
**Web** : http://www.vozko.com
**Activity** : Manufacturer, Exporter
**Products** : *Hides and Skins* : Wet blue, Chrome crust, Vegetable crust,

*Leather* : Footwear – upper leather, Leathergoods leather, Footwear – lining leather, Upholstery leather, Garment leather, Gloving leather, Industrial leather, Split leather,

production (daily capacity is 80-100 tons of cattle hides) is capable to meet our customers' every requirement, and produces widest range of genuine leather types from the raw material being sourced domestically as well as from EU countries, North and South America and Asia. Our production uses the chemicals of the well-known chemical manufacturers in the world under control of our Italian Chief technologist. The tannery is well situated nearby main ports of Black sea.

**Raw Materials** : Bovine, Goat

MV-Invest

**Contact** : Constantin Lesnichy
Director

**Address** : Lunin av. 85,87510
Mariupol-
Ukraine

**Tel.** : +38 050 6605721 / 067 6124317
**Fax** : +38 0629 511029
**Email** : mv-invest@list.ru
**Web** :
**Activity** : Manufacturer, Importer, Exporter, Agent
**Products** : *Hides and Skins* : Wet salted, Wet blue, Chrome crust,

*Leather* : Footwear – upper leather, Other - leather, Footwear – lining leather, Industrial leather,

**Raw Materials** : Bovine, Sheep

Ukraine Footwear – lining leather, Footwear – upper leather, Industrial leather, Other - leather

# UNITED KINGDOM

Andrew Muirhead & Son Ltd

**Contact** : John Mc Morris
Sales Manager

**Address** : 273-289 Dunn Street
Glasgow-G40 3EA
United Kingdom

**Tel.** : +44 (0)141 554 3724
**Fax** : +44 (0)141 554 4741
**Email** : sales@muirhead.co.uk
**Web** : http://www.muirhead.co.uk
**Activity** : Manufacturer
**Products** : *Leather* : Upholstery leather,

Muirhead has more than 160 years of expertise in leather manufacture and has a proven track record of innovation, service and flexibility. Its modern, fully automated Glasgow factory ensures consistent quality, time and time again alongside large runs it can also undertake smaller commissions of any size. Muirhead, founded in 1840, is one of Britain's leading upholstery leather companies. It supplies Britain's leading furniture upholstery manufacturers,as well as airlines, hotels, cars and cruise companies all over the world.

United Kingdom Upholstery leather

**Raw Materials** : Bovine

Brandler (UK) Ltd

**Contact** : Marcus or David Brandler
Director

**Address** : 20, Grove Place
Bedford-MK40 3JJ
United Kingdom

**Tel.** : +44 1234 270270
**Fax** : +44 1234 270273
**Email** : david@brandler.demon.co.uk
**Web** :
**Activity** : Importer, Exporter
**Products** : *Hides and Skins* : Wet blue, Chrome crust,

*Leather* : Footwear – upper leather, Leathergoods leather, Footwear – lining leather, Garment leather, Gloving leather,

Traders in Nigerian goat and sheepskin in wet blue, crust and finished. Own office in Nigeria.

United Kingdom Footwear – lining leather, Footwear – upper leather, Garment leather, Gloving leather, Leathergoods leather

**Raw Materials** : Sheep, Goat

Clayton of Chesterfield

| | | | | |
|---|---|---|---|---|
| **Address** | : | Clayton Street Tannery<br>Chesterfield. Derbyshire-S41 0DU<br>United Kingdom | | |
| **Tel.** | : | +44 1246 232863 | United Kingdom | Automotive leather, Industrial leather, Leathergoods leather, Other - leather, Sole leather, Split leather |
| **Fax** | : | +44 1246 207807 | | |
| **Email** | : | office@claytonleather.com | | |
| **Web** | : | http://www.claytonleather.com | | |
| **Activity** | : | Manufacturer | | |
| **Products** | : | *Hides and Skins* : Wet blue, Chrome crust, Vegetable crust, Other - hides and skins,<br><br>*Leather* : Leathergoods leather, Automotive leather, Other - leather, Sole leather, Industrial leather, Split leather, | | |

Daniels & Daniels

| | | | | | |
|---|---|---|---|---|---|
| **Contact** | : | Kit Daniels<br>Proprietor | Agents for leathers from all around the world selling into the English shoe and automotive markets. For the car trade a new dry finishing system for split leather for interior trim. For the shoe trade all types of upper and sole leather. Open to offers from manufacturers wishing to sell in the UK. | United Kingdom | Automotive leather, Footwear – lining leather, Footwear – upper leather, Leathergoods leather, Other - leather, Saddlery and harness leather, Sole leather, Split leather, Upholstery leather |
| **Address** | : | 7 Ashley Rd. Weston by Welland<br>Market Harborough<br>Leicestershire-LE16 8HR<br>United Kingdom | | | |
| **Tel.** | : | +44 1858 565 546 | | | |
| **Fax** | : | +44 1858 565 545 | | | |
| **Email** | : | kitd@danielsx2.freeserve.co.uk | | | |
| **Web** | : | | | | |
| **Activity** | : | Agent | | | |
| **Products** | : | *Hides and Skins* : Wet blue, Chrome crust,<br><br>*Leather* : Footwear – upper leather, Leathergoods leather, Automotive leather, Other - leather, Footwear – lining leather, Sole leather, Upholstery leather, Saddlery and harness leather, Split leather | | | |

Dermatech International Ltd

| | | | | |
|---|---|---|---|---|
| **Address** | : | Turnberry House, 1404/1410<br>High Road - Whetstone<br>London-N20 9BH<br>United Kingdom | United Kingdom | Footwear – upper leather, Garment leather, Gloving leather, Leathergoods |
| **Activity** | : | Manufacturer | | |
| **Products** | : | *Leather* : Footwear – upper leather, | | |

Leathergoods leather, Garment leather, Gloving leather, | leather

**Raw Materials** : Bovine, Sheep, Goat

Devonport Leathers Ltd

**Contact** : M. Chowdhry
Director

**Address** : 111 Reedley Road
Stoke Bishop
Bristol-BS9 1BE
United Kingdom

**Tel.** : +44 117 968 70 29
**Fax** : +44 117 968 51 08

**Email** : devonport@btinternet.com
**Web** :

**Activity** : Wholesaler, Manufacturer, Importer, Exporter, Agent

**Products** : *Hides and Skins* : Air/Frame dried, Limed, Pickled, Wet blue, Chrome crust, Vegetable crust, Other - hides and skins,

*Leather* : Footwear – upper leather, Leathergoods leather, Footwear – lining leather, Sole leather, Upholstery leather, Garment leather, Gloving leather, Saddlery and harness leather, Industrial leather, Split leather,

*Footwear* : Men's shoes, Children shoes, Boots, Safety, Sport, Military, Shoe components,

*Garments and Gloves* : Jacket, coats, Trousers, Skirts, Motorcycling, Fashion gloves, Sport gloves, Industrial gloves,

*Leather Goods* : Large leather goods, Belts, Furniture,

United Kingdom

Footwear – lining leather, Footwear – upper leather, Garment leather, Gloving leather, Industrial leather, Leathergoods leather, Saddlery and harness leather, Sole leather, Split leather, Upholstery leather

**Raw Materials** : Bovine, Goat, Pig, Other

F. Moxham & Son

**Contact** : Leonard Moxham
Owner/Manager

United Kingdom

Split leather

**Address** : 43, HR. Market St. Kearsley
Bolton
Lancashire-BL4 8HQ
United Kingdom
**Tel.** : +44 1204 573 342
**Fax** : +44 1204 573 342
**Email** :
**Web** :
**Activity** : Retailer, Manufacturer, Exporter
**Products** : *Leather* : Split leather,

*Leather Goods* : Other - leather goods,

**Raw Materials** : Sheep, Other (Chamois)

Fenland Sheepskin Co Ltd

United Kingdom

Footwear – lining leather, Garment leather, Other - leather

Geoffrey R. Cox

**Contact** : Brian Jones
Director
**Address** : Axe Rd. Colley
Lane Industrial Estate
Bridgwater, Somerset-TA6 5LN
United Kingdom
**Tel.** : +44 1278 427586
**Fax** : +44 1278 444165
**Email** : sales@fenland.com
**Web** : http://www.fenland.com
**Activity** : Manufacturer
**Products** : *Leather* : Other - leather, Footwear – lining leather, Garment leather,

*Garments and Gloves* : Jacket, coats,

*Leather Goods* : Car components, Other - leather goods,

**Raw Materials** : Sheep

Tanners of wool on sheep and lambskin for decoration, furniture, garment and auto industry. Baby fleeces and skins for medical use. Producers of "Aqualamb" waterproof sheepskin for the footwear and garment industry.

United Kingdom

Garment leather, Other - leather, Split leather

Hutchings & Harding Ltd

**Contact** : John Ettling
Managing Director

United Kingdom

Footwear – lining leather, Leathergoods

leather, Other - leather

**Address** : 161-163 High Street
Sawston
Cambridge-CB2 4HN
United Kingdom

**Tel.** : +44 1223 832 281
**Fax** : +44 1223 836 401
**Email** : handh@chamois.com
**Web** : http://www.chamois.com
**Activity** : Manufacturer
**Products** : *Hides and Skins* : Pickled,

*Leather* : Leathergoods leather, Other - leather, Footwear – lining leather,

**Raw Materials** : Sheep, Other

Joseph Clayton & Sons (Chesterfield) Ltd.

**Contact** : A. Barrie Birkin
General Manager

**Address** : Clayton Street Tannery
Chesterfield-S41 0DU
United Kingdom

Tanners since 1840 of thick speciality leathers suitable for industry, saddlery, sports balls, leather floors and wall tiles.

**Tel.** : +44 (0)1246 232863
**Fax** : +44 (0)1246 207087
**Email** : office@claytonleather.com
**Web** : http://www.claytonleather.com
**Activity** : Manufacturer
**Products** : *Leather* : Other - leather, Sole leather, Saddlery and harness leather, Industrial leather,

*Chemicals* : Tanning, Waterproofing,

*Machinery* : Wet working,

United Kingdom

Industrial leather, Other - leather, Saddlery and harness leather, Sole leather

**Raw Materials** : Bovine

Kent Chamois Co Ltd

**Contact** : Jerry Salaman

**Address** : .
P.O. Box 16

**Tel.** : +44 1892 837070
**Fax** : +44 1892 837030
**Email** : jerry@carcare.co.uk
**Web** : http://www.carcare.co.uk

United Kingdom

Other - leather

**Email** : jerry@carcare.co.uk
**Web** : http://www.carcare.co.uk
**Activity** : Manufacturer, Importer, Exporter
**Products** : *Leather* : Other - leather,

**Raw Materials** : Sheep

L.H. Nichols Ltd.

| | | | | |
|---|---|---|---|---|
| **Address** | : | Nautilus Works, Reckleford<br>Yeovil, Somerset-BA21 4EL<br>United Kingdom | | |
| **Tel.** | : | +44 1935 476 288 | United Kingdom | Garment leather, Gloving leather, Other - leather |
| **Fax** | : | +44 1935 431 474 | | |
| **Email** | : | office@lhnichols.com | | |
| **Web** | : | http://www.lhnichols.com | | |
| **Activity** | : | Manufacturer | | |
| **Products** | : | *Hides and Skins* : Wet salted, Dry salted, Air/Frame dried,<br><br>*Leather* : Other - leather, Garment leather, Gloving leather, | | |

Leather Solution - SONYS

| | | | | |
|---|---|---|---|---|
| **Address** | : | 55 Edge Lane Stretford<br>Mancester-M32 8PA<br>United Kingdom | | |
| **Tel.** | : | +44 7747 684 777 / 161 865 93 08 | United Kingdom | Footwear – lining leather, Footwear – upper leather, Garment leather, Sole leather, Split leather |
| **Fax** | : | | | |
| **Email** | : | uksonys@yahoo.co.uk | | |
| **Web** | : | http://www.ec21.com/sonys | | |
| **Activity** | : | Wholesaler, Manufacturer, Importer, Exporter, Agent | | |
| **Products** | : | *Hides and Skins* : Dry salted, Pickled, Wet blue, Chrome crust,<br><br>*Leather* : Footwear – upper leather, Footwear – lining leather, Sole leather | | |

gloves, Industrial gloves, Other - garments,

*Leather Goods* : Small leather goods,

**Raw Materials** : Sheep, Goat, Pig

Metropolitan Leather Co Ltd

**Contact** : Roy Winnard
Managing Director

**Address** : Cottingham Way
Thrapston
Kettering-NN144PL
United Kingdom

**Tel.** : +44 1832 732 216
**Fax** : +44 1832 732 808

**Email** : roy@metropolitanleather.com
**Web** : http://www.metropolitanleather.com

**Activity** : Manufacturer, Importer, Exporter

**Products** : *Hides and Skins* : Chrome crust, Vegetable crust,

*Leather* : Footwear – upper leather, Leathergoods leather, Automotive leather, Footwear – lining leather, Sole leather, Upholstery leather, Garment leather, Gloving leather, Saddlery and harness leather, Industrial leather,

**Raw Materials** : Bovine, Sheep, Goat, Pig

Metropolitan Leather supply a wide range of leathers, saddlery, bridle work, luggage, harness, shoe upholstery, small leathergoods are all catered for. Our finishing department can colour match to client's patterns. We also have massive stocks of redundant leathers at low prices suitable for shoes, boots and leathergoods. Our orthopaedic range of leathers is used for the manufacture of strapping and corrective footwear and prosthesis linings. We produce a leather suitable for police and military belts, cross belts and gun holsters.

United Kingdom

Automotive leather, Footwear – lining leather, Footwear – upper leather, Garment leather, Gloving leather, Industrial leather, Leathergoods leather, Saddlery and harness leather, Sole leather, Upholstery leather

Nitech International Leather

United Kingdom

Footwear – lining leather, Footwear – upper leather, Gloving leather

Pittards Plc

**Contact** : Florence Vaughan

**Address** : Sherborne Road
Somerset

**Tel.** : +44 1823 474 321
**Fax** : +44 1823 427 145

United Kingdom

Footwear – lining leather, Footwear – upper leather, Gloving leather, Industrial leather.

**Tel.** : +44 1823 474 321
**Fax** : +44 1823 427 145
**Email** : glovenquire@pittards.com
**Web** : http://www.pittardsleather.com
**Activity** : Manufacturer
**Products** : *Hides and Skins* : Wet salted, Pickled, Wet blue,

*Leather* : Footwear – upper leather, Leathergoods leather, Footwear – lining leather, Gloving leather, Saddlery and harness leather, Industrial leather,

**Raw Materials** : Bovine, Sheep, Goat

Leathergoods leather, Saddlery and harness leather

Ryan Leathers Ltd

**Address** : 33 Wadeson Street
London-E2 9DR
United Kingdom

**Tel.** : +44 0208 983 11 82
**Fax** : +44 0208 983 14 83
**Email** : barry@ryanleathers.com
**Web** : http://www.ryanleathers.com
**Activity** : Importer, Exporter, Agent
**Products** : *Leather* : Footwear – upper leather, Leathergoods leather, Automotive leather, Footwear – lining leather, Upholstery leather, Garment leather,

United Kingdom

Automotive leather, Footwear – lining leather, Footwear – upper leather, Garment leather, Leathergoods leather, Upholstery leather

Sharp, Samuel (Curriers) Ltd

**Contact** : Roger Dear
General manager

**Address** : The Stocks. Cosgrove
Milton Keynes-MK19 7JD
United Kingdom

**Tel.** : +44 1908 560 179
**Fax** : +44 1908 260 285
**Email** : office@sharpleather.com
**Web** : http://www.sharpleather.com
**Activity** : Manufacturer
**Products** : *Leather* : Leathergoods leather, Saddlery and harness leather,

**Raw Materials** : Bovine

A four hundred year old company finishing vegetable tanned leather by hand, mainly for the equestrian trade. Using techniques that maintain the natural appeal of the material, the company prides itself on the quality of its product.

United Kingdom

Leathergoods leather, Saddlery and harness leather

Walter Reginald Group Ltd

| | | | | |
|---|---|---|---|---|
| **Address** | : | Unit 6, 100 The Highway<br>London-E1W 2BX<br>United Kingdom | United Kingdom | Footwear – upper leather, Garment leather, Leathergoods leather, Upholstery leather |
| **Tel.** | : | +44 20 7481 2233 | | |
| **Fax** | : | +44 20 7481 2255 | | |
| **Email** | : | walter.reginald@btconnect.com | | |
| **Web** | : | http://www.walterreginald.com | | |
| **Activity** | : | Importer, Exporter, Agent | | |
| **Products** | : | *Leather* : Footwear – upper leather, Leathergoods leather, Upholstery leather, Garment leather, | | |

William Cowley

| | | | | | |
|---|---|---|---|---|---|
| **Contact** | : | Willem Visscher<br>Manager | Established in 1870. We make Parchment and Vellum for writing, printing, illuminating, bookbinding, furniture, architectural covering and drum heads. Skins of goat, sheep and calf are traditionally hand cured to make a very high quality, unique, immensely strong and long lasting Parchment. Also Alum Tawed leather for specialist bookbinding. | United Kingdom | Other - leather |
| **Address** | : | Parchment & Vellum Works,<br>97 Caldecote St. Newport Pagnell<br>Buckinghamshire-MK16 ODB<br>United Kingdom | | | |
| **Tel.** | : | +44 1908 610 038 | | | |
| **Fax** | : | +44 1908 611 071 | | | |
| **Email** | : | | | | |
| **Web** | : | | | | |
| **Activity** | : | Wholesaler, Retailer, Manufacturer, Exporter | | | |
| **Products** | : | *Leather* : Other - leather, | | | |
| **Raw Materials** | : | Sheep, Goat, Other | | | |

Yarwood Leather Ltd

| | | | | | |
|---|---|---|---|---|---|
| **Contact** | : | Andrew Young<br>Managing Director | We are the UK's largest upholstery leather distributor offering a complete range of upholstery leather in an exciting range of colours and textures. We have products suitable for domestic and contract furniture,auto,aviation and marine industries. The entire spectrum is covered, from pure anilines to fully pigmented articles. Sampling and bespoke colour matching services are available. Yarwood's products are the first choice of | United Kingdom | Automotive leather, Footwear – upper leather, Other - leather, Upholstery leather |
| **Address** | : | Treefield Industrial Estate,<br>Gelderd Road<br>Morley<br>Leeds, West Yorkshire-LS27 7JU<br>United Kingdom | | | |
| **Tel.** | : | +44 113 252 1014 | | | |
| **Fax** | : | +44 113 252 7391 | | | |
| **Email** | : | sales@yarwood.co.uk | | | |
| **Web** | : | http://www.yarwood.co.uk | | | |
| **Activity** | : | Wholesaler, Manufacturer, Importer, Exporter | | | |

**Products** : *Hides and Skins* : Wet blue,

*Leather* : Footwear – upper leather, Automotive leather, Other - leather, Upholstery leather,

*Leather Goods* : Furniture, Car components, Other - leather goods,

**Raw Materials** : Bovine

# PROFESSIONAL ASSOCAITIONS

## AUSTRIA

Fachverband der Lederverarbeitenden Industrie
**Contact** :

**Address** : Wiedner Hauptstrasse 63,
P.O. Box 63
Vienna-1045
Austria

**Tel.** +43 1 50105 3453
**Fax** :: +43 1 50 20 62 78

**Email** fvleder@wkoesk.wk.or.at

## BELGIUM

COTANCE (The European Leather Industry Organisation)
**Contact** :

**Address** : 3, rue Belliard
Brussels-1040
Belgium **Tel.**
**Fax** :
: +32 2 512 7703
+32 2 512 9157 **Email**
**Web** :
: cotance@euroleather.com
http://www.euroleather.com

European Confederation of the Footwear Industry (CEC)
**Contact** : Roeland Smets
Managing Director

CEC is known as the official representative body of the European Footwear Industry. CEC represents all major national footwear federations of the European Union and also observing footwear manufacturers of the E.U. and 10 observer federations are represented by the European Confederation of the Footwear Industry.

**Address** : 53, rue Francois Bossaerts
Brussels-1030
Belgium **Tel.**
**Fax** :
: +32 2 736 58 10
+32 2 736 12 76 **Email**
**Web** :
: cec@vidac.be
http://www.cecshoe.be

Fédération Belge de l'Industrie de la Chaussure A.S.B.L.
**Contact** :

**Address** : 53, rue François Bossaertstraat
Bruxelles-1030
Belgium **Tel.**
**Fax** :
: +32 2 73 52 701
+32 2 73 61 276 **Email**
**Web** :
: febic@vidac.be
http://www.febic.be

**BULGARIA**

Alliance of Skin Producers
**Contact** :

**Address** : Solun, 4
Jambol-8600
Bulgaria **Tel.**
**Fax** :
: +359 46 31079
+359 46 31027

**Email**
: yumax@atil.net

**CZECH REPUBLIC**

Czech Footwear Association
**Contact** :

**Address** : Tr. T. Bati 4
Zlín-762 02
Czech Republic **Tel.**
**Fax** :
: +420 577 525 230

+420 577 435 411 **Email**
**Web** :
: info@leatherindustry.cz
http://www.leatherindustry.cz/

## FINLAND

Association of Fashion Retailers in Finland

**Address** : Mariankatu 26 B 14
Helsinki-00170
Finland **Tel.**
**Fax** :
: +358 9 68447300
+358 9 68447344 **Email**
**Web** :
: muotikaupanliitto@moutikapanliitto.fi
http://www.muotikaupanliitto.fi

Association of Finnish Shoe and Leather Industries

**Address** : Kenkä- ja nahkateollisuus ry
Eteläranta 10, 7th floor
Helsinki-00130
Finland **Tel.**
**Fax** :
: +358 9 172 841
+358 9 179 588

## FRANCE

Assoc. Franç. Ingénieurs Chim. et Techniciens Industries du Cuir

**Address** : 4, rue Hermann Frenkel
P.O. Box 7003
Lyon cedex 07-69342
France **Tel.**
**Fax** :
: +33 4727 61010
+33 4727 61001 **Email**
**Web** :
: afictic@ctc.fr
http://www.ctc.fr/AFICTIC/

Conseil National du Cuir

**Address** : 109 rue du Faubourg Saint-Honoré
Paris cedex 08-75373
France **Tel.**
**Fax** :

: +33 1 43 59 05 69
+33 1 43 59 30 02 **Email**
**Web** ::
http://www.lescreateursfrancaisducuir.org

Fédération Française de la Chaussure

**Address** : 51, rue de Miromesnil
Paris-75008
France **Tel.**
**Fax** :
: +33 1 44 71 71 71
+33 1 44 71 04 04 **Email**
**Web** :
: chaussuredefrance@telepost.fr
http://www.chaussuredefrance.com

Fédération Française de la Maroquinerie

**Address** : 21, rue du Mont Thabor
Paris-75001
France **Tel.**
**Fax** :
: +33 1 42 44 22 44
+33 1 42 44 22 45 **Email**
**Web** :
: maroquinerie.française@wanadoo.fr
http://www.ff-maroquinerie.fr

Fédération Française de la Tannerie Mégisserie

**Address** : 122, Rue de Provence
Paris-75008
France **Tel.**
**Fax** :
: +33 1 45229645
+33 1 42933744 **Email**
**Web** :
: fftm@leatherfrance.com
http://www.leatherfrance.com

## GERMANY

Bundesverband Lederwaren und Kunststofferzeugnisse e.V.

**Address** : Waldstr. 44
P.O. Box 10 20 55
Offenbach am Main-63065
Germany

**Tel. Fax** :

: +49 69 88 7250
+49 69 81 2810

**Email Web** :
: info@lederwarenverband.de
http://www.lederwarenverband.de

Hauptverband der Deutschen Schuhindustrie e v.

**Address** : Waldstrasse 44
Offenbach-63065
Germany

**Tel. Fax** :
: +49 69 829 7410
+49 69 812 810

**Email**
**Web** :
: info@hds-schuh.de
http://www.hds-schuh.de

V.D.M.A. Garment and Leather Technology Association

| | | |
|---|---|---|
| **Address** | : | Richard-Strauss-Straße 56 / III<br>Munich-81677<br>Germany |
| **Tel.** | : | +49 69 66 03 1522 |
| **Fax** | : | +49 69 66 03 1675 |
| **Email** | : | josef.reingen@vdma.org |
| **Web** | : | http://www.vdma.org/ |

Verband der Deutschen Lederindustrie eV

**Address** : Fuchstanzstrasse, 61
Frankfurt-60489
Germany
**Tel.**
**Fax** :
: +49 699 784 3141
+49 697 880 0009
**Email:** info@vdl-web.de
**Web** :
http://www.vdl-web.de

Verband der Deutschen Lederindustri

| | | |
|---|---|---|
| **Address** | : | Fuchstanzstr. 61<br>Frankfurt am Main-60489 |
| **Tel.** | : | +49 6997843141 |
| **Fax** | : | +49 6978800009 |
| **Email** | : | info@vdl-web.de |
| **Web** | : | http://www.vdl-web.de |

| | | |
|---|---|---|
| **Email** | : | info@vdl-web.de |
| **Web** | : | http://www.vdl-web.de |

Wirtschaftsverband Häute / Leder e.V.
**Contact** : Paul J. Reusch
Managing Director

Under the umbrella of the registered Hide/Leather Trade Organisation there are organised the following special sections: - joint specialists for Leather wholesale and foreign trade - joint specialists for Hides and Skins wholesale and foreign trade - ISCOP - International Shoe Components Producers Several member companies are exhibiting at Asia Pacific Leather Fair in Hong Kong, Shoe and Leather in Guangzhou and all China Leather Exhibition in Shangai. You may find them at the German pavillons or at their individual stands. If you got any questions or further inquiries regarding the trade of leather, hides, skins or shoe components you should get in touch with us.

**Address** : Blumenstrasse 18
Backnang-71522
Germany **Tel.**
**Fax** :
: +49 7191 980 060
+49 7191 980 070

## GREECE

ELSEVIE Hellenic Association of Footwear Manufacturers & Exporters

| | | |
|---|---|---|
| **Address** | : | Pinelopis Delta 27<br>Neo Psyhiko-154 51<br>Greece |
| **Tel.** | : | +30 210 6725 295 |
| **Fax** | : | +30 210 6744 497 |
| **Email** | : | elsevie@hellasnet.gr |
| **Web** | : | |

## HUNGARY

Association for Leather and Shoe Industry BCE
**Address** : Gizella ut. 24-26
Budapest XIV-1143
Hungary
**Tel. Fax**
:
: +36 1 221 9327
+36 1 221 9327
**Email**
**Web**
:
: bce@axelero.hu
http://web.axelero.hu/bcegy/

## IRELAND

Federation of Irish Footwear Manufacturers
**Address** : c/o Blackthorn Shoes Ltd, Coe's Rd.
Industrial Estate
Dundalk Co Louth-
Ireland
**Tel.**
**Fax**
:
: +353 42 34 74 11 23
+353 42 33 371

## ITALY

AIMPES Associazione Italiana Manifatturieri Pelli e Succedanei

**Address** : V.le Beatrice D'Este, 43
Milan-20122
Italy

**Tel.** : +39 02 584 511
**Fax** : +39 02 584 51320

**Email** : segreteria@mipel.com
**Web** : http://www.aimpes.it

Associazione Calzaturieri di Parabiagio -Footware Association-

**Contact** : Banfi Massimo
**Address** : Piazza della vittoria
Palazzo comunale
Parabiagio-20155
Italy
**Tel.** : +39 0331 551 335
**Fax** : +39 0331 556 765
**Email** : assocap@assocap.com
**Web** :

Associazione Conciatori

**Address** : Via Buoni 2
Santa Croce sull'Arno. PI-56029
Italy

**Tel.** : +39 0571 366 310
**Fax** : +39 0571 366 231

**Email** : info@assoconciatori.com
**Web** : http://www.assoconciatori.com

Associazione Italiane dei Chimici del Cuoio

| | | |
|---|---|---|
| **Address** | : | Via San Tommaso, 67<br>Santa Croce Sull'Arno-56029<br>Italy |
| **Tel.** | : | +39 0571 35625 |
| **Fax** | : | +39 0571 35625 |
| **Email** | : | info@aicc.it |
| **Web** | : | http://www.aicc.it |

Associazione Nazionale Calzaturieri Italiani (ANCI)

| | | |
|---|---|---|
| **Address** | : | Via Monte Rosa 21<br>Milan-20149<br>Italy |
| **Tel.** | : | +39 02 438 291 |
| **Fax** | : | +39 02 4800 5833 |
| **Email** | : | info@anci-calzature.com |
| **Web** | : | http://www.anci-calzature.com |

Associazione Promotori Vendite Calzature

| | | |
|---|---|---|
| **Address** | : | Via Matteotti 38<br>Vigevano-27029<br>Italy |
| **Tel.** | : | +39 45 581 800 |
| **Fax** | : | +39 45 584 996 |

Associazione Promozione della Cultura e Tecnica Calzaturira

| | | |
|---|---|---|
| **Contact** | : | Marcello Pizzuti<br>President |
| **Address** | : | Via Boncore 132/a<br>Montegranaro - AP-63014<br>Italy |
| **Tel.** | : | +39 0734 993 280 |
| **Fax** | : | +39 0734 993 280 |

ASSOMAC

| | | |
|---|---|---|
| **Contact** | : | Mario Pucci<br>Director, International Relations |
| **Address** | : | Via Matteotti 4/a<br>P.O. Box 113<br>Vigevano (PV)-27029<br>Italy |
| **Tel.** | : | +39 0381 78883 |
| **Fax** | : | +39 0381 88602 |
| **Email** | : | pucci@assomac.it |
| **Web** | : | http://www.assomac.it |

Consorzio Europa 2000

**Address** : Via G. Lorca 6
Santa Croce S/A (PI)-56029
Italy

**Tel.** : +39 571 366 406
**Fax** : +39 571 366 409

**Email** : nobel@nobel.it
**Web** :

European Fashion Designer's Asso.

**Address** : Via B. Franceschini 5
Firenze-50142
Italy

**Tel.** : +39 055 7398 932
**Fax** : +39 055 7398 935

**Email** : obiemoda@iol.it
**Web** :

UNIC - Unione Nazionale Industria Conciaria

**Contact** : Sergio F. Conti

**Address** : Via Brisa, 3
Milano-21023
Italy

**Tel.** : +39 02 880 77 11
**Fax** : +39 02 720 000 72

**Email** : unic@unic.it
**Web** : http://www.unic.it

Unione Nazionale Accesori e Componenti per la Calzatura

**Address** : Via Brisa 3
Milano-20123
Italy

**Tel.** : +39 02 8807711
**Fax** : +39 02 860032

**Email** : info@unac.it
**Web** : http://www.unac.it

## NETHERLANDS

Federatie van de Nederlandse Schoenfabrikanten

**Address** : Reitseplein 1
Tilburg-5037

**Tel.** : +31 13 594 4263
**Fax** : +31 13 594 4749

**Email** : info@shoenfederatie.nl
**Web** : http://www.shoeplaza.nl/sites/fns

**Email** : info@shoenfederatie.nl
**Web** : http://www.shoeplaza.nl/sites/fns

Federatie van de Nederlandse Lederfabrikanten
**Contact** :
**Address** : .
P.O. Box 90154
Tilburg-5000 LG
Netherlands
**Tel.**
**Fax**
:
: +31 135944778
+31 135944749
**Email**
**Web**
:
: fnl@wispa.nl
http://www.lederfabrikanten.nl

The Dutch Federation of tanners represents companies in the Leather Industry for almost 75 years. Since the foundation of the Federation in 1927, FNL stands for the interests of the associated members and is the discussion partner towards many official parties that can influence the leather industry. The Dutch leather industry has undergone a great sanitation the last few years. That´s one of the reasons why the number of tanneries in the Netherlands has dropped to about 20. The Dutch leather industry has invested a lot in environmental friendly machinery and modern production methods. A couple of reasons for these investments are: * The strict environmental laws in the Netherlands; * The innovative character of the Dutch Leather industry; * The severe competition in the leather industry world-wide; * The demand for a high quality of leather.

Vereniging van Nederlandse Huidenhandelaren
**Address** : Westhavendijk 48
Steenbergen-4651 VZ
Netherlands
**Tel.**
**Fax**
:
: +31 167 540778
+31 167 540779
**Email**
**Web**
:
: ktm@kaptein.demon.nl

**PORTUGAL**

Associaçao Portuguesa dos Industrials de Curtumes
**Address** : Av. Ferñao de Magalhaes 460-5
Porto-4300
Portugal
**Tel.**
**Fax**
:
: +351 22 5374115
+351 22 5372065
**Email**
**Web** :

: apic@mail.telepac.pt
http://www.apic.pt

Associação Portuguesa dos Industriais de Curtumes APIC
**Address** : Av. Fernao de Magalhaes 460 - 5º
Porto-4300
Portugal
**Tel.**
**Fax** :
: +351 2253 74115
+351 2253 72065
**Email**
**Web** :
: apic@mail.telepac.pt
http://www.apic.pt

## ROMANIA

Association of Romanian Shoe Producers
**Contact** : Ioan Oprita
President
**Address** : Str.Stefan cel Mare, 58
Timisoara-1900
Romania
**Tel.**
**Fax** :
: +40 256 190 301
+40 256 190 427

## RUSSIAN FEDERATION

National Footwear Association of Russia
**Address** : Building 3, Myasnitskaya str.24
Moscow-101000
Russian Federation **Tel.**
**Fax** :
: +7 095 924 7564
+7 095 928 7171 **Email**
**Web** :
: info@nfar.ru
http://www.nfar.ru/engl/struc.php

## SLOVAKIA

Association of Leather & Shoe Industries of the Slovak Republic
**Contact** : Stefan Sulo
Executive President

The Association of Leather and Shoe Industry of the Slovak Republic (AL&SI), headquartered at Bratislava, was established by the founding members' general meeting on 2 November 1992. As a legal entity the Slovak Leather and Footwear Association has been in existence since 1st

January 1993 when its regular registration was made. At present, the AL&SI comprises 20 major footwear companies concerned with both manufacture and sale of footwear, shoe materials and components in the territory of the Slovak Republic. The number of member companies' employees is about 5 thousand. AL&SI associates entrepreneurial organizations and interest groups established by entrepreneurs and organizations in the field of leather and shoe industry in the Slovak Republic . The Slovak Leather and Footwear Association was created as an interest group to safeguard and defend its members' interests and secure their co-ordinated and unified course of action. A member of the AL&SI may be also the organi

**Address** : Nám. J. Herdu 1
Trnava-91822
Slovakia **Tel.**
**Fax** :
: +421 33 550 1282
+421 33 550 1282 **Email**
**Web** :
: zkop@zkop.sk
http://www.zkop.sk

## SLOVENIA

Chamber of Commerce and Industry Textiles/Clothing/Leather Products
**Contact** :

**Address** : Dimiceva 13
Ljubljana-1504
Slovenia **Tel.**
**Fax** :
: +386 1 58 98 000
+386 1 58 98 100/200 **Email**
**Web** :
: infolink@gzs.si
http://www.gzs.si

## SPAIN

Acexpiel - Leather Industry Assoc. of Spain for Foreign Trade

**Contact** : Laura Siurana
Asst. to General Manager ACEXPIEL's main aim is to promote Spanish tanneries. As organiser of Spanish pavilions in the biggest professional trade shows as well as international trade missions, our organisation through its actions wants to play a role in positioning Spanish tanners on the highest possible level in our sector's international market. You can have a look to the services we offer to our members through our website : www.spanishtanners.com

**Address** : Valencia, 359, 3rd Floor
Barcelona-08009
Spain
**Tel.**
**Fax** :
: +34 93 45 93 396
+34 93 45 85 061

**Email**
**Web** :
: leather@leather-spain.com
http://www.leather-spain.com

AEC

**Contact** : Laura Aliaga Martinez
Trade Officer We represent the 80% of Spanish companies of machinery and footwear components. Helping to promote the products of our associates all over the world is one of our main goals. Whenever an international buyer requires any kind of information regarding Spanish market, AEC is the best partner as we help to identify companies that will fulfill their needs. Nowadays we act for more than 250 manufacturers of soles, heels, toe puffs, leather, sheets, insoles, machinery for footwear manufacturing, etc. If any doubt arises please do not hesitate to contact us.

APICT Asociación Provincial de Industriales del Calzado de Toledo

**Contact** : La Asociación Provincial de Industriales del Calzado de Toledo se constituye en 1977 con la intención de aglutinar a los industriales del calzado de la provincia y representar sus intereses a todos los niveles. En la actualidad podemos afirmar que más del 90% de la producción provincial y al menos un 80% de las fábricas de calzado toledanas están integradas en nuestra Asociación.

**Address** : Avenida San Crispín, 105
Fuensalida-45510
Spain
**Tel.**
**Fax** :
: +34 925 784953
+34 925 784913
**Email**
**Web** :
: apict@inescop.es
http://apict.castillalamancha.es/

ASEFMA Asocia. Esp. de Fabricantes Marroq. Articulos de Viaje y Afines

**Contact** : La Asociación Española de Fabricantes de Marroquinería, Artículos de Viaje y Afines es el órgano de coordinación y representación que defiende los intereses generales y comunes de todos los empresarios de los distintos subsectores de la Marroquinería Española y de las industrias afines al sector que quieran, voluntariamente, adherirse a ella, fomentando el espíritu de solidaridad entre sus miembros, con el fin de favorecer el progreso económico y social de los sectores que la componen.

**Address** : Marquès de la Ensenada, 2
Madrid-28004
Spain
**Tel.**
**Fax** :

: +34 91 319 34 90
+34 91 319 07 37
**Email**
**Web** :
: asefma@asefma.com
http://www.asefma.com

Asocia. Prof. de Fabricantes de Calzado y Zapatillas Vulcanizados
**Contact** : Francisco Ballesta López
Presidente
**Address** : Avda. Europa, 4 y 5
Polígono Industrial Las Salinas
Alhama de Murcia-30840
Spain
**Tel.**
**Fax** :
: +34 968 63 01 62 / 22 00
+34 968 63 22 66

Asociac. de Fabricantes Auxiliares de Calzado de Baleares A.F.A.C.A.

Asociac. de Industrias del Calzado y Conexas de La Rioja AICCOR
**Contact** : Manuel Abad Urquijo
Presidente
**Address** : San Blas, 2 -1º C
Arnedo-26580
Spain
**Tel.**
**Fax** :
: +34 941 38 13 32
+34 941 38 09 64

Asociac. Provinc. de Industr. del Calzado de Valverde del Cam. APICAL
**Address** : Valle de la Fuente, 80-A
Valverde del Camino-21600
Spain
**Tel.**
**Fax** :
: +34 959 551 651
+34 959 551 651
**Email**
**Web** :
: apical@inescop.es

Asociac. Provincial de Fabricantes de Calzado y Afines (ASPROFA)
**Contact** : Antonio López García
Presidente

**Address** : Corredera 26 Pral.
Planta 1 - Aptdo 68
Almansa-02640
Spain
**Tel.**
**Fax** :
: +34 967 34 11 58
+34 967 34 11 62
**Email**
**Web** :
: asprofa@inescop.es

Asociación Comarcal de Fabricantes de Calzado (ASOCAL)
**Contact** : Jaime Rebollar Cueco
Presidente
**Address** : Pedro Viruela, 26 Bajos Aptdo. 33
Vall de Uxó-12600
Spain
**Tel.**
**Fax** :
: +34 964 69 64 52
+34 964 66 62 03
**Email**
**Web** :
: vxasocia@vallduixo.infoville.net

Asociación de Fabricantes de Calzado de Menorca
**Contact** : Jaime Rebollar Cueco
Presidente
**Address** : Pedro Viruela, 26 Bajos Aptdo. 33
Vall de Uxó-12600
Spain
**Tel.**
**Fax** :
: +34 964 69 64 52
+34 964 66 62 03
**Email**
**Web** :
: vxasocia@vallduixo.infoville.net

Asociación de Fabricantes de Calzado y Afines de Zaragoza y Pcia
**Address** : Carretera Aranda, 12
Illueca, Zaragoza-50250
Spain
**Tel.**
**Fax** :
: +34 976 822696
+34 976 548086

**Email**
**Web**
:
:
afcya@inescop.es

Asociación de Industriales del Calzado del Valle de Elda AICVE
**Address** : Avda. de Chapí, 13-Entlo.
Elda, Alicante-03600
Spain

Asociación de la Industria de la Piel para el Comercio Exterior
**Address** : Calle Valencia, 359,3°
Barcelona-08009
Spain
**Tel.**
**Fax**
:
:
+34 93 459 3396
+34 93 458 5061
**Email**
**Web**
:
:
inform@leather-spain.com
http://www.leather-spain.com/esp/CECacexpiel.asp

Asociación Española de Empresas de Componentes para el Calzado AEAC
**Address** : C/. Cap. Antonio Mena
25-Entlo. Izda
Elche-03201
Spain
**Tel.**
**Fax**
:
:
+34 6 546 01 58
+34 6 546 60 33
**Email**
**Web**
:
:
aeac@aeac.es
http://www.sho.es/aeac/

Asociación Española de Técnicos de la Industria del Calzado A.E.T.I.C.
**Address** : Poligono Industrial Campo Alto
Apdo 253
Elda-03600
Spain
**Tel.**
**Fax**
:
:
+34 96 539 5213
+34 96 538 1045

Asociación Química Española de la Industria del Cuero

**Address** : c/ Gran Via de los Corts Catalanes
608,8,C
Barcelona-08007
Spain
**Tel.**
**Fax**
:
:
+34 933024893
+34 933426395
**Email**
**Web**
:
:
aqeic@valles.com
http://www.valles.com/aqeic/

CAVEX Asociación de Exportadores de Calzado de la Comunidad Valenciana

**Contact** : La Agrupación de Exportadores de Calzado de la Comunidad Valenciana (CAVEX) se constituyó como asociación en 1987. CAVEX nació con el objetivo primordial de defender los intereses de este colectivo, haciendo un esfuerzo especial en dos aspectos: - Mejorar las estrategias y técnicas de comercialización - Promocionar de forma colectiva las ofertas individuales de los asociados en los mercados comunes de exportación.

**Address** : Explanada, 3 2º-A
Alicante-03002
Spain
**Tel.**
**Fax** :
: +34 965 20 64 43
+34 965 20 64 60
**Email**
**Web** :
: cavex@inescop.es

Confederación Española de Curtidores (CEC)
**Address** : Calle Valencia, 359 3°
Barcelona-08009
Spain
**Tel.**
**Fax**
:
:
+34 93 459 3396
+34 93 458 5061
**Email**
**Web**
:
:
content@paso-paso.com
http://www.leather-spain.com

FECUREX Asoc. Esp. de Com. Exterior de Empresarios Fabric. de Curtidos

**Contact** : María Corts Constituida como Asociación de exportadores vinculada a FECUR, cuya actividad organizadora de acciones de comercio exterior ha tenido, desde sus inicios, el objetivo de convertirse en una entidad de servicios promocionales del comercio internacional de las empresas de curtidos y sectores afines.

**Address** : Barón de Carcer 17-10
Valencia-46001
Spain
**Tel.**
**Fax** :
: +34 96 351 01 53
+34 96 351 00 81
**Email**
**Web** :
: fecurex@clavei.es
http://www.abserver.es/fecur/fecurex.htm

Federación Española de Empresarios de Curtidos (FECUR)
**Address** : Baron de Carcer 17-10
Valencia-46001
Spain
**Tel.**
**Fax** :
: +34 96 352 38 78
+34 96 352 34 13
**Email**
**Web** :
: arec.es@inescop.es
http://www.abserver.es/fecur

FICE Federación de Industrias del Calzado Español
**Address** : Nuñez de Balboa 116-3°
Ofic. 5 y 6
Madrid-28006
Spain **Tel.**
**Fax** :
: +34 91 562 70 01
+34 91 562 00 94 **Email**
**Web** :
: fice@inescop.es

International Union of Shoe Industry Technicians
**Address** : c/o INESCOP, Poligono Industrial
"Campo Alto", Elda
Alicante-03600
Spain **Tel.**
**Fax** :
: +34 965 395 213
+34 965 381 045 **Email**
**Web** :
: uitic@uitic.org
http://www.uitic.org

## SWEDEN

Swedish Federation of Footwear Industry

**Address** : c/o Arbesko
P.O. Box 1642
Örebro-70116
Sweden

**Tel.**
**Fax** :
: +46 19 30 66 00
+46 19 30 66 50

Swedish Shoemakers Association

**Address** : Tyskbagargat 7
Stockholm-11443
Sweden

**Tel.**
**Fax** : +46 8 6620 696
**Email**
**Web** :
: info@skomakare.com
http://www.skomakare.com

## SWITZERLAND

Asociación Española de Técnicos de la Industria del Calzado A.E.T.I.C.
**Address** : Poligono Industrial Campo Alto
Apdo 253
Elda-03600
Spain
**Tel.**
**Fax** :
: +34 96 539 5213
+34 96 538 1045

Asociación Química Española de la Industria del Cuero
**Address** : c/ Gran Via de los Corts Catalanes
608,8,C
Barcelona-08007
Spain
**Tel.**
**Fax** :
: +34 933024893
+34 933426395
**Email**
**Web** :
: aqeic@valles.com
http://www.valles.com/aqeic/

CAVEX Asociación de Exportadores de Calzado de la Comunidad Valenciana

**Contact** : La Agrupación de Exportadores de Calzado de la Comunidad Valenciana (CAVEX) se constituyó como asociación en 1987. CAVEX nació con el objetivo primordial de defender los intereses de este colectivo, haciendo un esfuerzo especial en dos aspectos: - Mejorar las estrategias y técnicas de comercialización - Promocionar de forma colectiva las ofertas individuales de los asociados en los mercados comunes de exportación.

**Address** : Explanada, 3 2º-A
Alicante-03002
Spain
**Tel.**
**Fax** :
: +34 965 20 64 43
+34 965 20 64 60
**Email**
**Web** :
: cavex@inescop.es

Confederación Española de Curtidores (CEC)
**Address** : Calle Valencia, 359 3°
Barcelona-08009
Spain
**Tel.**
**Fax** :

:
+34 93 458 5061
**Email**
**Web**
:
http://www.leather-spain.com

+34 93 459 3396

:
content@paso-paso.com

FECUREX Asoc. Esp. de Com. Exterior de Empresarios Fabric. de Curtidos

**Contact** : María Corts Constituida como Asociación de exportadores vinculada a FECUR, cuya actividad organizadora de acciones de comercio exterior ha tenido, desde sus inicios, el objetivo de convertirse en una entidad de servicios promocionales del comercio internacional de las empresas de curtidos y sectores afines.

**Address** : Barón de Carcer 17-10
Valencia-46001
Spain
**Tel.**
**Fax** :
: +34 96 351 01 53
+34 96 351 00 81
**Email**
**Web** :
: fecurex@clavei.es
http://www.abserver.es/fecur/fecurex.htm

Federación Española de Empresarios de Curtidos (FECUR)
**Address** : Baron de Carcer 17-10
Valencia-46001
Spain
**Tel.**
**Fax**
:
+34 96 352 34 13
**Email**
**Web**
:
http://www.abserver.es/fecur

:
+34 96 352 38 78

:
arec.es@inescop.es

FICE Federación de Industrias del Calzado Español

**Address** : Nuñez de Balboa 116-3°
Ofic. 5 y 6
Madrid-28006
Spain **Tel.**
**Fax** :
: +34 91 562 70 01
+34 91 562 00 94 **Email**
**Web** :
: fice@inescop.es

International Union of Shoe Industry Technicians

**Address** : c/o INESCOP, Poligono Industrial
"Campo Alto", Elda
Alicante-03600
Spain **Tel.**
**Fax** :
: +34 965 395 213
+34 965 381 045 **Email**
**Web** :
: uitic@uitic.org
http://www.uitic.org

## SWEDEN

Swedish Federation of Footwear Industry

**Address** : c/o Arbesko
P.O. Box 1642
Örebro-70116
Sweden

**Tel.**
**Fax** :
: +46 19 30 66 00
+46 19 30 66 50

Swedish Shoemakers Association

**Address** : Tyskbagargat 7
Stockholm-11443
Sweden

**Tel.**
**Fax** : +46 8 6620 696
**Email**
**Web** :
: info@skomakare.com
http://www.skomakare.com

## SWITZERLAND

**Address** : c/o INESCOP, Poligono Industrial
"Campo Alto", Elda
Alicante-03600
Spain **Tel.**
**Fax** :
: +34 965 395 213
+34 965 381 045 **Email**
**Web** :
: uitic@uitic.org
http://www.uitic.org

## SWEDEN

Swedish Federation of Footwear Industry

**Address** : c/o Arbesko
P.O. Box 1642
Örebro-70116
Sweden

**Tel.**
**Fax** :
: +46 19 30 66 00
+46 19 30 66 50

Swedish Shoemakers Association

**Address** : Tyskbagargat 7
Stockholm-11443
Sweden

**Tel.**
**Fax** : +46 8 6620 696
**Email**
**Web** :
: info@skomakare.com
http://www.skomakare.com

## SWITZERLAND

Swedish Federation of Footwear Industry

**Address** : c/o Arbesko
P.O. Box 1642
Örebro-70116
Sweden

**Tel.**
**Fax** :
: +46 19 30 66 00
+46 19 30 66 50

Swedish Shoemakers Association

**Address** : Tyskbagargat 7
Stockholm-11443
Sweden

**Tel.**
**Fax** : +46 8 6620 696
**Email**
**Web** :
: info@skomakare.com
http://www.skomakare.com

## SWITZERLAND

Räber Leder AG Lederhandlung - Lederzurichtesei

**Address** : Seebodenstrasse 4
Küssnacht-6403
Switzerland

**Tel.**
**Fax** :
: +41 850 2424
+41 850 1400

**Email**
**Web** :
: reaber@leder.ch
http://www.leder.ch

## UKRAINE

Ukrainian Leather and Shoe Union

**Address** : B.Zhitomirskaya Str., 21 off. 13
Kiev-010125
Ukraine

**Tel.** +38 044 228-0614
**Email**
**Web** :
: leather@ukr.net
http://www.leatherua.com

Ukraine

## UNITED KINGDOM

British Chemical Distributors & Traders Association Ltd
**Address** : Suffolk House, George St,
Croydon, Surrey-CR0 0YN
United Kingdom
**Tel.**
**Fax**
:
: +44 20 8686 4545
+44 20 8688 7768

British Footwear Association
**Address** : 3 Burystead Place
Wellingborough
Northants-NN8 1AH
United Kingdom
**Tel.**
**Fax**
:
: +44 1933 229 005
+44 1933 225 009
**Email**
**Web**
:
: bfa@easynet.co.uk
http://www.britfoot.com

British Glove Association
**Contact** : Colleen Swan
Secretariat
**Address** : c/o Crane & Partners, Sussex House
8-10 Homesdale Road
Bromley, Kent-BR2 9LZ
United Kingdom

**Tel.**
**Fax** :
: +44 20 8464 0131
+44 20 8464 6018
**Email**
**Web** :
: info@gloveassociation.org
http://www.gloveassociation.org

Fellmongers Association, The
**Address** : 3 Weavers Lane, Bramhall
Stockport, Cheshire-SK7 2DE
United Kingdom
**Tel.**
**Fax** :
: +44 161439 6446
+44 161 439 6446
**Email**
**Web** :
: alan@cosultfca.freeserve.co.uk

Independent Footwear Retailers Association (IFRA)
**Address** : c/o Arthur Spencer-Bolland
Banbury
P.O. Box 123
Oxon-OX15 6WB
United Kingdom
**Tel.**
**Fax** :
: +44 01295 738 726
+44 01295 738 275
**Email**
**Web** :
: ifra@shoeshop.org.uk
http://www.shoeshop.org.uk

Instock Footwear Suppliers Association
**Address** : Marlone House,
Churchill Way, Fleckney
Leicester, Leicestershire-LE8 8UD
United Kingdom
**Tel.**
**Fax** :
: +44 1162403232
+44 1162402762

International Council of Hides, Skins & Leather Traders Ass.

International Council of Tanners (ICT)

Leicester & County Footwear Manufacturer' Association
**Contact** :

**Address** : Willoughby House.
57 Sycamore St. Blaby
Leicester, Leicestershire-LE8 4FL
United Kingdom **Tel.**
**Fax** :
: +44 1162733399
+44 1162737494

National Union of Knitwear. Footwear & Apparel Trades
**Contact** :

**Address** : 55 New Walk
Leicester. Leicestershire-LE17EB
United Kingdom **Tel.**
**Fax** :
: +44 116 255 6703
+44 116 254 4406 **Email**
**Web** :
: head-office@kfat.org.uk,
http://www.poptel.org.uk/kfat/

Oil & Colour Chemists' Association
**Contact** :

**Address** : Priory House. 967 Harrow Rd
Wembley.
Middlesex-HA0 2SF
United Kingdom **Tel.**
**Fax** :
: +44 20 8908 1086
+44 20 8908 1219 **Email**
**Web** :
: gensec@occa.org.uk
http://www.occa.org.uk

Skin Hide and Leather Traders Association
**Contact** :

**Address** : c/o Secretariat Andaco Ltd
Douglas House, Douglas Rd, Melrose
Roxburghshire, Scotland-TD6 9QT
United Kingdom **Tel.**
**Fax** :
: +44 1896 82 22 33
+44 1896 82 33 44 **Email**
**Web** :
: offices@andaco.com
http://www.shalta.org

Society of Master Saddlers (UK) Ltd
**ontact** : Hazel Morley

**Address** : Kettles Farm, Mickfield
Stowmarket.
Suffolk-IP14 6BY
United Kingdom **Tel.**
**Fax** :
: +44 1449 711 642

+44 1449 711 642 **Email**
**Web** :
: enquiries@mastersaddlers.co.uk
http://www.mastersaddlers.co.uk

Tanning Extract Producers' Federation Ltd

**Address** : The Old School House, Bridge Rd
Hunton Bridge, Kings Langley
Hertfordshire-WD4 8SZ
United Kingdom **Tel.**
**Fax** :
: +44 1923264060
+44 1923261414

The Boot and Shoe Manufacturers' Association
**Contact** : Michael Gilbert
Chief Executive

**Address** : 25/26 Bloomsbury Square
London-WC1A 2PL
United Kingdom **Tel.**
**Fax** :
: +44 020 7612 7757
+44 020 7436 4663 **Email**
**Web** :
: basma@basma.com
http://www.basma.com

The British Luggage and Leathergoods Association
**Contact** :

**Address** : Federation Hous, 10 Vyse st.
Hockley
Birmingham-
United Kingdom **Tel.**
**Fax** :
: +44 121 236 2657
+44 121 236 3921 **Email**
**Web** :
:
http://www.blla.org.uk

The Real Sheepskin Association
**Contact** :
**Address** : 60 Main Rd. Hackleton
Northampton
Northamptonshire-NN7 2AB
United Kingdom
**Tel.**
**Fax** :
: +44 1604 870 703
+44 1604 870 430
**Email**
**Web** :
: rsa@easisider.com
http://www.realsheepskin.org.uk

# TRAINING AND RESEARCH INSTITUTES

CLO/CLR Ctre de Rech. techn.des les Tannerie, Chaussure, Pantoufles

**Address** : 53, rue François Bossaertsstraat
Bruxelles-1030
Belgium **Tel.**
**Fax** :
: +32 2 735 27 01
+32 2 736 12 76

**Email**: febic@vidac.be

Belgium

Dansk Teknologisk Institut
**Address** : Gregersensvej
P.O. Box 141
Taastrup-2630
Denmark
**Tel.**
**Fax** :
: +45 72202000
+45 72202019
**Email**
**Web** :
: info@teknologisk.dk
http://www.danishtechnology.dk

Denmark

VTT Technical Research Centre of Finland

**Contact** : VTT, Technical Research Centre of Finland is a non profit, impartial expert organization that carries out technical and technoeconomic research and development work. VTT's objective is to improve welfare of society and competitiveness of its customers. VTT has six research units: 1) VTT Electronics offers technology services for companies utilizing electronic technologies in their businesses. 2) VTT's Information Technology offers its client companies to derive maximum benefit from the rapid progress in microelectronics, information technology and media technology. 3) VTT 's Building and Transport cover aspects of the built environment. 4) VTT Processes is a technology partner for energy and process industries. 5) VTT Industrial Systems aims to enhance the competitiveness of companies and develop technological knowledge. 6) VTT Biotechnology uses biotechnology and biological materials to develop innovative processes and products.

**Address** : .
P.O. Box 1000
Espoo-02044 VTT
Finland
**Tel.**
**Fax** :
: +358 9 4561
+358 9 456 7000
**Email**
**Web** :
: kirjaamo@vtt.fi
http://www.vtt.fi

Finland

Centre Technique du Cuir, Chaussure, Maroquinerie

**Contact** : Expert en chaussure, maroquinerie et cuir, le Groupe CTC accompagne depuis plus de 40 ans les Fournisseurs, Industriels et Distributeurs dans l'amélioration de leur performance grâce à ses multiples atouts : - 120 collaborateurs - consultants, formateurs, chercheurs, techniciens et inspecteurs - aux savoir-faire riches et en constante évolution, - Un programme annuel de R&D et un système d'Intelligence Economique, qui enrichissent sans cesse cette expertise, - Une implantation internationale en expansion, qui affirme la vocation du Groupe CTC d'être au coeur des marchés mondiaux, - Des actions collectives et prestations en : Analyses de matériaux et de produits finis Conseil et Analyses en environnement Inspection de produits Intelligence Economique Formation Conseil en informatique Recherche et normalisation Conseil en production et aide à l'innovation

**Address** : 4, rue Hermann Frenkel
P.O. Box 7003
Lyon cedex 07-69367
France
**Tel.**
**Fax** :
: +33 472 76 10 10
+33 472 76 10 00
**Email**
**Web** :
: contact@ctcgroupe.com
http://www.ctcgroupe.com

France

Institut Colbert
**Address** : Domaine Universitaire - Choletais
Rue du Bordage Fontaine
Cholet-49300
France
**Tel.**
**Fax** :
: +33 241 49 22 56
+33 241 49 22 57
**Email**
**Web** :
: colbert@cnam-paysdelaloire.fr
http://www.institut-colbert.fr

France

Lycée d'Alembert GRETA de la mode
**Address** : 22, sente des Dorées
Paris-75019
France
**Tel.**
**Fax** :
: +33 1 42 08 04 10
+33 1 42 01 20 44
**Email**
**Web** :

: dal@lycee-dalembert-paris.org
http://lyc-dalembert.scola.ac-paris.fr/

France

Lycée de la Mode
**Address** : 20, rue du Carteron
P.O. Box 2124
Cholet-49321
France
**Tel.**
**Fax**
:
: +33 2 41 71 00 53
+33 2 41 71 28 55
**Email**
**Web**
:
: equipe.lycee@lycee-mode.com
http://www.lycee-mode.com

France

Lycée Turquetil GRETA de la mode
**Address** : 18, passage Turquetil
Paris-75011
France
**Tel.**
**Fax**
:
: +33 1 43 70 20 13
+33 1 43 70 52 28
**Email**
**Web**
:
:
http://greta-mode.scola.ac-paris.fr/

France

Forschungsinstitut für Leder und Kunststoffbahnen (FILK)

**Contact** : Matthias Dittrich
General Project Management activities: research and development in: -tanning processing and methods for process control, -dyeing and finishing technologies, -environmental control, -assurance of quality, complete chemical and physical material testing and analysis services of the Test Lab: - tests of leather and collagen - tests of plastic sheets - emission tests - further methods: FTIR, NIR, UV, Vis, GC, GC/MS, HPLC, HPTLC, SEM, EDX, DSC, TGA, photo-DSC, XPS, TMA, BET,etc. - expert opinions products: - Freiberg Hide Powder for the gravimetric analysis of tannin extracts

**Address** : Meissner Ring 1
P.O. Box 1144
Freiberg-09581
Germany
**Tel.**
**Fax** :
: +49 3731 3660
+49 3731 366-130
**Email**
**Web** :

: mailbox@filkfreiberg.de
http://www.filkfreiberg.de

Germany

Lederinstitut Gerberschule Reutlingen
**Address** : Erwin-Seiz-Str. 9
Reutlingen-72764
Germany
**Tel.**
**Fax**
:
: +49 71211623-0
+49 7121162311
**Email**
**Web**
:
: lgr@lgr-reutlingen.de
http://www.lgr-reutlingen.de

Germany

Prüf-und-forschungsinstitut für die Schuhherstellung e V.
**Address** : P.O. Box 2225
Pirmasens-0-66930
Germany
**Tel.**
**Fax**
:
: +49 6331 7 40 16
+49 6331 7 45 07

Germany

ELKEDE Technology and Design Centre SA
**Contact** :
**Address** : 12th KM Athens Lamıa National Road
Metamorphosis
Athens-144 52
Greece
**Tel.**
**Fax**
:
: +30 210 285 55 80
+30 210 284 64 71
**Email**
**Web**
:
: elkede@elkede.gr
http://www.elkede.gr

ELKEDE is a multi-technological and educational institute focusing on leather technology. Through its specialized and fully equipped modern laboratories, ELKEDE can perform a large range of quality control tests for leather and footwear sectors. Moreover, though its pilot plant tannery, ELKEDE participates a large number of E.U. projects in order to improve the technological standards and to enhance the competitiveness of the Greek Leather industry. Through an environmental friendly policy, ELKEDE solves the environmental problems of the leather sector and transfers the art of leather making though its educational courses, providing highly qualified human and technological assistance in the lêather and footwear sectors.

Greece

BIMEO Testing & Research Ltd Co

**Address** : .
P.O. Box
Ujpest-1325
Hungary
**Tel.**
**Fax**
:
+36 1369 6251
:
+36 1369 1058
**Email**
**Web**
:
bimeo@bimeo.hu
:
http://www.bimeo.hu

Hungary

AICC Associazione Italiana del Chimici del Cuoio
**Address** : Via San Tommaso, 67
Santa Croce Sull'Arno-56029
Italy
**Tel.**
**Fax**
:
+39 0571 35625
:
+39 0571 35625
**Email**
**Web**
:
info@aicc.it
:
http://www.aicc.it

Italy

ARS Arpel Group Srl
**Address** : Via Nievo, 33
Milano-20145
Italy
**Tel.**
**Fax**
:
+39 02 31 9121
:
+39 02 33 611 619
**Email**
**Web**
:
arsarpel@arsarpel.it
:
http://www.arsarpel.it

Italy

Centro Italiano Materiali di Applicazione Calzaturiera CIMAC
**Address** : C. so G. Brodolini, 19
Vigevano (PV)-27029
Italy
**Tel.**
**Fax**
:
+39 0381 84722
:
+39 0381 73393
**Email**
**Web**
:
cimac@cimacpv.it
:
http://www.cimacpv.it

Italy

CERCAL Research Center and International Footwear School
**Address** : Via dell' Indipendenza, 12
San Mauro Pascoli (FO)-47030
Italy
**Tel.**
**Fax**
:
:
+39 541 932 965/930 771
+39 541 932 999
**Email**
**Web**
:
:
cercal@cercal.org
http://www.cercal.org

Italy

CESECA Centro Servizi Calzaturiero
**Address** : Via Piaggiori Basso, 212
P.O. Box 55018
Segromigno in Monte LUCCA-
Italy
**Tel.**
**Fax**
:
:
+39 0583 929537
+39 0583 926310
**Email**
**Web**
:
:
segreteria@ceseca.it
http://www.ceseca.it

Italy

Fashion Institute Moda Pelle
**Address** : Via IV Novembre 54
Settimo Milanese-20159
Italy
**Tel.**
**Fax**
:
:
+39 02 33553 207
+39 02 33501 391
**Email**
**Web**
:
:
fashioninstitute@modapelle.com
http://www.modapelle.com

Italy

Instituto di certificacione della Qualita per l'Industria Conciaria
**Address** : Via Brisa, 3
Milan-20123
Italy
**Tel.**
**Fax**
:
:
+39 02 8807711
+39 0272000072
**Email**
**Web**
:

: info@icec.it
http://www.icec.it

Italy

Istituto Tecnico Industriale di Stato per la Chimica Conciaria
**Address** : Via le Vicenza
Arzignano (VI)-36071
Italy
**Tel.**
**Fax**
: +39 0444 670441/672016
: +39 0444 450920
**Email**
**Web**
: info@istitutoconciario.com
: http://www.istitutoconciario.com

Italy

Polimoda
**Address** : Villa Strozzi
Via Pisana, 77
Firenze-50143
Italy
**Tel.**
**Fax**
: +39 055 739 96 28
: +39 055 700 287
**Email**
**Web**
: info@polimoda.com
: http://www.polimoda.com/

Italy

Politecnico Intern. per lo Sviluppo Industriale ed Economico PISIE
**Address** : Via della Scala, 11
Firenze-50123
Italy
**Tel.**
**Fax**
: +39 055 2658178
: +39 055 2646000
**Email**
**Web**
: pisie@pisie.it
: http://www.pisie.it

Italy

Stazione Sperimentale Industria del le Pelli e delle Materie Concianti
**Address** : Via Poggioreale 39
Naples-I-80143
Italy
**Tel.**
**Fax**
: +39 0815979100
: +39 081265574

**Email**
**Web**
:
:
ssip@iol.it

Italy

CLPO Centralne Laboratorium Obuwniczego w Krakowie
**Address** : Central laboratory of shoe Idstry.
ul. Zakopianska 9
Kraków-30-418
Poland
**Tel.**
**Fax**
:
:
+48 12 266 65 22/35 11
+48 12 266 91 54
**Email**
**Web**
:
:
clpo@clpo.com.pl
http://www.clpo.com.pl

Poland

Centro Tecnologico do Calçado (CTC)
**Address** : Rua de Fundoes
Devesa Velha
S. Joao de Madeira-3700 121
Portugal
**Tel.**
**Fax**
:
:
+351 256 830 950
+351 256 832 554
**Email**
**Web**
:
:
ctc@mail.ctcalcado.pt
http://www.ctcalcado.pt

Portugal

Centro Tecnologico dos Industrias do Couros
**Address** : San Pedro
Alcana-2380
Portugal
**Tel.**
**Fax**
:
:
+35 124 988 15 77/989 13 16
+35 124 988 13 90
**Email**
**Web**
:
:
ctic@mail.telepac.pt
http://www.apic.pt/ctic

Portugal

European Union of Research Institutes for Shoes
**Address** : CTC Centro Tecnologico Calçado
Rua de Fundoes Devesa Velha
S. Joao de Madeira-3700-121
Portugal

**Tel.**
**Fax**
:
:
+351 256 830 950
+351 256 832 554
**Email**
**Web**
:
:
ctc@mail.telepac.pt

Portugal

Zavod IRCUO - Technological Center for Leather and Shoe Industry
**Address** : Savska loka, 21
Kranj-4000
Slovenia
**Tel.**
**Fax**
:
:
+386 4 201 4629
+386 4 201 4506
**Email**
**Web**
:
:
klemen.pibernik@zavod-ircuo.si
http://www.zavod-ircuo.si

Slovenia

Asociación de Investigación de las Indus. del Curtido y Anexas (AIICA)
**Contact** : José María Adzet
Director de Investigación
**Address** : Avda. Pla de la Massa, s/n.,
P.O. Box 58
Igualada, Barcelona-08700
Spain
**Tel.**
**Fax**
:
:
+34 93 805 53 88
+34 93 805 06 18
**Email**
**Web**
:
:
info@aiica.com
http://www.aiica.com

AIICA es la Asociación de Investigación de las Industrias del Curtido y Anexas, cuya actividad se centra en la investigación aplicada del cuero: · Asesoramiento técnico : Calidad y productividad · Gestión Medioambiental · Servicios analíticos : Ensayos químicos y físicos · Divulgación tecnológica : Organización de Symposiums y Mesas redondas · Cursillos de formación · Desarrollo de actividades de I+D+I. Está acreditada por la "Junta de Residus de la Generalitat de Catalunya" y en el año 2015 implantó el sistema EMAS. Aparte del sector curtidos, que es prioritario en nuestras actividades, colaboramos con el sector químico, textil y papel.

Spain

Escuela de Tenería de Igualada
**Contact** :
**Address** : Plaza del Rey, 15
Igualada-08700
Spain

**Tel.**
**Fax**
:
:
+34 93 803 5300
+34 93 803 1589
**Email**
**Web**
:
:
euetii@euetii.upc.es
http://www.euetii.upc.es

La EUETII - Escuela de Tenería de Igualada es un centro de enseñanza superior y universitaria y centro de referencia de enseñanza de las técnicas relacionadas con la curtición. Ofrecemos los cursos de Técnico Diplomado en Curtidos (se requiere bachillerato), Ingeniería Técnica Industrial especialidad en Química Industrial, y un Máster en Curtidos. Disponemos de una planta piloto de curtidos donde nuestros alumnos realizan las prácticas y además la ponemos a disposición de las empresas. También disponemos de un laboratorio de análisis acreditado donde principalmente se hacen análisis para empresas del sector de curtidos. También es un centro de referencia en investigación en curtidos y tecnologías limpias y estamos abiertos a colaborar con otros centros de investigación en curtidos.

Spain

Institut Quimic de Sarriá
**Address** : c/ Via Augusta 390
Barcelona-08017
Spain
**Tel.**
**Fax**
:
:
+34 932 672 000
+34 932 056 266
**Email**
**Web**
:
:
secre@iqs.url.es
http://www.iqs.es

Spain

Instituto Tecnologico del Calzado y Conexas (INESCOP)
**Address** : Polígono Industrial
Campo Alto
P.O. Box 253
Elda-03600
Spain
**Tel.**
**Fax**
:
:
+34 965395213
+34 965381045
**Email**
**Web**
:
:
info@inescop.es
http://www.inescop.es

Spain

Nordeconsult Sweden AB

**Contact** : Stefan Rydin
Chief Executive Officer Nordeconsult Sweden AB is a leading provider of consulting services in the fields of environmental technology and engineering for the leather industry.

**Address** : Sofiaparken 3C
Lund-
Sweden
**Tel.**
**Fax** :
: +46 70 6803860 / +46 46 2405924
+46 46 2402477
**Email**
**Web** :
: stefan.rydin@nordeconsult.com
http://www.nordeconsult.com

Sweden

Anthony Vrahimis Ltd

**Contact** : Anthony Vrahimis
Director design consultancy that produce leather architectural interiors. variouse courses in bespoke handbag design and making.

**Address** : 13 Tollington Way
London-N7 6RG
United Kingdom
**Tel.**
**Fax** :
: +44 020 7686 0001
+44 020 7686 0002
**Email**
**Web** :
: mail@anthonyvr.com
http://www.anthonyvr.com

United Kingdom

BLC Leather Technology Centre Ltd
**Address** : Leather Trade House
Kings Park Road-Moulton Park
Northampton-NN3 6JD
United Kingdom
**Tel.**
**Fax** :
: +44 1604 679999
+44 1604 679998
**Email**
**Web** :
: info@blcleathertech.com
http://www.blcleathertech.com

United Kingdom

British School of Leather Technology
**Address** : University College Northampton
Boughton Green Road
Northampton-NN2 7AL
United Kingdom
**Tel.**
**Fax** :

: +44 1604 735 500
+44 1604 711 183
**Email**
**Web** :
: bslt@northampton.ac.uk
http://www.leathernet.com/bslt

United Kingdom

Cordwainers College London College of Fashion
**Address** : 20 John Prince's Street
London-W1G 0BJ
United Kingdom

**Email**
**Web** :
: l.oatham@lcf.linst.ac.uk
http://www.lcf.linst.ac.uk/cms.cgi/site

United Kingdom

Footwear Training Centre The Wellingborough College
**Address** : Church Street
Wellingborough
Northamptonshire-NN8 4PD
United Kingdom
**Tel.**
**Fax** :
: +44 1933224165
+44 1933441832
**Email**
**Web** :
: http://www.emnet.co.uk/Colleges/TheWellingborough

United Kingdom

ITS Intertek Testing Services UK Footwear & Leathergoods Testing
**Address** : Centre Court
Meridian Business Park
Leicester-LE19 WR
United Kingdom
**Tel.**
**Fax** :
: +44 116 263 0330 / 9611
+44 116 263 0311
**Email**
**Web** :
: labtest.uk@intertek.com
http://www.intertek-labtest.com/

United Kingdom

Leather Conservation Centre
**Address** : University College Campus
Boughton Green Rd - Moulton Park
Northamptonshire-NN2 7AN
United Kingdom
**Tel.**
**Fax** :

: +44 1604719766
+44 1604719649
**Email**
**Web**
:
: lcc@northampton.ac.uk

United Kingdom

Leather Wise Ltd.

**Contact** : Christine Powley-Williams
Director Leather Wise Ltd provides professional problem solving and arbitration services relating to leather and leather products and bespoke training courses on all aspects of leather production/technology and use of leather in consumer products.

**Address** : Moulton Park Business Centre
Redhouse Road, Moulton Park
Northampton-NN3 6AQ
United Kingdom
**Tel.**
**Fax** :
: +44 1604 497 568 / 9
+44 1604 497 569
**Email**
**Web** :
: info@leatherwise.co.uk
http://www.leatherwise.co.uk

United Kingdom

Naturel Resources Institute University of Greenwich at Medway
**Address** : Central Avenue
Chatham Maritime
Chatham. Kent-ME4 4TB
United Kingdom
**Tel.**
**Fax**
:
: +44 1634880088
+44 1634880077
**Email**
**Web**
:
: nri@greenwich.ac.uk
http://www.nri.org

United Kingdom

SATRA Footwear Technology Centre
**Address** : SATRA House, Rockingham Rd
Kettering
Northamptonshire-NN16 9JH
United Kingdom
**Tel.**
**Fax**
:
: +44 1536410000
+44 1536410626
**Email**
**Web** :

info@satra.co.uk
http://www.satra.co.uk

United Kingdom

W2O Environment Ltd
**Contact** : Wolfram Scholz
Head of Environmental Services

Environmental consulting training and research for the leather industry.

**Address** : 58 Cecil Road
Queens Park
Northampton-NN2 6PQ
United Kingdom **Tel.**
**Fax** :
: +44 1604 478 415
+44 1604 478 415

**Email**
**Web** :
: info@w2oenvironment.net
http://www.w2oenvironment.net

United Kingdom

# SUPPLEMENTS

## LEATHER RELATED SITES

| | |
|---|---|
| www.all-about-leather.co.uk | UK site offering advice on leather care |
| www.iultcs.org | International Union of Leather Technologists and Chemists Societies |
| www.ichslta.org | International Council of Hide and Skin Traders' Associations |
| www.euroleather.com | European Tanners Association (COTANCE) |
| www.worldleather.co.uk | "World Leather" - a specialist leather journal |
| www.leatherbiz.com | A commercial site related to World Leather |
| www.samsetter.org | A site publishing articles from "Leather" - a specialist leather journal |
| www.limeblast.org | A site publishing articles from "Leather" - a specialist leather journal |
| www.leathernet.com | A commercial site giving information about leather |
| www.blcleathertech.com/fair | European project funded site covering quality of hides and skins |
| www.fao.org | Food and Agriculture Organisation of the United Nations - information and statistics on animal and meat production |
| www.leathercouncil.org/fair | FAIR Project: Concerted Action Ref CT 97-3940 |

## LEATHER INDUSTRY GLOSSARY

#### AGEING

The process by which certain types of leather are at some stage of manufacture allowed to lie in piles to "age".

#### ALUM TANNING

A process of tanning with alum, used in combination with salt, egg yolk and other substances. Used for the original feathery golf balls. "In 1845 we more than doubled that. Hard work it was. I can still smell the leather, feel the heat. We used to use a chest clamp to literally compress and push those goose down feathers into the ball. Of course you cut six strips of bull hide and you soaked it in alum and of course you took three of 'em and stitched them inside out there, and the feathers went back in, and you compressed and compressed, and the idea being that as the leather shrinks as it dries out and the feathers expand. Then that gives you the compression." Quoted by Wally Uihlein, Sept 1998, at St.Andrews Golf Congress.

#### ALUTA

Roman name for tawed (alum tanned) leather. Aluta was used for sails in Venice, and for shoe uppers in ancient Greece.

#### ANILINE LEATHER

Leather which retains its colour only from dyestuffs rather than from pigment, and as a consequence looks more natural.

### Bag and case leather

A general term for the leathers used in travelling bags and suitcases. It does not include the light leathers employed for women's fancy handbags. The staple material for bag and case leather is cowhide.

### Bag Leather

A form of vegetable tannage in which the skins are sewn together in pairs to form bags and floated in tan liquor. This method avoids drawn grain and gives good spread of leather.

### Basil

Bark tanned pickled sheepskins.

### Bating

The process prior to tanning proper where the fibres of a hide or skin which have been plumped or swollen by liming are reduced and softened, thus assuring pliability in the product. The word is a form of "abate" in the sense of reduce.

### Beamhouse

The area of the tannery where the unhairing and liming processes are carried out. Before modern machinery the processes of fleshing, scudding and others were carried out over specially designed wooden beams using curved two handled knives with sharp or blunted edge according to the operation. Hence the name.

### Belt leather

Leather used for the leather going into men's clothing belts.

### Belting leather

Leather employed for the transmission of power for machinery. The great bulk of this leather is made from the butts of high-grade cattle hides. In Europe a certain amount of buffalo hide is also used.

### Boarding

A process of finishing a side or skin by folding it with the grain side in and rubbing the surface together under pressure. Gives a distinct look, and creates "box" look when done two ways and "willow" when done only in one direction.

### Bougie Leather

Leather from the town of Bougie in North east Algeria. Famous in the fifteenth century.

### Box Calf or box sides

Calf or side leather which has been boarded in two directions.

### Buffing

Sandpapering the leather with sandpaper or emery paper for various reasons such as the creation of a suede like nap on suede, a nubuck finish on grain, or for the preparation of corrected grain leather. Sometimes done on the flesh side to tidy up its appearance.

### Cabretta Leather

A wrongly named hair sheep. When the Portuguese first went to Brazil they mistook the indigenous hairsheep for goats and called them cabrettas (kids). The skins were exported to the USA by the Blue Funnel Line (later the Booth Group) and the name cabretta stayed with them. Now all hairsheep skins have taken the generic name cabretta. Much used in footwear leather and sport glove leather.

### California Banknotes

In "Two Years Before the Mast" Richard Henry Dana describes how he sailed from Boston to California in 1834 to collect hides. He explains how hides are dried and loaded onto the ships before returning to the East Coast. Since California had nothing else of wealth at that time the dried hides were known as "California Banknotes". "The hides are brought down dry, or they will not be received. When taken from the animal they have holes cut in the ends, and are staked out, and thus dried in the sun without shrinking. They are then doubled once, lengthwise, with the hair side usually in, and sent down upon mules or in carts, and piled above high-water mark: and then we take them upon our heads, one at a time, or two, if they are small, and wade out with them and through them into the boat." On page 140 of the book detailed at the end is a fine description of the full cure process used to prepare the hides for a wait of over a year before they would get back to Boston around the Cape for tanning. Hides were valued in Boston at 12 and a half cents a pound dry salted and the captain got 1% commission. Ships would spend nearly a year collecting and accumulating hides up and down the California cost to make the journey worthwhile. On Dana's ship they brought back 40,000 hides.

### Carding Leather

A special type of side leather used on the cards of cotton machinery. The leather lies flat against the beds of the cards, the teeth being forced through.

### Chamois leather

A soft leather originally made from the skins of the Alpine antelope known as the chamois but at the present time from the fleshers of sheepskins. Certain grades used to be used in gloves and fancy articles but the staple employment is for cleaning and polishing, primarily automobile. Chamois is characterised by an ability to absorb at least three times its own weight of water. Shoemakers, but unlike cordwainers they work with old leather.Cobblers are essentially repairers.

### Combing leather

The name applied to the leather used on the combing rolls of cotton machinery and manufactured of calfskin or side leather.

### Conditioning

When leather is dried after retanning, dyeing and fatliquoring the fibres tend to stick together and the leather is hard. The fibres are separated and the leather softened by staking. Staking is best done at about 18% humidity and so a little humidity has to be put into the dry leather. This is most commonly done by a water spray and then piling the leather long enough for the moisture to even out. Adjusting the moisture content before staking in this way is called conditioning.

### Cordovan

The shell of a horse hide, often tanned with a sulphur tannage.As such it was a soft vegetable tanned leather first made in Cordoba in Spain, and followed by goat, sheep and pigskin leathers with a similar formula.Cordovan leather has good wearing characteristics, and I non porous.The horse product still tends to be called “shell cordoban leather”.

### CORDOVAN LEATHER

Developed in Spain in the 8th century, when the Moors arrived in Spain. Made from the skin of the mouflon (Ovis Musimom). This hair sheep now only survives in Corsica and Sardinia. It was tanned with alum and later with alum (Koninklijke Bibliotheek says sumac was not introduced until the 15 th century). Best brilliant scarlet type was tawed with alum and dyed with kermes.

### CORDWAINERS

From Cordovan leather. At first made many types of leather articles. In Middle Ages specialised in Shoes. Cordwainer is from the French word "cordonnier" and came to England in 1066 with the Norman Invasion.After Cordoba fell in the 12 th century English Crusaders brought back this alum tanned goat skin.It was considered the highest quality shoe leather in Europe. Cordwainers work only with new leathers.

### CORRECTED GRAIN

Chrome tanned side leather which is buffed with emery paper on the grain side to remove defects and then has a plastic resin and pigment finish built up on the leather. Used for shoe upper leather.

### CRUPP LEATHER

A semicircular portion of leather taken from the butt of stuffed vegetable tanned horse hide.

### CRUST

Leather dried after tanning. Since chrome leather dried immediately after tannage will go hard, change charge and become difficult to rewet, this drying normally takes place after a basic retanning and fatliquoring. Leather is frequently traded world wide in this state, although tanners normally prefer to buy wet blue or pickle which gives them more flexibility of processing.

### CURRYING

A term practically equivalent to dressing and finishing, but confined chiefly to heavy leather (Latin corredare, to prepare or dress).

### DELIMING

A process preparatory to tanning proper to reduce the swollen and rigid fibres of a hide or skin after liming.

### DONGOLA TANNAGE

a. A vegetable and alum tannage developed in Gloversville, New York, in the 1860's to compete with the expensive kid tannage for gloves. Used hair sheep. Dongola is a town in the Sudan, and there is a breed of hair sheep named after it. "Dongola, strictly speaking, is alum, salt, and gambier only, used together in one solution. Dongola is especially applied to glazed and dull kid. For full dongola the process is commenced in very weak gambier liquor, with the full proportion of alum and salt, and the gambier is gradually strengthened. Dull dongola is ironed like kid in the finish. It is said to be sometimes glazed with a blood seasoning, and then dulled by a mixture of soap and oil, followed by slating with a smooth round -edged slicker, but it is generally sized". b. Dongola tannage.- gambier, alum, and salt make what is known as dongola leather. There are many modifications of this process. Fine leather is made by tanning the skins first in gambier or quebracho liquor, and then giving them an alum and salt re-tannage. For 200 average skins, a mixture is prepared of 5lb. of alum, 9lb. of salt, 24lb of flour, 10lb. of egg-yokes, or a corresponding quantity of sulphonated oil, and 8 to 10 gallons of water. The flour is made into paste with cold water. The alum and salt are dissolved in part of the water, and the flour paste is slowly stirred into the solution. The oil or the egg-yoke mixed with warm water is next added, and the whole mixture is thoroughly stirred. The tanned skins are drummed with this mixture one hour, then dried, colored and finished, thus making soft, durable leather. This mixture may also be used on untanned skins as come from the bate or drench. They should be drummed with it, dried, kept in crust for some time, then wet-back and tanned with chrome liquor, the result being soft durable leather. The combination tannage of gambier, alum, and salt can also be applied in the following manner: The bated and washed skins are placed in gambier liquor in a paddle. From 3 to 5lb. of gambier are used for one dozen skins. After they have started to absorb the gambier, from 8 to 16 oz. of alum and 8 oz. of salt are added to the liquor, for each dozen skins, and the paddling is continued until the tannage is complete, which takes 18 to 36 hours. The leather is then washed in warm water to remove the adhering tan, next fatliquored with acid fat-liquor, dried, wet-back, colored, dried again, and finished. After the alum and salt have been added it is customary to put the skins, together with the tanning liquor, into a drum and run them for a few hours or until thoroughly tanned. Some soluble oil may also be added to the liquor and applied to the leather toward the end of the tanning process. Excellent leather is also made by taking the skins out of the gambier liquor when they are well struck through, striking them out and then drumming them with a paste of water, flour, alum, salt, and either egg-yoke or soluble oil, drying and then coloring them with a basic dye and titanium-potassium oxalate. The color of the leather can be modified by adding a solution of fustic or other dyewood to the gambier liquor, and the entire process may be reversed. The skins may be first drummed with alum and salt and then tanned with gambier. Heavy skins may be tanned with gambier, alum, and salt. After the leather is dry, it can be colored with acid or basic dies: and, if not fatliquored immediately after tanning, drummed with acid fatliquor or with an emulsion of oil and soap, staked and finished.

### DRENCHING

A process for reducing the plumped fibres of a hide or skin. It accomplishes approximately the same purpose as bating and basically in the same way - that is, through soaking in a fermenting solution. Some authorities, however,, restrict the term bating to the process using ferments of manures and the term drenching to that using damp sawdust, bran, middlings, or a solution of lactic acid or some other chemical having a similar action.

### DRUMS

The collective term for the rotary vessel in which many processes of tanning are now carried out.

### ECRASE

Usually highly polished goatskin leathers showing differences in colour tone coinciding with the natural goatskin grain.

### EXTRACTV

A solution of a tanning material, normally vegetable.

### FATLIQUORING

Using fats and oils in appropriate mixes to lubricate and soften the fibre structure of leather, given the leather the required softness for its eventual end use.

### FOOTBALL LEATHER

Leather for covering the outside of soccer balls. Originally made of pigskin, then of cattlehide splits, and more recently of PU laminated splits. Lately leather has been somewhat replaced by full synthetics.

### Flesher

The flesh piece from a thick woolly sheep which has been split into two layers. Used to make chamois. The grain is made into a skiver. Sometimes for cost and easy maintenance the material is part tanned and then split. The grain is then called a pliver. The flesh created in this latter way will not make true chamois.

### Frizing

The process of removing the grain of a skin by exposure to a strong lime liquor over an exceptionally long period,, sometimes as much as eight weeks. Such skins, after tanning are finished on the fine fibres under the grain. This is the method used in the manufacture of mocha glove leather and of certain classes of buckskin. (11)

### Full grain leather

Leather whose grain has not been sandpapered or buffed to hide defects.

### Glove Leather

A self-explanatory term which, however, covers two rather distinct classes: the leather going into utilitarian or work-gloves and made of a variety of hides and skins, of which the most important are horsehides, cattlehide splits, calfskins and pigskins; and the leather going into dress-gloves, including those for street, riding, driving, and sports wear. the latter is tanned predominately from sheep and lambskins; but there is a considerable item made of deerskin and a small one of pigskin, while an important item for the highest grades of women's fine gloves is tanned in a few countries of Europe from kidskins.

### Guilds (Gilds)

Western European trade associations, grew strongly in the 12th and 13th centuries to protect and promote trade groups. Data from the Brewers' Company in London show that their were at least 14 different guilds concerned with leather listed in London in 1422).

### Handlers

One of the series of pits or vats in which heavy leathers are tanned with bark or vegetable extracts. They are usually worked with stronger liquors than the suspenders, but with weaker liquors than the layers.

### Heavy Leathers

A term distinguishing sole leather, belting leather, and harness leather proper from other classes which are referred to collectively as light leathers.

### Helvetia Leather

Oil tanned hide from which not all the excess grease is removed.

### Hydraulic leathers

A collective term sometimes used for the cattle hide leathers, chiefly rawhide and combination tannages, employed in pump valves, as piston packing, oils seals and so forth.

### In the hair; in the wool; in the raw

A group of more or less equivalent terms used to describe stock that has not yet undergone any of the processes of leather manufacture.

### In the Rough; In the Crust; In the White; In the Blue

A group of approximately equivalent terms used to describe stock which has been tanned,, but not finished. In the rough or rough tanned is most commonly applied to vegetable tanned cattle hide leathers; in the crust and in the white to vegetable, alum or formaldehyde tanned sheepskins and lambskins; and in the blue to chrome tanned skins particularly goatskins. The use of the term in the white needs to be distinguished from that mentioned in the following definition. See also Wet White and Wet Blue.

### In the White; In the Pickle

Two roughly equivalent terms used to describe stock which has undergone the processes preliminary to tanning, but has not been actually tanned. Historically in the pickle is restricted to sheepskins and lambskins; in the white, in this sense, is used for practically all other classes of hides and skins.

### Japanning

A process of preparing the oil for, and the process of, manufacturing patent leather.

### Larrigan Leather

An American speciality made of light cattle hide and used in the manufacture of the heavy moccasins worn by lumbermen to guard against slipping when walking on wet logs.

### Latigo Leather

The Spanish word latigo means a whiplash and this leather was originally tanned for that purpose; but as a technical term in the present day American trade, latigo means the straps used for cinching saddles of the McClellan, cowboy and Mexican types. This leather is usually prepared from cattlehides by a combination tannage.

### Layers

The last set of vats or pits in which heavy leather is tanned, containing the strongest liquor. The hides in these pits are laid flat - originally with layers of tan bark between them.

### Leather

For the avoidance of all ambiguities and doubts, which may and do grow upon the definition and interpretation of this word leather, it is enacted, and declared by these presents, that the hides and skins of ox, steer, bull, cow, calf, deer, red and fallow, goats and sheep being tanned or tawed, and every salt hide is, shall be, and ever hath been reputed and taken for leather. Act of Parliament. UK year 1604. (2)

### Light Leather

Leather for clothing, gloving and shoe uppers mostly chrome tanned.

### Liming

A process preliminary to tanning, which serves one or both of two purposes: (1) to loosen the hair or wool on a hide or skin, preparatory to dehairing; and (2) to plump or swell the fibres as of the processes necessary to prepare the substance for the action of the tan liquors. Liming is always required for the latter of these purposes.

### PADDLES

A name applied to certain types of machinery with rotating arms, which are used in various tanning operations for agitating hides or skins in process. Use more water than drums, allowing larger floats and consequently gentler action. Mostly used in the soaking and liming areas.

### PAINTING

A process for loosening hair or wool (usually the latter) which is employed with skins whose protective covering is so valuable as to make it desirable to avoid injuring it by soaking in a lime liquor. The process is carried out by painting the flesh side of a skin with a depilatory substance, containing sodium sulphide or arsenic. Nowadays this is the usual method with sheepskins bearing the higher grades of wool. Before it was invented, such skins were usually dehaired by sweating.

### PARCHMENT

See Pergamum.

### PASTING

A method of drying where wet leather is pasted onto a glass or steel plate and then allowed to dry in controlled conditions - often a tunnel with various chambers adjusted to fit the planned removal of moisture. Most used with side leather. Holds the area well, but if not well retanned the leather can feel hard and empty. There is a danger of the paste damaging the grain or interfering with the finish. US tanners are most skilled in this drying method.

### PELT

This word means, strictly speaking, any kind of skin (Latin pellis, related to the German felle, a skin, and the English word fell, now preserved only in fellmonger). The word is somewhat loosely used in the leather industry, but its only common applications nowadays are to sheepskins in two or three slightly differing senses: to the skin proper, to distinguish it from the wool that grows on it; to dewooled sheepskins, as a pickled pelt or a fellmongered; or in some countries to a woolskin bearing the shortest recognised staple.

### PERGAMUM

Town near Izmir (Smyrna) in Asia Minor. Parchment (from Latin "carta Pergamena") supposedly first made there in 3rd cent BC. When the King of Pergamus was building a great library in rivalry with the library of the King of Egypt in Alexandria, the latter placed an embargo on the exportation of papyrus from Egypt to hamper competition. The King of Pergamus thereupon perfected the manufacture of parchment for the making of books.

A more comprehensive discussion of this is given by the Koninklijke Bibliotheek.Since it is very interesting I quote from their website: Parchment was used chiefly for writing, first on a scroll - as is still the case in Israel - and from the second century BC onwards in book form. To make a book, the rectangular cut sheets might be folded one or more times. The skins of sheep and goats from the areas round the Mediterranean were rarely more than 50 cm long by 40 cm wide. In northern regions we find larger skins and also calfskins being used to make books. The term pergamena is first used in the Edict of Diocletian (301 AD); until that time the term membrana had been used. It is generally accepted that the use of a new term indicates a new or modified product, but so little is known about the parchment of those days that it is impossible to say with any certainty whether this was the case here.

One of our few informants about pre-Christian times is the (unreliable) Roman historian Pliny. He writes that the king of Pergamon (in present-day Turkey), Eumenes II (197-159 BC), was forced to look for alternative writing materials when the import of papyrus from Egypt was suspended. This is supposed to have led to the invention of parchment. Although parchment had been known at least eight hundred years before this date, Pergamon did have a reputation for good quality parchment in classical antiquity. The great change occurred around the fourth century AD, when people started manufacturing parchment using lime water. Until the fourth century skins were mostly treated with salt, flour and other vegetable products that were used to remove the hairs and to prepare the skin. The lime water method may have been introduced by Jews and Arabs to Spain in the early Middle Ages, after which it spread throughout the rest of Europe. Jewish parchment was lightly tanned on the surface with vegetable tannins. Another technique, the splitting of skins, was also known to the Jews and Arabs, even before the Middle Ages. In the West the traditional procedure to obtain the required thickness was to shave the full skin.

Formulas and depictions of parchment manufacturing have come down to us, especially from the late Middle Ages. There is considerable correspondencebetween these mediaeval formulas and those used by modern parchment makers, and even the processing and tools have not changed fundamentally. For the most part, parchment manufacture is still a matter of handwork.

### Picker Leather

The picker is the mechanism on either side of a power loom that throws the sharp pointed shuttle and receives it again as it is thrown back. For arming this mechanism, long experience has found nothing equal to a special, very tough leather, usually rawhide - either cattle or buffalo. Such picker leather is made extensively in the North of England and in parts of the USA, partly from native cattle hides and partly from imported buffalo hides.

### Pickling

A preliminary process for preparing hides and skins for tanning, largely by adjusting the pH with acid and controlling the swelling with salt. It is also use as stable way of holding material, after unhairing, for transport between plants and countries and for trading.

### Retanning

A process subsequent to the main tannage when the character of the leather is adjusted by the addition of further alternate types of tanning material. Thus synthetic or vegetable tans may be added to a chrome leather to adjust certain characteristics.

### Roans

Sumac tanned sheepskins.

### Rockers

A device for the continuous agitation of hides when suspended in pits or vats in order to hasten the operation of the liquors.

### Rolling

One of the final operations in the manufacture of sole leather, by which it is given a smooth surface and even thickness.

### Russia Leather

Leather characterised by its odour. "Anglo Russias" are skins treated with birch tar oil to imitate the smell of Russia leather. "The Russians have manufactured for a long time a variety of red leather called Juncten. This leather has an agreeable and characteristic odor, does not mould even in damp places, and is not attacked by insects.

### Russia Leather

Originally and properly calfskin shoe leather, dressed with birch oil and distinguished by its odour rather than its appearance.

### Santa Croce..

..... Igualada, Vic, Alcanena, Solofra, Lyon, Arzignano, Guadalajara, Kano, Northampton, Ambur, Ranipet, Vaniyambada, Millau, Kano, Graulhet, Mazamet, Gloversville Some of the places in the world which are centres for the leather industry

### Samm, sammying

The mechanical extraction of moisture from leather after a processing stage. Most normally done on wet blue after chrome tanning, using a machine which carries the leather through felts.

### Scud

A film or deposit of waste matter appearing on the surface of leather in process after certain operations, esp. bating.

### Scudding

One of the preliminary processes preparatory to tanning. After bating or drenching the excess fermenting materials, together with dirt, fatty matter, hair follicles, short hairs, and glandular tissue, are worked out of the hide or skin.Mostly done by hand using a blunt two-handed knife over a curved beam. Can be done by machine.

### Setting out

This mechanical process is used at various stages in the finishing of leather to counteract the shrinking and stiffening resulting form the processes that have gone before.Most common after retanning, fatliquoring and dyeing. Normally done by machine using a knifed cylinder with blunted blades. Some modern machines combine sammying and setting and some incorporate a heated roller to help set the grain in a smooth tight configuration. Striking out is a similar process for heavy, vegetable tanned leather.

### Shagreen

From Turkish "saghri" and means the croup of a beast. Originally made in Persia from hides of asses, horses and camel, probably untanned. Seeds of a species of Chenopodium were trampled into the skin when it was moist and shaken out when it dried, thus leaving granular indentations. The material was then stained. In the 17th cent and later, shagreen was made either of finely granulated shark skin or of the skin of a ray fish, whose pearl like papillae were ground flat, leaving a lovely pattern.

### Side Leather

Large hides are cut in half down the backbone to make them easier to handle in the tannery. Each piece is called a side. Most shoe leather made from cattle hides is produced as side leather, while most upholstery leather produced from hides is processed as whole hides. Increasingly the cutting of hides into sides is done after tanning, at the wet blue stage.

### Skirting Leather

A specialised cattlehide leather used for the skirts or hanging portions of saddles that come between the legs of the rider and a horse's flanks.

### Skivers

The grain of the wool sheepskin when it has been split in order to prepare a suede leather for manufacture into chamois leather. Normally tanned with vegetable materials for use as in shoe lining, bookbinding or leathergoods.

### Slat

Vegetable tanned sheepskin produced from a skin whose wool has been removed by the sweating process. Mazamet in France is a famous source of slats.

### Splits

The lower flesh side section of a hide (normally) or a skin after it has been split. Normally made into a suede split.

### Staking

Mechanical softening of leather. Done by hand by pulling skins over a moon shaped knife, but mostly by machines of which tow types are common. The old "grab" staker with crocodile jaws which come together at a point where the operator offers the hide or skin and pulls the leather away from him while he restrains it carefully and the vibrating through feed machine invented in Czechoslovakia in the sixties. The former is more precise, but is also more labour intensive and skilled, while if not used carefully will lead to tearing and loss of area.

### Stocks

A wooden device previously used in oil tannages especially for chamois. Two wooden hammers pound the oil into the leather prior to hanging in a hot room for the oil to oxidise. The hammers are driven by an eccentric wheel. This process is now done in drums where temperature and humidity can be carefully controlled.

### Strop Leather

The leather from which razor strops are made. The best grades are tanned from the shells of horse hides.

### Suede

The finish produced by running the surface of leather on an emery wheel, with the result of ruffling up the fibres and giving it a "nappy" appearance. The grain of leather may be suede finished (called nubuck) but the process is more appropriate to flesh or split surfaces. The name was applied (originally in France) to a glove leather of Swedish origin and only later to the finish that characterised the material.

### Suspenders

One series of vats or pits used in tanning heavy leathers, the hides being hung so as to be exposed as freely as possible to the action of the liquor. The suspender pits usually contain the weakest liquor, and the hides are treated in them before passing to the handlers and layers.

### SWAMP

An area near the Manhattan side of Brooklyn bridge just south of the current City Hall set aside for tanning in 1664. Remained for 275 years.

### SWEATING

A process for loosening the hair or wool on a hide or skin by hanging the pieces near together in a close atmosphere, thus encouraging bacterial action. It has now become comparatively rare, being confined to out of the way places or primitive industries, and to a few special trades like that centering about Mazamet in France.

### TAWING

The old English term applied to the process of making leather with alum to distinguish it from tanning in a strict sense, the latter term having been originally confined to leather making with vegetable tanning agents. The English word has now become nearly obsolete, but in French the distinction between tannage and megissage is still strictly drawn.

### TACKING

A process of stretching leather at certain stages in the manufacture by tacking it on a frame or board. the method seems crude and slow, but is very effective for counteracting the shrinkage which follows certain operations, without applying excessive strains on particular portions of a piece.

### TOGGLING

A modernised method of tacking to dry leather, using toggles to hold the leather instead of nails. Originally the toggles were fixed into holes in a perforated metal plate which was put in an oven. More modern machines find and clip the leather mechanically.

### VACUUM DRYING

A method of drying leather taking advantage of the fact that moisture evaporates more quickly under vacuum. The wet leather is laid out on a wet steel plate (often slicked, a form of hand setting out) and the vacuum head brought down. After retanning and fatliquoring the leather can be dried to either 30% and then hang dried or in some circumstances fully dried direct. Drying only takes two to five minutes. A newer use of vacuum drying involves using a rubber base instead of stainless steel. While the leather is under vacuum this rubber base expands outwards, stretching the leather out from its centre. I have seen a page of newspaper pulled into jigsaw-sized pieces by this machine. It is not so good for taking out large amounts of moisture but good for the drying after conditioning and staking of soft leathers. Avoid using it just for area gain.

### VELLUM

Vellum is practically the same thing as parchment but is made of calfskin. The word is derived from the Latin vitulus, a calf, whence our word veal. Drum leather is a specialised form variety of vellum, made nowadays in diminished quantities for the purpose indicated by its name. (11)

### WET BLUE

Chrome tanned leather. Chrome tanning creates a blue colour in the leather and there is a natural safe resting stage just after tanning when the leather is both wet and blue. A significant stage in which leather is traded semi-processed worldwide.

### WET WHITE

Hides and skins with the hair or wool removed and preserved after a light aluminium tannage. More stable than pickle. Increasingly used as an intermediate stage for transporting and selling hides and skins.

# GLOBAL BUSINESS LIBRARY
# (PRICE $149.95)

| ISBN | TITLE |
|---|---|
| 1433017938 | Global Adoption Guide |
| 1433000024 | Global Aeronautical Industry Handbook |
| 1433017946 | Global Air Freight Companies Directory |
| 1433017954 | Global Airports Handbook |
| 1433020343 | Global Airports Handbook: Regulations and Business Opportunities |
| 1433017962 | Global Aviation & Aerospace Industry Handbook, Vol.1 Europe |
| 1433017962 | Global Aviation & Aerospace Industry Handbook, Vol.2 USA |
| 1433017970 | Global Aviation Industry Handbook |
| 1433017989 | Global Aviation Training Institutions Directory |
| 1433017997 | Global Banking Laws and Regulations Handbook |
| 1433018004 | Global Business and Industrial Directories Publishers Handbook |
| 1433018012 | Global Business Associations Handbook |
| 1433018020 | Global Business Contacts Directory |
| 1433018039 | Global Business Lawyer Associations and Arbitration Centers Handbook |
| 1433018047 | Global Central Banks Directory |
| 1433018055 | Global Chambers of Commerce Directory - USA |
| 1433018063 | Global Chambers of Commerce Directory - World |
| 1433018071 | Global Civil Air Navigation Regulations and Opportunities Handbook |
| 143301808X | Global Counter Terrorism Operations & Programs Handbook |
| 1433018098 | Global Counter-Terrorism Handbook |
| 1433018101 | Global Credit Unions Handbook |
| 143301811X | Global Customs Laws and Trade Regulations Handbook |
| 1433018128 | Global E-Commerce Business Guide |
| 1433018136 | Global E-Commerce Business Law Handbook |
| 1433018144 | Global E-Commerce Laws and Regulations Handbook |
| 1433018152 | Global Economic Financial and Development Organizations Directory |
| 1433018160 | Global Embassy Directory (Asian Countries) |
| 1433018179 | Global Embassy Directory (EU Countries) |
| 1433018187 | Global Embassy Directory (European Countries) |
| 1433018195 | Global Embassy Directory (US, Canada Latin American Countries) |
| 1433018209 | Global Embassy Directory (US, Canada Latin American Countries) |
| 1433018217 | Global Environmental Profiles Handbook |
| 1433018225 | Global Export-Import Procedures and Contacts Handbook |
| 1433018233 | Global Fishing Industry Handbook |
| 1433018241 | Global Foreign Investment Law Handbook |

| | |
|---|---|
| 143301825X | Global Foreign Policy Handbook |
| 1433018268 | Global Foreign Trade Barriers to the US Products and Services Exports Handbook |
| 1433018276 | Global Free Trade and Industrial Zones Law and Regulations Handbook |
| 1433021870 | Global Helicopter Industry & Transportation Handbook |
| 1433018284 | Global Humanitarian Customs Regulations Handbook |
| 1433018292 | Global International & Slavic Libraries Directory |
| 1433018306 | Global Investment Funds Directory |
| 1433018314 | Global Investment Promotional Agencies Handbook |
| 1433018322 | Global Islamic Countries Handbook |
| 1433018330 | Global IT & Telecom Market Export and Business Opportunities Handbook |
| 1433018349 | Global Law Firms Directory, Volume 1 |
| 1433018357 | Global Leather and Footwear Industry Handbook |
| 1433018365 | Global Leather Exporters & Importers Directory |
| 1433018373 | Global Mining and Mineral Industry Government Agencies Directory |
| 1433018381 | Global Mining, Oil and Gas Industry Directory |
| 143301839X | Global Mobile & Cellular Communications Industry Directory |
| 1433018403 | Global Money Laundering Law Handbook |
| 1433018411 | Global National Intelligence and Security Agencies Handbook |
| 143301842X | Global National Libraries Directory: EUROPE |
| 1433018438 | Global Non Profit Organizations Directory |
| 1433018446 | Global Offshore Business and Investment Contacts Handbook |
| 1433018454 | Global Offshore Business Laws and Regulations Handbook |
| 1433018462 | Global Offshore Financial Services Providers Directory |
| 1433018470 | Global Offshore Investment and Business Guide |
| 1433019744 | Global Offshore Tax Guide (Volume 1) |
| 1433019752 | Global Offshore Tax Guide (Volume 2) |
| 1433019760 | Global Oil & Gas Industry Directory |
| 1433060574 | Global Parliament Libraries Directory |
| 1433019779 | Global Pharmaceutical Industry Directory |
| 1433019787 | Global Privatization Laws and Regulations Handbook. Vol. 1 United States |
| 1433019795 | Global Privatization Laws and Regulations Handbook. Vol. 1. Eastern Europe |
| 1433019809 | Global Privatization Laws and Regulations Handbook. Vol. 10. Pacific Countries |
| 1433019817 | Global Privatization Laws and Regulations Handbook. Vol. 11. China |
| 1433019825 | Global Privatization Laws and Regulations Handbook. Vol. 2. Russia and NIS |
| 1433019833 | Global Privatization Laws and Regulations Handbook. Vol. 3. European Union |
| 1433019841 | Global Privatization Laws and Regulations Handbook. Vol. 4. Africa |
| 143301985X | Global Privatization Laws and Regulations Handbook. Vol. 5. Central Asia |
| 1433019868 | Global Privatization Laws and Regulations Handbook. Vol. 5. South Asia |
| 1433019876 | Global Privatization Laws and Regulations Handbook. Vol. 6. South America |
| 1433019884 | Global Privatization Laws and Regulations Handbook. Vol. 7. Middle East and Arabic Countries |
| 1433019892 | Global Privatization Laws and Regulations Handbook. Vol. 8. Central America & Mexico |
| 1433019906 | Global Privatization Laws and Regulations Handbook. Vol. 9. Caribbean Countries |
| 1433019914 | Global Privatization Programs and Opportunities Handbook Vol. 1 Africa |
| 1433019922 | Global Privatization Programs and Opportunities Handbook Vol. 2 Asia |

| | |
|---|---|
| 1433019930 | Global Privatization Programs and Opportunities Handbook Vol. 3 Latin America |
| 1433019949 | Global Privatization Programs and Opportunities Handbook Vol. 4 Pacific Countries |
| 1433019957 | Global Privatization Programs and Opportunities Handbook Vol. 5 Caribbean |
| 1433019965 | Global Privatization Programs and Opportunities Handbook Vol. 6 Europe |
| 1433019973 | Global Privatization Programs and Opportunities Handbook Vol. 7 Russia and NIS |
| 1433019981 | Global Professional Internet Advertising Handbook |
| 143301999X | Global Publishers Directory |
| 1433060930 | Global Recent Economic and Political Developments Yearbook |
| 1433020009 | Global Satellite Communications Organization Handbook |
| 1433020017 | Global Sea Food Industry Directory |
| 1433020025 | Global Seafood Industry Handbook |
| 1433020033 | Global Senate Handbook |
| 1433020041 | Global Shipbuilding Industry Handbook. Vol 1. Asia |
| 143302005X | Global Shipbuilding Industry Handbook. Vol 2.Americas |
| 1433020068 | Global Shipbuilding Industry Handbook. Vol 3.Europe |
| 1433020076 | Global Shipbuilding Industry Handbook. Vol 4.Russia and Eastern Europe |
| 1433020084 | Global Space Programs and Organizations Handbook |
| 1433020092 | Global Special Operation Forces Handbook |
| 1433020106 | Global Stem Cell Research Programs Handbook |
| 1433020114 | Global Stock Exchange Directory |
| 1433020122 | Global Tax Guide, Volume 1 Asia |
| 1433020130 | Global Tax Guide, Volume 2 Europe |
| 1433020149 | Global Tax Guide, Volume 3 Latin America |
| 1433020157 | Global Tax Guide, Volume 4 Eastern Europe |
| 1433020165 | Global Tax Guide, Volume 5 Caribbean |
| 1433020173 | Global Tax Guide, Volume 6 Pacific Islands |
| 1433020181 | Global Telecom Industry Business Opportunities Handbook |
| 143302019X | Global Telecom Industry Handbook Regulations and Contacts VOL 2 |
| 1433020203 | Global Telecom Industry Handbook: Regulations and Contacts VOL 1 |
| 1433020211 | Global Telecommication Handbook: Investment & Business Opportunities |
| 143302022X | Global Telecommunication Privatization Handbook |
| 1433020238 | Global Terrorism Attacks Encyclopedic Handbook |
| 1433020246 | Global Terrorism Organizations Yearbook |
| 1433020254 | Global Trade & Business Show Directory Vol. 1 |
| 1433020262 | Global Trade & Business Show Directory Vol. 2 |
| 1433020270 | Global Trade and Business a Atlas |
| 1433020289 | Global Transportation Business Contacts Handbook |
| 1433020297 | Global Transportation Contacts Directory |
| 1433020300 | Global US Economic Assistance Guide |
| 1433020319 | Global US Emigration Guide |
| 1433020327 | Global Wireless Telecom Communication Handbook: Companies and Operations |
| 1433020335 | Global World Trade Centers Directory |

38. Common Fund for Commodities Handbook
39. Common Market for Eastern and Southern Africa (COMESA) Handbook
40. Cooperation Council for the Arab States of the Gulf (GCC) Handbook
41. Council of the Baltic Sea States (CBSS) Handbook
42. Council of Europe Development Bank (CEB) Handbook
43. East African Development Bank (EADB) Handbook
44. Eastern Caribbean Central Bank (ECCB) Handbook
45. Economic Community of West African States (ECOWAS) Handbook
46. Economic Cooperation Organization (ECO) Handbook
47. European Bank for Reconstruction and Development (EBRD) Handbook
48. European Central Bank (ECB) Handbook
49. European Free Trade Association (EFTA) Handbook
50. European Investment Bank (EIB) Handbook
51. European Investment Fund (EIF) Handbook
52. European Union, The (EC) Handbook
53. Financial Fund for the Development of the River Plate Basin (FONPLATA) Handbook
54. Food and Agriculture Organization of the United Nations (FAO) Handbook
55. Fund for Co-operation, Compensation and Development (ECOWAS Fund) Handbook
56. Inter-American Development Bank (IDB) Handbook
57. Inter-American Institute for Cooperation on Agriculture (IICA) Handbook
58. Inter-Arab Investment Guarantee Corporation (IAIGC) Handbook
59. International Atomic Energy Regulations Handbook
60. International Civil Aviation Regulations Handbook
61. International Cocoa Production and Trade Regulations Handbook
62. International Coffee Production and Trade Regulations Handbook
63. International Confederation of Free Trade Unions (ICFTU) Handbook
64. International Cotton Advisory Committee (ICAC) Handbook
65. International Fund for Agricultural Development (IFAD) Handbook
66. International Grains Council Handbook
67. International Labour Organization (ILO) Handbook
68. International Lead and Zinc Study Group Handbook
69. International Monetary Fund (IMF) Handbook
70. International Olive Oil Council (IOOC) Handbook
71. International Rubber Study Group Handbook
72. International Sugar Organization (ISO) Handbook
73. International Telecommunications Union (ITU) Handbook
74. International Tropical Timber Organization (ITTO) Handbook
75. Islamic Development Bank Group (IsDB) Handbook
76. Islamic Research and Training Institute (IRTI) Handbook
77. Joint Vienna Institute (JVI) Handbook
78. Kuwait Fund for Arab Economic Development Handbook
79. Lake Chad Basin Commission (LCBC) Handbook
80. Latin American Association of Development Financing Institutions (ALIDE) Handbook
81. Latin American Economic System (SELA) Handbook
82. Latin American Energy Organization (OLADE) Handbook
83. Latin American Export Bank (BLADEX) Handbook
84. Latin American Integration Association (ALADI) Handbook
85. Latin American Reserve Fund (LARF) Handbook
86. League of Arab States Handbook
87. Mekong River Commission (MRC) Handbook
88. Nordic Development Fund (NDF) Handbook

89. Nordic Investment Bank (NIB) Handbook
90. OPEC Fund for International Development Handbook
91. Organisation for Economic Co-operation and Development (OECD) Handbook
92. Organisation of Eastern Caribbean States (OECS) Handbook
93. Organization of American States (OAS) Handbook
94. Organization of Arab Petroleum Exporting Countries (OAPEC) Handbook
95. Organization of the Petroleum Exporting Countries (OPEC) Handbook
96. Pacific Financial Technical Assistance Centre Handbook
97. Pacific Islands Forum Secretariat Handbook
98. Pan American Health Organization (PAHO) Handbook
99. Regional Association of Oil and Natural Gas Companies in Latin America and the Caribbean (ARPEL) Handbook
100. Regional Electrical Integration Commission (CIER) Handbook
101. Saudi Fund for Development (SFD) Handbook
102. Secretariat for Central American Economic Integration (SIECA) Handbook
103. Secretariat of the Pacific Community Handbook
104. Sectorial Commission for the Common Market of the South (MERCOSUR) - Uruguay Handbook
105. South Asian Association for Regional Cooperation (SAARC) Handbook
106. South-East Asian Central Banks (SEACEN) Research and Training Centre Handbook
107. Training Centre for Regional Integration (CEFIR) Handbook
108. United Nations African Institute for Economic Development and Planning (IDEP) Handbook
109. United Nations Conference on Trade and Development (UNCTAD) Handbook
110. United Nations Development Program (UNDP) Handbook
111. United Nations Economic and Social Commission for Asia and the Pacific (ESCAP) Handbook
112. Asian and Pacific Centre for Transfer of Technology (APCTT) Handbook
113. Regional Coordination Centre for Research and Development of Coarse Grains, Pulses, Roots and Tuber Crops in the Humid Tropics of Asia and the Pacific (ESCAP CGPRT Centre) Handbook
114. Statistical Institute for Asia and the Pacific (SIAP) Handbook
115. United Nations Economic and Social Commission for Western Asia (ESCWA) Handbook
116. United Nations Economic Commission for Africa (UNECA) Handbook
117. United Nations Economic Commission for Europe (UN/ECE) Handbook
118. United Nations Economic Commission for Latin America and the Caribbean (ECLAC) Handbook
119. United Nations Educational, Scientific and Cultural Organization (UNESCO) Handbook
120. United Nations Industrial Development Organization (UNIDO) Handbook
121. United Nations Latin American and Caribbean Institute for Economic and Social Planning (ILPES) Handbook
122. World Postal Service Handbook: Volume 1 Strategic information and basic regulations
123. West African Development Bank (BOAD) Handbook
124. West Africa Economic and Monetary Union Handbook
125. World Bank Group Handbook
126. World Food Program (WFP) Handbook
127. World Health Organization (WHO) Handbook
128. World Trade Organization (WTO) Handbook

www.ingramcontent.com/pod-product-compliance
Ingram Content Group UK Ltd.
Pitfield, Milton Keynes, MK11 3LW, UK
UKHW051509290926
15471UKWH00008B/1522

9 781438 719627